IMPROVE YOUR

CRITICAL
THINKING
& REFLECTIVE
SKILLS

HOW TO IMPROVE YOUR CRITICAL THINKING & REFLECTIVE SKILLS

**KATHLEEN McMILLAN &
JONATHAN WEYERS**

PEARSON

Harlow, England • London • New York • Boston • San Francisco • Toronto • Sydney
Auckland • Singapore • Hong Kong • Tokyo • Seoul • Taipei • New Delhi
Cape Town • São Paulo • Mexico City • Madrid • Amsterdam • Munich • Paris • Milan

Pearson Education Limited
Edinburgh Gate
Harlow
Essex CM20 2JE
England

and Associated Companies throughout the world

Visit us on the World Wide Web at:
www.pearson.com/uk

First published 2013

© Pearson Education Limited 2013

ISBN 978-0-273-77332-0

British Library Cataloguing-in-Publication Data
A catalogue record for this book is available from the British Library

Library of Congress Cataloging-in-Publication Data
A catalog record for this book is available from the Library of Congress

ARP impression 98

Typeset in 9.5/13 pt Helvetica Neue Pro Roman by 3
Printed in Great Britain by Ashford Colour Press Ltd.

SMARTER STUDY SKILLS

Instant answers to your most pressing university skills problems and queries

Are there any secrets to successful study?

The simple answer is 'yes' – there are some essential skills, tips and techniques that can help you to improve your performance and success in all areas of your university studies.

These handy, easy-to-use guides to the most common areas where most students need help, contain accessible, straightforward practical tips and instant solutions that provide you with the tools and techniques that will enable you to improve your performance and get better results – and better grades!

Each book in the series allows you to assess and address a particular set of skills and strategies, in crucial areas of your studies. Each book then delivers practical, no-nonsense tips, techniques and strategies that will enable you to significantly improve your abilities and performance in time to make a difference.

The books in the series are:

- *How to Write Essays and Assignments*
- *How to Write Dissertations and Project Reports*
- *How to Argue*
- *How to Improve Your Maths Skills*
- *How to Use Statistics*
- *How to Succeed in Exams and Assessments*
- *How to Cite, Reference and Avoid Plagiarism at University*
- *How to Improve Your Critical Thinking and Reflective Skills*

For complete handbooks covering all of these study skills and more:

- *The Study Skills Book*
- *Study Skills for International Students*

Get smart, get a head start!

CONTENTS

Preface and acknowledgements   ix
How to use this book   xi

INTRODUCTION

1 **Key concepts and processes** – how thinking, reflection and
   creativity involve important skills   3

KEY APPROACHES TO THINKING

2 **Critical thinking** – how to develop a logical approach to
   analysis and problem-solving   17

3 **Reflective thinking** – how to evaluate your feelings in
   academic contexts   30

4 **Creative thinking** – how to generate innovative and original
   ideas   43

CRITICAL THINKING IN PRACTICE

5 **Arriving at a viewpoint** – how to sift fact and opinion to
   arrive at a position on a topic   55

6 **Supporting or opposing an argument** – how to express
   your point of view through discussion and debate   64

7 **Interpreting and manipulating data** – how to approach
   graphs, tables, formulae and basic statistics   76

8 **Decision-making and work-planning** – how to make
   choices, plan ahead and prioritise   91

9 **Group effort and collaboration** – how to enhance your
   contribution to teamwork   104

EVALUATING THE IDEAS OF OTHERS

10 **Evaluating information sources** – how to filter and select
    reliable material   119

11 **Effective academic reading** – how to read efficiently and
    with understanding   129

12 **Note-making from texts** – how to create effective notes for
later reference   142

13 **Plagiarism and copyright infringement** – how to avoid being
accused of 'stealing' the ideas and work of others   154

14 **Citing and listing references** – how to refer appropriately to
the work of others   164

PUTTING YOUR THINKING INTO WORDS

15 **Tackling a writing assignment** – how to respond to the
specified task   187

16 **Academic writing style** – how to adopt appropriate language
conventions   197

17 **General writing structures** – how to select and shape your
content appropriately   210

18 **Writing about reflection** – how to structure and report your
thoughts   224

19 **Editing and presenting your assignment** – how to review
your own work and follow academic style conventions   235

FORWARD THINKING

20 **Exploiting feedback** – how to learn from what lecturers think
of your work   247

21 **Preparing for employment** – how to transfer your thinking
skills to a career   254

References and further reading   267
Glossary of key terms   270

PREFACE AND ACKNOWLEDGEMENTS

We are pleased that you have chosen *How to Improve Your Critical Thinking and Reflective Skills* and hope that it will provide you with a deeper understanding of the thought processes used in university learning. We have included a range of tips and suggestions to help you to develop relevant skills. These cover methodical thinking, when a logical approach is required; reflective thinking, when self-analysis is expected; and creative thinking, when you need to be innovative. We have tried to make the book as practical and jargon-free as possible, and have avoided a theoretical treatment of logic or behaviour. The book takes you through the full process of applying thought. It will help you to analyse the ideas of others and put your own notions into words. We also show you how to make the most of feedback from staff and how to let potential employers know about your thinking skills. We hope this book will meet your needs – regardless of your experience and background.

We would like to offer our sincere thanks to many people who have influenced us and contributed to the development and production of this book. Numerous students over the years have helped us to test our ideas, especially those whose written work we have commented upon, supervised and assessed. We are grateful to the following colleagues and friends who have helped us directly or indirectly: Margaret Adamson, Michael Allardice, the late John Berridge, Stuart Cross, Margaret Forest, Andy Jackson, Bill Kirton, Eric Monaghan, Neil Paterson, Jane Prior, Fiona O'Donnell, Dorothy Smith, Gordon Spark, Amanda Whitehead, David Walker and David Wishart. Also, we acknowledge those at other universities who have helped frame our thoughts, particularly our good friends Rob Reed, Nicki Hedge and Esther Daborn. We owe a special debt to the senior colleagues who encouraged various projects that contributed to this book, and who allowed us the freedom to pursue this avenue of scholarship, especially Robin Adamson, Chris Carter, Ian Francis, Rod Herbert and David Swinfen. At Pearson Education, we have had excellent advice and support from Steve Temblett, Rob Cottee and Philippa Fiszzon. Finally, we would like to say thanks to our long-suffering but nevertheless enthusiastic families, Derek, Keith, Nolwenn, Fiona, Tom and Eilidh; and Mary, Paul and James, all of whom helped in various capacities.

Kathleen McMillan and Jonathan Weyers

Publisher's acknowledgements

We are grateful to the following for permission to reproduce copyright material:

Figure 3.1 The reflective cycle, from *Learning by Doing: A guide to teaching and learning methods*, Further Education Unit, Oxford Polytechnic (Gibbs, G. 1988); Table 3.2 from 'Marking Criteria for Assessing Portfolios submitted for the Qualification in Forensic Psychology (Stage 2)' (available 26/02/12 as the document QFP marking criteria from http://www.bps.org.uk/careers-education-training/society-qualifications/forensic-psychology/qfp-2011-documents/qualificati).

In some instances we have been unable to trace the owners of copyright material, and we would appreciate any information that would enable us to do so.

HOW TO USE THIS BOOK

Each chapter in *How to Improve Your Critical Thinking and Reflective Skills* has been organised and designed to be as clear and simple as possible. The chapters are self-contained and deal with particular aspects of the subject matter so that you can read the book through from beginning to end, or in sections, or dip into specific chapters as you need them.

At the start of each chapter, you'll find a brief paragraph and a **Key topics** list that lets you know what is included. There is also a list of **Key terms** at this point that highlight words that may be new to you or may be used in a particular way in the chapter. Should you be uncertain about the meaning of these words, you will find definitions in the **Glossary** at the end of the book.

Within each chapter, the text is laid out to help you absorb the key concepts easily, using headings and bulleted lists to enable you to find what you need. Relevant examples are contained in figures, tables and boxes which complement the text. The inset boxes are of three types:

Smart tip boxes emphasise key advice that we think will be particularly useful to you.

Information boxes provide additional information that will broaden your understanding by giving examples and definitions.

Query boxes raise questions for you to consider about your personal approach to the topic.

At the end of each chapter, there's a **Practical tips** section with additional suggestions for action. You should regard this as a menu from which to select the ideas that appeal to you and your learning style.

Finally, the **And now** box provides three suggestions for possible follow-up action as you consider ideas further.

INTRODUCTION

1

KEY CONCEPTS AND PROCESSES

How thinking, reflection and creativity involve important skills

We routinely think without really contemplating what we are doing. However, in academic contexts there are benefits from a deeper understanding of the various modes of thinking, including reflection and creativity. An insight into the relevant concepts and skills can help to improve learning. Moreover, advanced thinking skills are highly valued by employers, so being able to communicate and evidence these attributes is essential.

KEY TOPICS

→ What do we mean by critical thinking?

→ What do we mean by reflection?

→ What do we mean by creative thinking?

→ Other modes of thinking and allied skills

→ Why thinking skills are important

KEY TERMS

Creative thinking   Critical thinking   Criticism   Curriculum vitae
Metacognition   Reflective thinking   Transcript

Having a deeper understanding of how you think and reflect will help you feel more confident in your studies and ensure you are equipped to perform better. Beyond this, it is important to grasp the value of 'thinking skills' as a product of your higher education experience. Increasingly, students are expected to be able to convince potential employers through their transcript, curriculum vitae and letter of application that they can demonstrate their abilities in this area.

WHAT DO WE MEAN BY CRITICAL THINKING?

Critical thinking means different things to different people. In a university context, the term is generally used to describe the ability to analyse a problem and present a solution to it. The word 'critical' implies that your intelligence is applied to a specific issue or problem and that a weighing-up of options is an integral part of the process.

Critical thinking is...

- Incisive, seeing through complexity and obscurity
- Logical, deploying evidence towards a clear position
- Deep, involving higher level skills of analysis, synthesis and judgement

Critical thinking is not...

- Disorganised, being a haphazard collection of ideas
- Prejudiced, ignoring evidence on one side of an issue
- Unsubstantiated, failing to take account of evidence

Critical thinking is applied in many different scenarios, for example, in dialogue, when writing and when tackling personal issues. The focus in this book will mainly be on its use in academic situations, such as essay-writing, research, problem-solving and producing exam answers. However, it is important to recognise its value in other circumstances, as these may well be typical of the workplace where you might be expected to apply the graduate skills you have developed in academic exercises.

Critical thought and criticism

The use of the word 'criticism' in academic contexts is different from that in normal conversational English. In the latter, it is commonplace for the verb 'to criticise' to carry negative connotations, as in finding fault. It is important to realise that in the academic sphere, this is not the case. Here, 'criticism' means seeing (and explaining) both the positive and negative aspects of an issue. The aim is to arrive at (and discuss) a balanced view of a topic rather than create a one-sided treatment of the topic.

Here are some examples of situations where critical thinking may be required:

Personal decision-making:

- You decide to purchase a new model of mobile phone with associated contract: you will need to investigate the market and balance the features of all the options against their cost, taking account of your budget.

- You wish to choose a new extra-curricular activity: before selecting a suitable means of participating, this may involve weighing up your interests and motivations, the time you can commit and what you might gain from the experience.

- You need to apply for a part-time job to refresh your finances: this might involve evaluating how available positions might suit your experience and skills, taking account of location, hours and wages and the potential effect on your studies, relationships and curriculum vitae.

Academic tasks:

- In preparation for a tutorial, you are expected to arrive at a viewpoint on a specified issue: you will need to research the matter, gauge what others have to say about it, synthesise your own position, and plan what tactics to adopt when arguing in its defence.

- You are set a complex numerical problem as part of your studies: you will need to identify the nature of the problem, decide what theory and associated mathematical models may be relevant, apply a suitable formula to the data provided and present your answer in the required format.

- An exam requires you to write an answer in limited time: having chosen a topic, you will need to brainstorm possible content, focus on relevance, decide on an outline structure and commit to writing – all within a few minutes.

Three further examples are outlined in Table 1.1 and critical thinking is considered in greater detail in Chapter 2.

Table 1.1 Some examples where thinking skills might be required. In all three examples, some fact-finding underpins the thinking and decision-making process. There is also the need to weigh the pros and cons of different aspects given this information. In all cases there is also a personal element to the decision-making process. Finally, there is always action and an outcome – and without this conclusion, the thinking effort would be wasted.

1 A personal matter

Julie needs to rent a flat for the new academic year. This involves a three-way compromise, balanced between: cost of rent, distance from university and her own personal checklist of important facilities (for example, an *en suite* bathroom is a must). If she needs to pay more to get a closer, better flat, she will need to decide what sacrifices might be made from her limited budget to pay for this. Her approach is to make a table of the different factors of personal importance and weigh up how each available flat would score in the different areas. Having created this grid, she decides to show it to her parents. The process of explaining her decision-making clarifies her own thoughts and the priorities she wishes to give to certain features of her student life. Having targeted a district, type of flat and budget, she is now able to make applications in good time to have the pick of the available accommodation that fits her requirements.

2 An academic challenge

Fabrice has been given an essay title for submission in three weeks' time, but cannot immediately see how to approach the topic, which requires that he defends a specific position on an issue. He needs to organise his work, allocating different periods for the separate elements of the task, and in particular needs to plan for extensive reading around the subject so he can master the language and concepts involved and see how others have approached this and analogous topics. He sets aside time in the evenings to visit the library and consult appropriate reference works, making notes in the form of a mind map (p. 149). This outlines the various schools of thought on the essay topic. He later uses these notes to develop an outline for his personal approach and as an aid for balancing his own viewpoint against other published stances on the issue. Using this essay plan, he finds it far easier to tackle the writing itself.

3 A tactical decision

Kevin has to choose a research project for his final year. The department has given him a list from which to choose. Some of the projects involve learning how to use a specific research technique; others entail working with supervisors whose approach he admires; while further topics might be interesting but extremely challenging in terms of producing results. He feels he should balance out the advantages of projects which will motivate him with those that will look good on his CV and potentially lead to a job. He makes a short-list of potential projects and supervisors, and then visits each potential supervisor in turn to discuss what research would be involved, and how this might qualify him for employment. He also makes an appointment to discuss job prospects with the university careers service. By the end of this process he has a more detailed and informed picture of his discipline and while there is an element of personal attraction to his eventual choice, he is persuaded that he will be able to access a range of interesting career paths with this experience.

WHAT DO WE MEAN BY REFLECTION?

The term reflection generally refers to the process where an individual evaluates an event or experience to arrive at a deeper understanding of the incident(s) and surrounding issues. In fact, we continually reflect as part of life: about conversational exchanges; news stories; or even the food we eat. You can see from this why it is considered to be an important part of the learning process. Reflection is a personal activity, but in university education it must be focused and take place within boundaries set by the academic context, especially when it is assessed.

Reflective thinking is...

- Personal, belonging to you as a individual
- Authentic, being a genuine image of your private thoughts
- Empowering, leading to new positions and actions

Reflective thinking is not...

- Self-indulgent, and a means of promoting your ego
- Dishonest, presenting a false picture of your feelings
- Imitative, being copied from others

Here are some examples of reflection in action:

Personal reflection:

- A friend comments on the slogan on your latest T-shirt: you then wonder how the clothes you wear might influence people's perception of you as a person.

- You enter a heated discussion in the pub and instinctively defend an extreme point of view: later, you think further about the other viewpoints that were expressed and their validity and modify your personal outlook as a result.

- You watch a movie and the plight of the main character in one scene strikes a chord with you: this makes you think about whether you could have handled a particular real-life situation in a different way.

Reflection as an everyday activity

A familiar experience will be the informal 'end of day review' that many people carry out just before going to sleep. It generally consists of setting and answering the following questions:

■ What happened today?
■ How did I react to events?
■ What were the consequences?
■ Could my responses have been improved?
■ How should I move on from my position?

Although often lacking in order and system, this appraisal of the day's events essentially contains the important elements of a more formal reflective process, and illustrates that we have the innate skills to carry this out in a more disciplined manner, and to communicate our thoughts to others.

Academic reflection:

● As part of training for professional engagement with a pupil, client or patient, you are asked to comment on your experience regarding a specific (mock or real) interaction that has taken place and detail how you might approach a similar scenario in future.

● As part of a teamwork exercise, you are asked to write about the experience, commenting on your own input, your interactions with other team members and how you might work with others in future.

● As part of personal development planning, you are asked to look back on the past academic year, evaluate how you have changed and set new goals for the future.

Reflection is considered further in Chapter 3.

Links between reflection and critical thinking

Many university lecturers regard reflective writing as evidence of reflective and critical thinking. In assessed reflective writing, they will expect you to be self-aware, analytical and able to situate your thoughts in the relevant academic and professional context.

WHAT DO WE MEAN BY CREATIVE THINKING?

Creativity and originality are words that encompass several strands of meaning. In the context of thinking, these include:

- novelty – meaning that no-one else has thought this way;
- invention – suggesting a new approach to the use of ideas, information or technology;
- imagination – signifying radical new thoughts or a jump in thinking;
- intuition – implying that solutions can appear spontaneously, without an apparent reasoning process;
- problem-solving – suggesting that there can be valuable outcomes from the process.

Creative thinking is...

- ■ Imaginative, being original and fresh
- ■ Idiosyncratic, drawing on a range of sources but being outside the normal pattern
- ■ Difficult to force, because it often arises spontaneously

Creative thinking is not...

- ■ Conventional, or following established patterns
- ■ Copied from others, or imitative
- ■ Safe, since it always carries an element of risk

Creativity is clearly to the fore in artistic subjects, where fresh ideas and innovation are especially prized. However, it is also highly regarded in most other subjects, where the term originality tends to be preferred. Typical situations where creative solutions will be valued include:

- finding a new perspective on a well-discussed academic issue;
- developing a new hypothesis to explain observations;
- developing the program coding for a computer application;
- finding an answer to an engineering or architectural problem;
- conceiving a new piece of art;
- designing a new consumer product;
- generating new examples to illustrate a viewpoint.

Many people find that creativity is difficult to produce on demand and that it often arises unpredictably. However, it is also accepted that putting your mind 'in the right place' can help you to produce inventive thought. Several techniques have been developed to promote originality and these are discussed in Chapter 4.

OTHER MODES OF THINKING AND ALLIED SKILLS

Certain specialised forms of thought process are particularly valued in specific subject disciplines. While some courses may focus and reward thinking of a particular type, it is useful to recognise that an element of several modes may be present in each task you are asked to complete and that certain features and skills are common across the categories.

Problem-solving

This mode of thinking involves a logical approach and elements of creating thinking in response to a specific scenario. The range of subjects requiring this thought process is wide, including those with a mathematical element such as engineering, many other sciences, but also design, computing and some disciplines dealing with 'people-problems' like social work or psychology. Relevant processes and techniques are discussed in Chapters 2 and 5.

Scientific and logical thinking

Thinking in which conclusions are strongly based on evidence or precedence are common in all the sciences and in subjects like medicine and law. The 'scientific method' and associated notions of evidence and proof are discussed in Chapter 5, while reasoning is covered in Chapter 6. Data analysis and manipulation (Ch 7) involve allied skills. Philosophy, of course, devotes an entire branch of study to logic (deemed to be too specialised to cover in this book).

Decision-making

This is a thinking skill that applies everywhere, but it is especially valued in administration and management, and hence is promoted in business-related subjects. There are many opportunities to practise it in academic life, for example, when choosing an essay or project topic or when participating in extra-curricular activities. Chapter 8 outlines the key methods used in arriving at a decision and associated skills such as planning and prioritising.

Group thinking

This is an important aspect of vocational subjects where teamwork is a key aspect of the workplace, but is also encouraged elsewhere through group projects. Putting several minds together to arrive at a collective outcome requires an understanding of team dynamics, empathy for the needs of others, a willingness to contribute to the common good and at times personal qualities such as leadership. This topic is covered in Chapter 9.

Skills allied to all modes of thinking include those involved in researching the ideas of others and their ethical treatment in your own writing (Chs 10–14). Your thoughts also need to be communicated, requiring a range of writing and editing skills (Chs 15–19).

WHY THINKING SKILLS ARE IMPORTANT

Having well-honed thinking skills is important in the modern world and has the potential to enrich your life experience. More than ever, there is a need to employ critical thought when responding to rapidly changing, complex events – and the escalating availability of information means that it is essential to be able to evaluate evidence confidently and quickly. To be an active member of today's society, you need to be able to digest facts and figures, arrive at a viewpoint on them and present a cogent position, either in writing or in speech.

Although you might not have thought about education in this way before, you have probably come to university or college with the underlying expectation that relevant thinking skills will be refined, tested and evaluated. Another way of looking at this is to state that your performance in higher education will not match your expectations and those of your lecturers *unless* your critical thinking skills improve in step with the learning outcomes at each level of study. Taking account of feedback (Ch 20) is vital to that process.

Increasingly, employers offer jobs to graduates on the basis that the thinking skills a candidate can demonstrate are transferable to the workplace and will add value to the business or activity. You will need a full understanding of these skills to be able to communicate your abilities effectively to a potential employer. You might be required to convey evidence about them in your application, your curriculum vitae, in written tests, and during interviews. This is discussed further in Chapter 21.

Which critical thinking skills are deemed important by employers?

This is a sample:

- Analysing problems and tasks
- Being numerate
- Carrying out information analysis
- Creative problem-solving
- Dealing with complex data
- Discussing and debating
- Managing time and prioritisation
- Planning work and project management
- Report-writing
- Retrieving information

 PRACTICAL TIPS FOR UNDERSTANDING THE ROLE OF THINKING IN YOUR STUDIES

Approach academic work with thinking processes in mind. For each assignment you are given, think carefully about the thinking skills being assessed. These may not be explicit.

Check that you have a full understanding of all the vocabulary surrounding thinking processes. Staff may use a word in the academic context to mean something slightly different from common usage. Look at the Glossary in this book (p. 270) or explanations such as those in Table 2.1 (page 18).

Look at the feedback on you work to see if it makes comments on the depth of your thinking. If necessary, speak to your lecturers about what you need to do in future.

 AND NOW ...

1.1 Think back to the last 'big' decision you made. It might have been choosing a university or degree subject, for example. Think back to the decision-making process and the analysis you made of the options. Also, think about how you have reflected on this decision since it was made. How have you learned from this experience? Would you do things differently now?

1.2 Look again at your course aims. These are usually published in an online or hard-copy handbook. To what extent do they define and explain the thinking skills expected of a graduate in your degree subject? Consider also the range of academic exercises in your subject. Again, you can find this out from the relevant handbook(s). What do the associated learning outcomes and assessment criteria tell you about the modes of thinking required for specific assignments?

1.3 Think about your future career possibilities. What sorts of general and specialised thinking skills are likely to be valued in these occupations? Can you link the answers to the questions in 1.2 to the answer you give? If not, you might consider taking on a new or different extra-curricular activity to augment your skills.

KEY APPROACHES TO THINKING

2

CRITICAL THINKING

How to develop a logical approach to analysis and problem-solving

The ability to think critically is probably the most transferable of the skills you will develop at university – and your future employers will expect you to be able use it to tackle professional challenges. This chapter introduces concepts, methods and pitfalls to watch out for when trying to improve your analytical capabilities.

KEY TOPICS

→ The importance of thinking skills for coursework

→ Thinking about thinking

→ How to approach a critical thinking task

→ Putting forward a balanced and unbiased analysis

→ Common pitfalls in thinking

KEY TERMS

Bias   Devil's advocate   Fallacy   Metacognition   Propaganda
Skewed   Value judgement

Critical thinking was defined in Chapter 1 as the ability to analyse a problem and present a solution to it. Many specialists think that critical thinking is a skill that you can develop through practice – and this assumption lies behind much university teaching. The aim of this chapter is to help you make the most of such opportunities through a deeper understanding of relevant thought processes.

Contexts for thinking critically

Examples of university work involving higher level thinking skills include:

- Essay-writing in the arts and social sciences
- Problem-based learning in medicine and nursing
- Engineering problems concerning machines and structures
- Case scenarios in law
- Project-based practical work in the sciences

THE IMPORTANCE OF THINKING SKILLS FOR COURSEWORK

Much of the course material and the assessed exercises at university will provide you with opportunities to cultivate your thinking skills. Lecturers will lead you through complex subjects, modelling patterns of investigative thought and research. They will expect you to absorb different approaches and ways of reaching a conclusion. Some of the tasks they will present to you will require similar logical processes. Table 2.1 presents some examples.

Table 2.1 Examples of assessed academic exercises and the types of critical thinking involved. Note that phrases like 'filter', 'analyse', 'evaluate', 'solve', or 'make conclusions' clearly encompass deeper levels of thought, but even superficially straightforward verbs such as 'organise', 'identify', 'describe', 'observe', or 'present' can involve complex reasoning.

Assessment exercise	Typical elements and subsidiary tasks, illustrating some of the important thought processes involved
Essay	You will need to research a particular topic; find relevant information; organise this within a coherent structure; and present evidence or a case in writing using a logical structure.
Tutorial	You will need to research a particular topic; filter out important and relevant information; summarise your thoughts verbally in a succinct, coherent fashion; answer specific questions from the tutor and other members of the group; respond to others' presentations and debate issues with them.
Numerical problem	You will need to read the text of the problem and identify the relevant pathway to a solution (this could be a specific equation); abstract the required numerical information from the text and transform it to the appropriate units; carry out error-free calculations; present your answer in the correct units; interpret your result in meaningful terms.

Assessment exercise	Typical elements and subsidiary tasks, illustrating some of the important thought processes involved
Problem-solving exercise	You will need to read the text of the problem and identify the key elements; find a relevant pathway or pathways to a solution; evaluate or carry out calculations; discuss advantages or disadvantages to different approaches; present your preferred approach or solution in writing.
Practical work	You will need to follow instructions faithfully; observe and note key features of a specimen/location or accurately note outcomes from an observation or experiment; filter out the relevant from the irrelevant; present your notes in a coherent form; analyse your results, sometimes using statistical techniques; make conclusions based on your findings; present these in a logical form.
Reflective writing	You will have to select an episode from the past; determine the key features and describe these coherently; analyse what happened; explain this, possibly with reference to a theoretical model or established pattern of behaviour; describe what the outcome means to you as a learner or developing professional.
Mock business report	You will carry out research on a specific company or area of business; select and present tables and graphical information about this in an easily digested form; analyse the data you have assembled; write about the key features of your research; identify key opportunities and action points arising from your analysis.
Teamwork	You will have to work with others on a specific task (for example, creating a poster); assign different tasks to members of the group; present and share ideas and information; develop an approach as a team; solve any problems that are encountered; complete the task on time; think about your relationship with other members of the team; present a reflective piece on your experience; assess your partners' performances.
Dissertation or literature survey	You may be asked to select an area for study or develop one for yourself; carry out reading and research in the subject area, typically by finding and selecting relevant articles and reviews covering relevant topics; read and analyse these sources, taking coherent notes; arrive at a stance on the central issue or topic and assemble evidence for and against your viewpoint; create an outline structure for your writing; write succinctly and clearly, ensuring that you quote and paraphrase appropriately; develop a logical conclusion and present this.
Research project	You may be asked to select an area for study or develop one for yourself; set a context for your investigation by reading relevant literature; carry out research in the subject area, typically by making observations or carrying out experiments; analyse your results in numerical form, presenting relevant tabular and graphical information; interpret your results for meaning, quoting from other sources when required.

For each piece of assessed work, you should receive feedback. It is vital to reflect on these comments to see how your performance is matching your lecturers' expectations.

Most of the assessed tasks will require you to lay out your analysis or argument in words. It is important to recognise that this is a key stage in critical thinking. Expressing your thoughts in spoken or written language requires you to:

- refine and clarify your thoughts;
- lay out the logic of your thinking so that it can be followed and understood;
- understand the connotations and meanings of phrases and words;
- find the right expressions to explain your meaning to others;
- use language to persuade.

It follows that the skills of speaking and writing are important for critical thinking and that these skills will be assessed just as much as your ability to arrive at a logical conclusion – and in some cases they may amount to the same thing.

 Always ask yourself questions

One of the keys to critical thinking is to ask 'why?' when coming across any new fact, concept or theory. Developing this habit of questioning means that you are constantly seeking the underlying reasons for things being the way they are. To develop the skill of thinking for yourself, you must rarely take anything for granted and seldom rely on someone else's views.

THINKING ABOUT THINKING

Benjamin Bloom, a noted educational psychologist, working with several colleagues, identified six different processes involved in thinking within education:

- knowledge acquisition;
- comprehension;
- application;
- analysis;

- synthesis;
- evaluation.

Bloom *et al.* (1956) showed that students naturally progressed through this scale of thought processing during their studies (Table 2.2). Looking at this table, you may recognise that your schoolwork mainly focused on knowledge, comprehension and application, while your university lecturers tend to expect more in terms of analysis, synthesis and evaluation. These expectations are sometimes closely linked to the instruction words used in academic assessments, and Table 2.2 provides a few examples. However, you should take care when interpreting these instructions, as processes and tasks may mean different things in different subjects. For example, while 'description' might imply a lower level activity in the sciences, it might involve high-level skills in a subject like architecture.

Table 2.2 **Classification of thinking processes by Bloom *et al.* (1956)**

Bloom's taxonomy of thinking processes (in ascending order of difficulty)	Typical question instructions
Knowledge. If you know a fact, you have it at your disposal and can *recall* or *recognise* it. This does not mean you necessarily understand it at a higher level.	• Define • Describe • Identify
Comprehension. To comprehend a fact means that you *understand* what it means.	• Contrast • Discuss • Interpret
Application. To apply a fact means that you can *put it to use*.	• Demonstrate • Calculate • Illustrate
Analysis. To analyse information means that you are able to *break it down into parts* and show how these components *fit together*.	• Analyse • Explain • Compare
Synthesis. To synthesise, you need to be able to *extract relevant facts* from a body of knowledge and use these to *address an issue in a novel way* or *create something new*.	• Compose • Create • Integrate
Evaluation. If you evaluate information, you *arrive at a judgement* based on its importance relative to the topic being addressed.	• Recommend • Support • Draw a conclusion

When you analyse the instructions used in writing assignments and other forms of assessment, you should take into account what type of thinking process the examiner has asked you to carry out, and try your best to reach the required level. To help you understand what might be required, Table 2.3 gives examples of thought processes you might experience in three representative areas of study.

Thinking about thinking in this way involves an advanced level of insight, known as 'metacognition'. Understanding thought processes at this 'higher' level will allow you to place your activities at a 'lower' level into context. Thus, rather than aimlessly trying to achieve a goal, you are able to recognise the type of activity necessary to meet your target and adopt methods that have previously been successful for that sort of task. In short, an awareness of academic thinking at this new level should aid you to perform better in all aspects of your studies.

Definition: metacognition

This has been defined as 'knowing about knowing'. In the context of this book, it includes understanding how you think and how you might apply different thinking processes to different tasks.

HOW TO APPROACH A CRITICAL THINKING TASK

How can you apply theory and technique to help you think better? Suppose you recognise that critical thinking is required to solve a specific problem. This could be an essay question set by one of your lecturers, an issue arising from problem-based learning, or even a domestic matter such as what type of car to buy or where best to rent a flat. The pointers below will help you to arrive at a logical answer. Although presented sequentially, you should regard this listing as a menu rather than a recipe – think about the different stages and how they might be useful for the specific issue under consideration and your own style of work. Adopt or reject them as you see fit, or, according to your needs, change their order.

- **Decide exactly what the problem is.** An important preliminary task is to make sure you have identified this properly. Write down a description of the problem or issue – if this is not already provided for you – taking care to be very precise with your wording. If a specific instruction has been given as part of the exercise, then

Table 2.3 Examples of Benjamin Bloom's taxonomy of thinking processes within representative university subjects

Bloom's categories of thinking processes (in ascending order of difficulty)	Law	Examples	
		Arts subjects, e.g. history or politics	Numerical subject e.g. engineering
Knowledge	You might know the name and date of a case, statute or treaty without understanding its relevance.	You might know that a river was an important geographical and political boundary in international relations, without being able to identify why.	You might be able to write down a particular mathematical equation, without understanding what the symbols mean or where it might be applied.
Comprehension	You would understand the principle of law contained in the legislation or case law, and its wider context.	You would understand that the river forms a natural barrier which can be easily identified and defended.	You would understand what the symbols in an equation mean and how and when to apply it.
Application	You would be able to identify situations to which the principle of law would apply.	You might use this knowledge to explain the terms of a peace treaty.	You would be able to use the equation to obtain a result, given background information.
Analysis	You could relate the facts of a particular scenario to the principle of law to uncover the extent of its application, using appropriate authority.	You could explain the importance of the river as a boundary as being of importance to the territorial gains/ losses for signatories to the peace treaty.	You could explain the theoretical process involved in deriving the equation.
Synthesis	By a process of reasoning and analogy, you could predict how the law might be applied under given circumstances.	You could identify this notion and relate it to the recurrence of this issue in later treaties or factors governing further hostilities and subsequent implications.	You could be able to take one equation, link it with another and arrive at a new mathematical relationship or conclusion.
Evaluation	You might be able to advise a client based on your own judgement, after weighing up and evaluating all available options.	You would be able to discuss whether the use of this boundary was an obstacle to resolving the terms of the treaty to the satisfaction of all parties.	You would be able to discuss the limitations of an equation based on its derivation and the underlying assumptions behind this.

analyse its phrasing carefully, to make sure you understand all possible meanings. If you are working in a group (Ch 9), then ideally all members should agree on the group's interpretation.

● **Organise your approach to the problem.** You might start with a 'brainstorm' (Ch 4) to identify potential solutions or viewpoints. This can be a solo or group activity and typically might consist of three phases:

1 **Open thinking.** Consider the issue or question from all possible angles or positions and write down everything you come up with. Don't worry at this stage about the relevance or importance of your ideas. A 'spider diagram' or 'mind map' (Ch 12) can be used to lay out your thoughts.

2 **Organisation.** Next, you should try to arrange your ideas into categories or subheadings, or group them as supporting or opposing a viewpoint.

3 **Analysis.** Now you need to decide about the relevance of the grouped points to the original problem. Reject trivial or irrelevant ideas and rank or prioritise those that seem relevant. This involves several further activities discussed below.

● **Obtain background information and check your comprehension of the facts.** You need to gather relevant information and ideas to support your viewpoint or position, provide examples or suggest a range of interpretations or approaches. You also need to ensure you fully understand the information you have gathered. This could be as simple as using dictionaries and technical works to find out the precise meaning of key words; it might involve discussing the ideas with your peers or a member of staff; or you could read a range of texts to see how others interpret your topic.

 Sharpening your research skills

Consult the following chapters for further information and practical tips:

■ Reading sources and note-taking: Chapter 11, Chapter 12

■ Analysing information: Chapter 5, Chapter 10

■ Avoiding plagiarism: Chapter 13

■ Collecting information that will allow you to cite your sources: Chapter 14

- **Check relevance.** Now consider the information you have gathered, your thoughts and how these might apply to your question. You may need to re-analyse the question. You will then need to marshal the evidence you have collected, for example: for or against a proposition; supporting or opposing an argument or theory. You may find it useful to prepare a table or grid to organise the information (Ch 12) – this will also help you balance your thoughts. Be ruthless in rejecting irrelevant or inconsequential material.

- **Think through your argument, and how you can support it.** Having considered relevant information and positions, you should arrive at a personal viewpoint (Ch 5), and then construct your discussion or conclusion around this. When writing about your conclusion, you must take care to avoid value judgements or other kinds of expression of opinion that are not supported by evidence or sources (p. 28). This is one reason why frequent citation and referencing is demanded in academic work (Chs 13 and 14).

- **Get cracking on your answer.** In many academic situations, this will be a written piece of work, and once you have decided on what you want to say, writing this up should be much easier. In other cases, the 'answer' may be action in terms of (say) a purchase or other decision.

Can a methodical approach also inspire you creatively?

Some tasks or problems require creative solutions. We all recognise that ideas often come to us when we are not even trying to think about the issues. Nevertheless, technique can sometimes help to create the right mental environment for inspiration. Chapter 4 provides some tips for achieving this.

PUTTING FORWARD A BALANCED AND UNBIASED ANALYSIS

In academic situations, the outcome of critical thinking should always be balanced. This means that due consideration must be given to all sides of a topic, before arriving at a personal viewpoint based on your interpretation of the evidence.

'Bias' is the opposite of such even-handedness and arises because a person's views are affected by such factors as:

- a specific past experience;
- their culture or ethnicity;
- their gender;
- having a strong political stance;
- looking at a small or skewed sample of sources;
- having a vested interest in a particular outcome.

Awareness, and especially self-awareness, is important in minimising some of these sources of bias. This is not always easy to achieve. However, if you try to read widely around the topic, you may become aware of a greater variety of possible viewpoints on relevant issues, and some of these sources will also draw attention to bias in others. This will help you become more alert to this possibility in your own position. Discussing issues with others is another way of gaining a wider perspective.

When writing up your assignment, you should make a determined effort to balance your discussion. You should mention the conclusions of others, but also provide well-argued reasons why you disagree. At the same time, you should always strive to be open-minded. Although you might admit to starting with preconceived ideas about a topic, you should try to be receptive to the ideas of others. You may find that your initial thoughts become altered by what you are reading and discussing.

 Think about opposing viewpoints

One way of ensuring balance is to take a 'Devil's advocate' stance at some point in your deliberations. In this context, this means artificially taking a view you might not agree with, so that you can reveal the strengths and weaknesses of your preferred argument.

The language you use can help you to achieve balance. In particular, try to avoid 'absolutes'. Be careful with words that imply that there are no exceptions, for example: 'always', 'never', 'all' and 'every'. These words can only be used if you wish to imply 100% certainty. Instead, it may be better to use the 'hedging' language typical of academic writing, such as 'this suggests', 'it may be', or 'it seems that' (see Table 16.2).

If you feel there is not enough evidence to support *any* conclusion, be prepared to suspend judgement. However, if your assignment requires you to arrive at a position on a subject, you should try your best to do this: you should avoid sitting on the fence and should come down on one side or the other, supporting your reasons with evidence (see **Ch 5**).

COMMON PITFALLS IN THINKING

Equally as important as understanding of the characteristics of deeper thinking is an awareness of the pitfalls of shallow thinking. Apart from bias, discussed above, here are some of the common bad habits and errors that we all make from time to time.

- **Rushing to conclusions** – in the context of general academic work, this means basing a view on very little reading around the subject. Also included in this category might be situations such as relying on too few observations or experiments; or not carrying out the necessary statistical analysis of results.
- **Generalising** – this means drawing a conclusion from one (or few) cases. An awareness of other possibilities is important to avoid this mistake.
- **Oversimplifying** – this means arriving at a conclusion that does not take account of potential complexities or other possible answers.
- **Personalising** – this means drawing conclusions based on your own experience or being subjective about an issue.
- **Thinking in terms of stereotypes** – here, the danger is of thinking in terms of 'standardised' ideas, especially about groups of people. This 'received wisdom' may come about due to one's upbringing, gender, ethnicity and so on, and involves basing an opinion on appearances, rather than the underlying facts.
- **Believing propaganda** – this is false or incomplete information that supports a particular political or moral view.

Being descriptive rather than analytical

This is regarded as a symptom of shallow thinking. Overly descriptive work, a common student error, relies too much on quotes, facts or statements. Being analytical, in contrast, involves explaining the importance and context of information and showing an understanding of what it means or implies.

- **Using fallacious arguments** – this means that there is a break in the logic of your argument or that something you are relying on in your argument is not true. This type of error is discussed further in Chapter 6.

- **Making value judgements** – These are statements that reflect the views and values of the speaker or writer rather than the objective reality of what is being assessed or considered. Value judgements often imply some sense of being pejorative (negative).

 Examples of value judgements

In the example: *'Australian wines are the best – they are full bodied and smooth'*, the assumption is made that the listener/reader will share the view that a good wine needs to be full bodied and smooth – a value judgement. Similar assumptions may be inherent in descriptive phrases. For example, if a person is sympathetic to a cause they may refer to those who support it as members of a 'pressure group'; if they disagree with the cause, then its members become 'militants'; similarly 'conservationists' versus 'tree-huggers'; 'freedom fighters' versus 'insurgents'.

As with bias, many of these errors can be avoided by reading more widely around your subject – either to take account of a greater selection of views, the way they have been presented, or the methods used to analyse findings. Look beneath the surface of what you read. It is important to decide whether sources are dealing with facts or opinions; examine any assumptions made, including your own; and think about the motivation of writers. Rather than restating and describing your sources, focus on what they *mean* by what they write.

 PRACTICAL TIPS FOR THINKING CRITICALLY

Focus on the task in hand. It is very easy to become distracted when reading around a subject, or when discussing problems with others. Take care not to waste too much time on preliminaries and start relevant action as quickly as possible.

Write down your thoughts. The act of writing your thoughts is important as this forces you to clarify them. Also, since ideas are often fleeting, it makes sense to ensure you have a permanent record. Reviewing what you have written makes you more critical and can lead you on to new ideas.

When quoting evidence, use appropriate citations. This is important as it shows you have read relevant source material and helps you avoid plagiarism (Ch 15). The conventions for citation vary among subjects, so consult course handbooks or other information and make sure you follow the instructions carefully, or you may lose marks.

Draw on the ideas and opinions of your peers and lecturers. Discussions with others can be very fruitful, revealing a range of interpretations that you might not have thought about yourself. You may find it useful to bounce ideas off others. Tutors can provide useful guidance once you have done some reading and are usually pleased to be asked for help.

Keep asking yourself questions. A good way to think more deeply is to ask questions, even after you feel a matter is resolved or you understand it well. Nearly all critical thinking is the result of asking questions.

 AND NOW . . .

2.1 Analyse the instruction words in past exam papers. Note which types of instruction words are commonly used. First check that you understand what is expected in relation to each word (see Table 2.2) then, taking into account the subject and the way in which it has been taught, what level of thinking you are expected to demonstrate in your exam answers. If you are in doubt, ask a lecturer to explain.

2.2 Practise seeing different sides of an argument. Choose a topic, perhaps one on which you have strong views (for example, a political matter, such as state support for private schooling; or an ethical one, such as the need for vivisection or abortion). Write down the supporting arguments for both sides of the issue, focusing on your least favoured option. This will help you see both sides of a debate as a matter of course.

2.3 Analyse the opinion and letters sections of a newspaper. These are often a rich source of writing with bias, prejudice and forms of fallacy. See if you can spot opinion columns or letters that are guilty of the common pitfalls in thinking described on pp. 27–8.

3

REFLECTIVE THINKING

How to evaluate your feelings in academic contexts

Reflection is frequently involved in learning. The overall process can be broken down into subsidiary elements, which reveals the individual skills required for proficiency. A range of frameworks are favoured for recording reflection in the different academic disciplines, each requiring a specific approach. In tackling these assignments, the relevant learning outcomes and marking criteria must always be taken into account.

KEY TOPICS

→ Academic contexts for reflection

→ Processes involved in reflection

→ Reflection in practice

→ Assessment of reflection

KEY TERMS

Blog   Extra-curricular activity   Learning journal   Learning outcome
Marking criteria   Metacognition   Objective   Personal development plan
Portfolio   Reflective thinking   Scenario   Sketchbook   Subjective

Reflection was defined in Chapter 1 as a process where an individual evaluates an event or experience to arrive at a deeper understanding of the incident and related issues. In this chapter the aim is to explore how this process is incorporated into university teaching, and to discuss how it is assessed.

ACADEMIC CONTEXTS FOR REFLECTION

It is part of human nature to learn continually from experience, generally becoming more proficient and wiser in our responses to events as we grow older. Reflection is thus an important part of being an effective learner (Ch 1). Academic life presents many situations where you can benefit from this form of introspection, including:

- reviewing your learning experiences, such as lectures, tutorials and practicals;
- analysing your subjective reactions to the topics in your course;
- analysing your experience of being assessed;
- reacting to feedback from staff;
- planning for your personal development;
- thinking about your career after graduation.

In addition, certain academic exercises are constructed to mimic experiences in the professions, allowing you to build specialist expertise by analysing your responses in relevant scenarios and develop effective patterns of behaviour. Your reflection in these instances may be assessed formally with the aim of developing the habit of continuing self-evaluation. Examples of these types of assignment might include:

- analysing classroom interactions for a novice teacher;
- evaluating client or court exchanges for a would-be lawyer or accountant;
- reviewing case management for a trainee social worker;
- reviewing texts for views on two political systems;
- reviewing patient treatment and relationships for student nurses, doctors or dentists.

Reflection as a professional activity

Students studying for vocational (professional) degrees will often find that opportunities for reflection are provided in their coursework and that this activity is assessed. This emphasis is because reflective behaviour is regarded as a key aspect of continuing professional development, ensuring that practitioners constantly review their patterns of work and keep up-to-date with developments in their field of expertise.

Table 3.1 Some examples of reflection in professional training

Discipline and scenario	Narrative on reflective exercise
Nursing John is a trainee nurse, taking part in a placement in a surgical ward, where he was contributing to the treatment of patients recovering from a range of operations.	John was allocated a specific patient, Edith, and asked to explore his role in her treatment and recovery. His report was required to provide background information about the patient's condition and the necessary surgical intervention. He was then expected to give details of his involvement in Edith's preparation for surgery and rehabilitation, including: monitoring vital signs; administration of drugs; wound dressing; dietary requirements; washing and toilet; dealing with relatives; and discharge from the ward. His account was expected to contain personal reflections on both his interactions with the patient and the success of the treatment.
Social work Hilda is a social work student and as part of her studies has been asked to shadow an experienced social worker for a day.	Hilda was expected to select one 'difficult' client from the case load of the qualified social worker, Brian, look into the background of the case, comment on the particular meeting she observed, and discuss with Brian how he thought the client's issues would eventually be resolved. Drawing on this information and experience, she was expected to reflect on how she would deal with this individual in future meetings to arrive at the best possible outcome.
Art and design Hui Zhong is studying jewellery and has been asked to assemble a sketchbook as part of a studio exercise with the title 'sunshine'.	Hui Zhong was expected to use the sources collected in her sketchbook to help her design and then make a piece of jewellery. In so doing, she was asked to reflect on what the sources meant to her and how she aimed to translate them into a jewellery item. Following the title of the exercise, she collected a range of images of the sun's rays breaking through clouds. To Hui Zhong, this image is associated with a positive change in the weather and hence is a cipher for optimism – and, she feels, an ideal sentiment for a customer buying a brooch for a new sweetheart. These thoughts led to others relating to the design ('billowing swirls' and 'sparkling shafts') and the materials (a mix of silver and gold) and hence to the sketch for a design and ultimately the manufacture of the piece itself.
Engineering Fisal is a product engineering student who has carried out an industry-sponsored project while in placement at a local manufacturing firm.	Fisal was accepted in a placement at Suqqit Pumps Ltd where he was asked to work with the manager of the production line, Jimmy. The engineering school staff met with Fisal and Jimmy at an early stage to discuss his project and together they defined a project to explore why a proportion of pumps were failing quality control by not meeting suction rate thresholds. Fisal dismantled the failing pumps and compared them with a sample of satisfactory units. He eventually discovered that there were flaws in one of the membranes in most of the failing pumps and suggested reasons for this and how it might be solved by a modification to the production process. His report was expected to provide an account of the project and the outcomes but also reflection on his working relationships while on placement and on the skills he needed to carry out the work successfully.

The selection of an episode to reflect upon may come after the event, as in the use of 'critical incidents' in nursing studies (p. 35). Sometimes a 'mock' situation is set up within the campus with students or actors playing roles within the scenario. In other cases, the training takes place in the workplace during a placement or internship in which case real patients or clients may be involved. Table 3.1 provides some examples taken from a cross-section of disciplines.

PROCESSES INVOLVED IN REFLECTION

The educational researcher Graham Gibbs described the different processes of reflection as part of a cyclical pattern of behaviour (Gibbs, 1988). This cycle (Figure 3.1) contains the following elements:

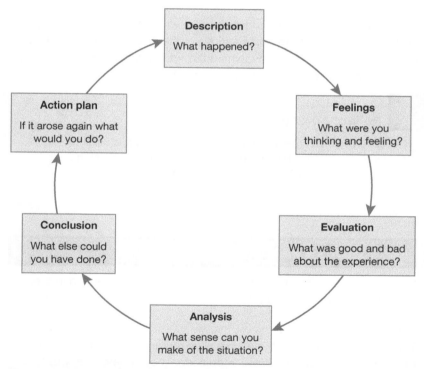

Figure 3.1 The reflective cycle described by Gibbs (1988)

1 **Description.** This requires your powers of observation and your ability to record the situation and associated events with accuracy and impartiality.

2 **Feelings.** Here, you are expected to record your reactions to events. This can be a difficult part of reflection because we are usually taught to depersonalise our thinking and writing when carrying out academic work.

3 **Evaluation.** Here, you are expected to weigh up the positive and negative aspects of the experience.

4 **Analysis.** This element of reflection requires you to benchmark your personal interactions against relevant theory or other published work.

5 **Conclusion.** This should be a summary of your current response to events, including discussion of what you learned and how you might respond in future.

6 **Action plan.** This is a method of formalising the outcome of your reflection.

The cyclical nature of the process occurs when the outcome of a prior cycle of reflection informs your actions in the next similar event. This is commonplace at university, where the educational process involves building on past learning and developing skills.

Reflection and metacognition

Reflection involves metacognition (p. 23), because it is used to construct meaning within an existing framework of understanding. This requires awareness of both the framework and its principles of operation.

REFLECTION IN PRACTICE

Various specialised types of reflective exercise are employed in the different academic disciplines.

The reflective report

This kind of assignment is used in a wide range of situations, often in response to a specific scenario or episode. They are especially used to analyse responses to 'set piece' professional training situations (p. 31). The report is often structured in sections, following the Gibbs cycle described above. However, this may be simplified, for example by combining 'evaluation' and analysis' into an 'interpretation' section.

Mapping process to report structure

Where the recommended structure for your reflective assignment differs from Gibbs' six subdivisions of reflective activity (Fig. 3.1), it may integrate some processes under a particular heading. If this is the case, you may find it useful to map the subdivisions in both schemes against each other to ensure you cover all aspects (see Table 18.2, p. 230, regarding content).

Critical incident analysis

Some disciplines, especially those in the caring professions, encourage reflective thinking by analysing what are called critical incidents – events regarded as difficult or personally challenging. These may feature matters of ethics, competence, or situations marked by conflict or aggression. They often involve elements of professional practice, communication, relationships, cultural customs, beliefs or emotions. Retrospective analysis can also apply to events with positive outcomes, for example, where a meeting went particularly well or where a patient was happy with the resolution of a problem. The purpose of the analysis is not to make personal criticisms of those involved in the incident but to examine ways in which the situation could have been dealt with more appropriately. In this way, students are encouraged to reflect on their own learning, professional competence, attitudes and beliefs.

The learning journal

In essence, this consists of a sequential diary of events and your reactions to them. A learning journal is typically used to record your experiences and your development during a focused spell of activity (for example, as a student teacher during a placement). The emphasis is on a personal analysis of what you have learned and how. You may be asked to provide an evaluation of your journal to self-assess your progress. This evaluation may itself be assessed by staff.

Keeping notes in this form ensures that you are actively involved in the learning process and that the outcomes are personalised to your needs. Rather than the lecturers dictating the agenda, it is you who takes control and who, through the reflective process, maximises the benefits of your experience. In some professions, an additional aim is to ensure that you start working as you should continue, developing the habits of a being a 'reflective practitioner' (Schön, 1983).

Critical incidents – an example from nursing

Nursing students may be asked to analyse an event that they have witnessed where actions taken were regarded, in the student's view, as inappropriate. For example, a hospital patient may have been allowed to shower without supervision and have fallen on the floor suffering a head injury. The ward was short-staffed and the patient was returned to bed without anyone checking to see whether the fall had been caused by slipping on the wet floor or by some momentary loss of consciousness. The student may have been either an observer or a participant in the incident and, as a trainee, is not meant to intervene directly. However, for the purposes of assessment, the student may use this critical incident for analysis in various respects such as:

■ explaining the reasons for the failure to monitor the patient in the shower;

■ identifying health and safety issues and duty of care;

■ noting possible medical conditions that might have contributed to the fall and how these should have been checked;

■ suggesting possible ways in which a similar situation ought to be dealt with and ways in which it could be avoided in future.

The blog

A blog (short for web-log) is an online record of your experiences which is intended to be shared with others. An advantage of this format is that images, videos and links to other websites are easily incorporated. Indeed, these may critical as a source of material for reflection. Another benefit of blogs is that they can include space for others to discuss the entries. This might be comments and guidance from your lecturer, or a debate among your peer group. Blogs that are truly open may attract comments from across the world. One disadvantage of blogs to watch out for is that they can absorb a lot of your time.

Different types of blogs involve a range of reflective content:

● a research blog may detail a continuing investigation of a topic by one person or a group, with relatively little reflective content;

● a diary blog will document events over a period of time and may contain some reflection;

- a creative blog may allow you to draw together source materials for your work and reflect on what these mean to you (see also sketchbook, below);
- a learning blog may be the online equivalent of a learning journal and focus strongly on the reflective element.

Blogger beware

You probably won't know when your blog is being consulted so you should assume that a peer or a staff member might be looking at it at any point. Take care when constructing and uploading your blog entries not to present incomplete and unchecked work. If anything in your blog is at all controversial or intensely personal, it is always a good idea to 'sit' on a draft overnight and re-read this in the cold light of another day before posting.

The sketchbook

In the creative arts, the sketchbook is a traditional method of assembling source materials and your thoughts about them with the aim of informing the artistic process. A wide range of visual materials can be included, for example:

- your own sketches;
- photos;
- images taken from magazines and other sources;
- magazine cuttings or fabric swatches showing particular colours or colour combinations;
- found objects;
- words from outside sources, such as quotes or song lyrics;
- your own notes, either reflective on the sources or technical, covering details of how you intend to choose and use an artistic medium.

Special aspects of reflection in the creative arts

- Helping the creative process (Ch 4)
- Allowing you to examine your work in a detached way
- Helping you to solve problems with your work, for example, where a design isn't working
- Documenting your progress as an artist
- Allowing you to demonstrate your originality
- Assisting you to explain your work, for example during a crit

A sketchbook can and should be a very personal thing, and thus may not be tuned to the expectations of your lecturers. You need to preserve your originality yet also meet the requirements of your course. Do not be worried if you feel your initial work falls short of your personal expectations or those of the course. This is all part of the development process, and it is often the way you work through this which is being both facilitated and accessed via the sketchbook.

Collecting source material for a sketchbook

You'll need to keep your eyes open and to be on the look-out continually for potential sources, not only for current exercises but also for exercises in the future. You'll also need a place to store these items prior to selecting items for the sketchbook.

The portfolio and e-portfolio

The term 'portfolio' is used as a catch-all that covers a wide range of methods for collating learning material and assessed work. The name derives from the word for a portable case for carrying loose papers; however, most portfolios these days are presented online and are known as e-portfolios. A *process portfolio* contains developmental material demonstrating the progression of your ability or of a specific project you are carrying out, while a *product portfolio* contains final versions of work submitted as part of your studies.

Examples of portfolio use include:

- storing or copying coursework, either completed or in development (this may be called a webfolio);
- as a medium for collaborating with project group members;
- sharing your work with others, such as a personal tutor or a potential employer;
- noting the outcomes of meetings with staff;
- as a means of collecting evidence of the development or achievement of certain skills;
- developing your curriculum vitae;
- logging your reflections as you move through your studies.

Sharing an e-portfolio

This is usually a process under your command, so draft or personal material is not available to staff or others. Take care that when you do share your work, you have double-checked the material and restricted access to areas you would rather keep private. You may wish to load your work in pdf format, so that others are unable to copy or modify it. This can be done in later versions of Microsoft Office using the *Save as > Save as type > PDF* command.

The work involved in assembling a high-quality e-portfolio may be extensive and should not be underestimated. Careful planning and time-management will be required (**Chs 8** and **15**).

The personal development plan

A personal development plan (or PDP) is used in many fields of study as part of a structured process to assist you to plan for the future by reflecting on your learning, performance and achievements. It may involve you thinking about your personality, education and potential career. Many professional bodies that validate degrees encourage PDP activities and there is a drive to introduce PDP schemes for most degrees.

The main aims of a PDP are to help you:

- record and reflect upon events in your education;
- review, plan and take responsibility for your personal development;
- identify personal goals and evaluate your progress towards them;
- become a more independent, confident and self-directed person;
- start your career planning and enhance your employability;
- mirror the process of continuing professional development in a future employment.

Your PDP may focus on both coursework and extra-curricular activities. While employers will rely on your university transcript as evidence of your academic success, they will also be interested in your non-academic achievements as an indicator of your personal qualities. A PDP is one mechanism for collecting evidence about these interests and for reflecting on them. Your PDP may be assessed and this will involve similar criteria to those used for other portfolios and for reflection in general (Table 3.2).

Keeping up with your PDP

The advantages of creating a PDP are clear to see, but the lengthy timescale of its development may mean that other tasks take priority. You should make a diary note to revisit the PDP on a regular basis. One stimulus for this may occur when you are searching for vacation work and an updated curriculum vitae is required.

ASSESSMENT OF REFLECTION

The subsidiary elements of reflection discussed on p. 33 provide a framework for assessment and you should recognise some or all of these aspects in the exercises you are asked to complete, even though the sections might have different titles and certain elements may be combined or omitted. The precise details will depend on the situation with which you are presented, the overall aims of your course and your lecturers' specific focus within the topic being covered.

How can such a personal matter as reflection be evaluated?

You may ask yourself how reflection can be fairly assessed, if the feelings it comprises are personal. Can your lecturers say what is right or wrong in that situation? Won't their views be subjective? The answer to this question is that it is generally the *process* of reflection that is evaluated, rather than the specific personal details. That said, there are clearly boundaries to what would be considered an appropriate professional response to events.

It is vital to consult at an early stage the learning outcomes and assessment criteria for any exercises involving reflection. These may be found in your course handbook. They indicate what you should try to achieve and what grades your lecturers will award for different qualities of work. They will allow you to orientate and plan your activity and gauge the depth of thinking required and how it should be displayed. Table 3.2 provides examples of both of these information sources.

Because reflection is personal, many students find it hard to find the right words or 'voice' to describe their experiences, and yet this is essential if the quality of your reflection is to be assessed as part of your studies. Chapter 18 examines the language of reflection and how this should be used for different formats of assessed work.

Table 3.2 Representative marking criteria for a reflective report – a practice diary in the field of forensic psychology. The criteria are mapped to the four levels of marks recognised by the British Psychological Society's Statutes.

Marking criteria
Distinction: Excellent work demonstrating the ability to work independently and competently across all of the competencies required for this Core Role. The exemplars (including the practice diary) demonstrate excellent organisation and provide a comprehensive illustration of how the candidate meets all of the requirements. Evidence that the candidate has employed a systematic approach to work undertaken and considered ethical issues. The supervision log, practice diary and summary statement all provide substantial evidence of reflective practice. Excellent presentation in accordance with the standards set.
Competence demonstrated: Satisfactory work demonstrating an adequate level of potential to work competently across the majority of competencies required for this Core Role. Work represented in the exemplar is clearly of a forensic nature and provides evidence of depth and breadth of experience. Evidence of reflective practice is provided through the supervision log and practice diary or summary statement. Ethical guidelines have been observed. Satisfactory presentation overall. Assessors may allow weaknesses in some competencies to be compensated for by other areas of strength.
Conditional pass: This mark is available only where clerical errors are identified, including issues such as signatures required on the supervision log; editing or clarification of tables; grammatical and typographical errors; referencing errors; any failure to anonymise third parties. The conditional pass work must be re-submitted within one month: hence recommendations for Conditional passes must be for clerical issues, and rectifiable within one month. Conditional passes are not designed for additional evidence collation/collection. Where this is wanted, the assessor should consider is it really needed? If yes, then a fail must be awarded. If it is not essential, it can be provided as a piece of advice and guidance as part of a pass report.
Competence not yet demonstrated: The work described in the exemplar is significantly flawed and demonstrates an inadequate level of competence. The following issues may be grounds for failure: • Ignoring key areas for assessment and intervention (where such work is not to be carried out, it should at least be recognised as a need/limitation) • Significant failure to observe ethical guidelines • Significantly flawed research or evaluation designs • Little or no evidence of reflective practice • Significant deviations from the exemplar plan (without sufficient explanation) • A lack of primary evidence (which can include the narrative account) • Insufficient time over the Core Role (while some slippage exists for the amount of 'days' required for each exemplar within a Core Role, the rough guide of three months per exemplar remains) • Presentation is poor and disorganised so that assessment is difficult.

Taken from 'Marking Criteria for Assessing Portfolios submitted for the Qualification in Forensic Psychology (Stage 2)' (available 26 February 2012 as the document *QFP marking criteria* from *http://www.bps.org.uk/careers-education-training/society-qualifications/forensic-psychology/qfp-2011-documents/qualificati*). An 'exemplar' is a report of a piece of work that demonstrates the candidate's competence. 'Core Role' refers to one of four specified areas of professional expertise.

Revisit the rationale for reflection. Although it is natural for students to focus on assessment, and to try to give a 'right answer' for assignments, it is important to realise that reflection is primarily a learning exercise, and as such should be viewed as an opportunity for self-development rather than one for gaining marks.

Keep the balance between description and analysis in mind. Many students fall into the trap of providing too much detail without looking at the bigger picture.

Ask a staff member for advice. If you are really uncertain about what you are writing, take a draft to your lecturer and ask for comments. He or she may be able to point out how phrasing can improve the content or further aspects where you might comment.

 AND NOW ...

3.1 Find out what methods of recording reflection will be used in your course. What skills will you need to use these formats? Is there any training or exploration you might carry out beforehand to facilitate their use and enhance your performance? For example, if a blog is to be hosted on a specific website platform, do you know your way around this and do you know how to use all its features?

3.2 Assess your ability to perform the different elements of reflection (as discussed on pp. 33 and 230). What skills will you need for these activities? Is there any training or exploration you might carry out beforehand to enhance your performance? For example, have you mastered the necessary language conventions (Ch 18)?

3.3 Review your PDP and the support for personal development planning that your institution provides. How well are you engaging with this framework? Have you used it to reflect on your progress so far – both in coursework and extra-curricular activities? How might you extract benefit from your PDP?

4

CREATIVE THINKING

How to generate innovative and original ideas

Creativity and originality are highly important attributes for academic studies and employment and they are often key elements of critical thinking. You will find many situations where creativity is required at university, from essay writing to poster design. A number of techniques have been suggested for sparking original thought.

KEY TOPICS

→ Being creative in academic study

→ What does it take to be creative?

→ Methods for stimulating innovative thinking

KEY TERMS

Brainstorming   Creativity   Freewriting   Interdisciplinary   Lateral thinking
Mood board   Originality   Paradigm   Sketchbook

Creativity is a multi-stranded activity with the common theme that it results in fresh approaches to problems (Ch 1). The status of innovative and creative output is particularly evident in artistic and design-led subjects, but it also has its place in studies of the humanities and sciences. It is seen as a key graduate attribute for many jobs (Ch 21).

What do people have say about creativity?

'Imagination is more important than knowledge.' (Albert Einstein)

'An essential aspect of creativity is not being afraid to fail.' (Edwin Land)

'Genius is one percent inspiration and ninety-nine percent perspiration.' (Thomas Edison)

BEING CREATIVE IN ACADEMIC STUDY

Finding a new way of looking at a topic or a novel solution to a problem is vital for the advancement of knowledge and understanding. For this reason, originality is a highly regarded quality in nearly all academic subjects. A close look at assessment criteria will often show you that finding a new perspective on a topic is used as an indicator of first-class work, regardless of discipline.

i Creativity, originality and appropriateness

In fine art and some forms of writing, the emphasis for creativity is on originality; however, in most practical subjects, including design, the additional criterion of appropriateness is assumed. Finding a *relevant* new idea is valued in most academic disciplines.

Original thinking tends to result in small-scale changes in academic understanding. Occasionally, however, major 'paradigm shifts' occur after important new ideas, concepts or discoveries come to the fore. These events sometimes involve a period of intense opposition from proponents of 'established' understanding. Even with small-scale changes in thinking, differences of opinion are part-and-parcel of academic debate (Ch 6) and often aid the development of an idea by requiring the proponents of different ideas to defend the logic of their position. Some of your assignments may require you to model this process, by inviting you to outline and discuss contrary viewpoints.

Many advances come from cross-fertilisation of ideas in interdisciplinary studies. Here, approaches and techniques developed for one field may find application in another, or a combination of methods and ideas from different areas may give rise to completely new thinking or a novel approach. You may recognise instances where this has occurred in your subject.

WHAT DOES IT TAKE TO BE CREATIVE?

Many new ideas involve 'lateral thinking', an expression first coined by Edward de Bono. This means jumping out of past thought patterns and concepts ('thinking out of the box'). It involves challenging the assumptions or limitations that apparently define a situation, and choosing a new perspective on the problem.

Not surprisingly, then, it is important to support free and unfettered thinking. This involves resisting or moving away from the influences of others' prior arguments or work, one's own preconceptions or apparent boundaries. Finding a personal route to liberate your thoughts is essential for switching on your creativity.

However, thinking with freedom should not be confused with being ignorant about your topic. New ideas rarely arise independently from a framework of understanding. This mental 'scaffolding' is important to understand the problem, the underlying principles and the language in which a solution might be described. You need to find a balance so your fresh ideas are not overly constrained by these influences.

Nor should you allow thoughts about practicalities to stifle your initial thoughts. What is required for creativity is an initial focus on the *generation* of ideas, without these being constrained by theory or feasibility. You should delay the process of selecting those ideas which are viable as a secondary process.

Overcoming barriers to creativity

Exercises requiring creativity are difficult for many students. Problems may arise due to:

- an incomplete understanding of the topic – making it feel difficult to synthesise something new
- being 'blocked' – not knowing how to generate ideas
- fear of failure – worrying that ideas will not be positively received
- perfectionism – feeling that what is produced should be perfect
- procrastination – delaying starting for a range of possible reasons including some of the above.

What is vital is to find a way of starting. Once into the work, things tend to proceed a lot more easily.

Your mind needs stimuli to come up with ideas. You can select these stimuli and try to focus your thoughts or set up conditions that support unpredictable new thinking. However, the results may not be immediate: sometimes original thoughts come in unusual places and at unexpected times. It is said that Archimedes' 'eureka' inspiration about measuring the density of gold came while he was having a bath, while Einstein is said to have conceived the Theory of General Relativity in a dream.

Reading and note-making as adjuncts to creativity

Sometimes when you have no ideas, it is because you lack the seed to grow them. At the start of an assignment, you might need to read around the subject to find out more about it. If stalled in the middle, finding a new source with a fresh approach might kick-start your own thinking. It is important not simply to read: you need to take notes, so you keep things active and retain your thoughts. Your notes should be of three main types:

1 notes about the subject material (Ch 12);

2 source details, so you can cite these and avoid plagiarism (Ch 13);

3 your own ideas, as these appear through association as you read.

It is a good idea to keep a written summary of the essay title or problem alongside these notes and refer to it from time to time, so that your mind remains connected with the problem.

METHODS FOR STIMULATING INNOVATIVE THINKING

From the preceding discussion, it seems that you can't easily 'force' creativity; all you can try to do is set up the right conditions to allow it to happen. A range of different techniques have been developed to help with this, each of which might suit different personality types. Try any that seem effective and attractive to you. There can be no guarantees with these methods, but they may help you move towards a solution for your particular task.

Tailoring your idea-generating approach to your learning style

First, try the short VARK questionnaire at *www.vark-learn.com* (created by Neil Fleming) to diagnose your learning preference. Then, following the tips on that website, try the following approaches:

- **Visual preference:** use doodles and drawings to spark ideas
- **Kinesthetic preference:** think while exercising or role-play the problem
- **Read–write preference:** try freewriting or word association
- **Aural preference:** discuss the problem with others
- **Multimodal preference:** attempt any or all of the above, especially those that particularly attract you

Brainstorming

This is probably the most-used technique for generating ideas. It means coming up with a range of thoughts about a topic before trying to make sense of them. The advertising executive Alex Osborn, who coined the term, proposed that the four keys to effective brainstorming are:

1 think of as many ideas as possible – the more you generate, the greater the chance of finding an answer;

2 encourage seemingly eccentric lines of thought – even your wildest ideas might give rise to further ideas and even solutions;

3 resist evaluating the ideas until later – the process of judgement may stifle your creativity;

4 look for associations between your ideas – this may give rise to new patterns of thinking.

Brainstorming as part of teamwork can be particularly effective as the group members exchange and build ideas together.

Note-making techniques for capturing your thoughts

Most people use a mind map (p. 149) to capture their ideas during brainstorming or when finding connections, and this method can also incorporate visual concepts. In tasks where the subject is directed (such as an essay), the title or description of the topic should be written out in the centre of the mindmap so it can be referred to continually. Other note-making techniques (Ch 12) may appeal for certain exercises.

Finding connections

This method is essentially a more focused approach to brainstorming. It involves three main phases. First, write down a short description of your problem (or, for an assignment, the topic or title). Second, try to tease out the different aspects of the problem. Ways of doing this include:

● focusing on each key word or phrase of the description or title in turn to see what thoughts arise;

● addressing the six journalists' queries 'Who?' 'What?' 'When?' 'Where?' 'Why?' 'How?' to the problem;

- viewing the topic from a range of different perspectives, perhaps the different sub-disciplines of your subject. An example of this could be a student writing a general essay in biology who could look at the topic from different angles such as its anatomy, biochemistry, biophysics, ecology, environment, evolution, genetics, physiology – and so on.

The third phase is to review and select from the ideas you have produced.

 Suggestions for finding connections

Here are some possible ways of connecting the words or phrases in your topic to other words and ideas:

- use the *Define: Word* function in your search engine to find definitions and alternative meanings
- use a dictionary or, better, a thesaurus – online, in book form or within a word-processor – to find associated words
- put each of the key words in your problem into a search engine and see what comes up
- do the above, but search for images or videos rather than websites

Making random associations

This technique is suited to relatively undirected tasks. It seeks to stimulate chaotic, unpredictable new thoughts about your core topic. First, write down the topic or brief. Now find 5–10 random unrelated words (nouns are best). You could do this, for example, by flicking through a dictionary, a newspaper, a series of websites, or via an online random word generator such as the one at creativitygames.net (available at ***http://creativitygames.net/random-word-generator***, last accessed 2/3/12). Now try to incorporate each word into a sentence about your topic. This forces you to think in spontaneous ways about it.

Freewriting

This approach aims to get ideas flowing by making you write quickly and continuously about your topic. It particularly helps those with writer's block. First, find an undisturbed location and decide on a specific period of time to spend on the exercise. Now, write down your topic theme and then start writing about it. Don't stop, just keep going, and write as speedily as you can. The idea is to capture a 'stream of consciousness'. Don't worry about what you are writing or why, nor its neatness, grammatical correctness or spelling. If the text seems to drift off-subject don't be concerned – just keep writing (but try to return to the main theme if you can). Finally, after your allocated time is up, review what you have written and select the interesting points. Use these ideas within a further freewriting or brainstorming exercise.

Going on a 'thought walk'

This is meant literally – going on a solo walk to focus on thinking. Perhaps surprisingly, many great thinkers have used this simple method, including Sigmund Freud. Several aspects of the approach may be valuable:

- it gives you undisturbed time and space to think;
- it gets blood circulating to your brain;
- it seems that while part of your brain focuses on the repetitive motor action of walking, another part is released to think;
- you may see random things or events on your walk that stimulate new thinking.

There are other variations on this theme, such as meditation, walking a labyrinth or having a workout in the gym.

Be ready to take notes wherever you are

It is a good idea to keep a portable notebook or recording device with you at all times to store your thoughts. You might also position a pen and pad near your bedside to capture any ideas that come during the night: inspiration at these times is easily forgotten.

Keeping ideas notebooks, sketchbooks, mood boards and inspiration boards

The straightforward reason for keeping an ideas notebook is to prevent valuable thoughts being forgotten. For written notes, a pocket or bag-sized book is best, so it can be carried with you for use at any time, for example, to note ideas that come when day-dreaming on public transport. Laptops, notepads and phones can also be used if preferred.

Sketchbooks (p. 37) are the artists' equivalent of a written ideas notebook and are also used to assist with the long-term development of a train of thought. Mood boards carry out a similar function. These are posters or collages containing many images, samples or text often pinned to a board or collected digitally. They tend to be used in design-based subjects to build a 'feel' behind a project.

Digital mood boards

These can be assembled using generic programs such as Microsoft's *PowerPoint* or Jasc Software's *Paint Shop Pro*. There are also simple online programs such as *Mosaic Maker* (available from ***http:// bighugelabs.com/mosaic.php*** [Accessed 29 February 2012]) and more specialised ones like *ImageSpark* (available from ***http://www. imgspark.com/*** [Accessed 29 February 2012]). A range of mobile phone apps (such as *Moodboard*) can be used to capture and store images on the move.

The key processes in creating a mood board are:

1 define the brief for the project;
2 source and collect items for your board;
3 review your items, associate them and annotate the clusters with your thoughts;
4 reject inappropriate material (but don't discard it immediately);
5 identify themes and put these ideas into words;
6 write a summary of your response to the brief.

An inspiration board is similar but is generally more diverse in nature and may not be directly associated with a current project – its aim is to assemble items that arouse creative thought in the owner, for example, things you like, people you admire, or places that stir feelings.

Doodling (aimless drawing) is a potentially valuable activity associated with keeping a notebook or sketchbook in which you simply create images that enter your thoughts and then build on them. The quality does not matter. In artistic subjects, this can lead to germs of ideas for images and designs. In subjects where the outcome is written, the technique can be used to free up the creative part of your brain.

Using visual cues as an alternative to the written word

The analogous activity to reading around the subject in artistic and design-related subjects is to absorb others' thoughts and solutions visually, for example, by:

- visiting an art gallery or museum in fine art
- looking at a range of buildings in architecture
- walking around shops (especially those whose style you admire) in design
- exploring new software in computing

Some of these prompts might assist with written assignments, too. However, whatever the subject, you should not use these activities as an excuse for procrastinating.

PRACTICAL TIPS FOR ENHANCING CREATIVITY

Think about the timing of your work. If it is late at night, or you have just eaten a large meal, you may feel tired and unimaginative. Instead, try working immediately you feel wide awake after a restful sleep or when your body (and brain) has been energised by light exercise.

Incubate the problem. This only works if you have time at your disposal. Simply start doing something else, other than thinking about your task. If there are routine elements to the assignment, such as writing out reference details, do these. Often a relevant idea will leap into your brain when the conscious part is focused on something else.

Be contrarian. Take on the role of someone attacking your own position. Alternatively, re-frame your favoured solution as if it were the complete opposite of the one you have been given, and then try to defend it. Either technique may reveal new avenues for you to pursue.

Never be afraid to fail and do not worry about finding the perfect solution. These allied feelings are barriers to action and to free thinking. Finding an incomplete or part-workable solution is often much better than nothing at all. It might spark a different way of thinking, and you'll never know this unless you try. Moreover, in some academic exercises, you might gain credit for putting forward an unsuccessful idea and then giving a reasoned explanation of why you rejected it.

4.1 Check that you have enough information to understand your problem and frame a solution. If this isn't the case, do a little more research. However, don't allow this activity to delay starting for too long.

4.2 Think about the environment where you do your thinking. Choose a place where you can avoid distractions and apply yourself wholeheartedly. Get away from the TV, switch off your mobile phone and don't visit social networking sites. Sometimes being in familiar places leads to the same old thought patterns (or lack of them). Go to a different studio, library or lab. Sit down at a café rather than at a desk. Visit an art gallery or museum. Going somewhere else could help you break out of a mental rut.

4.3 Talk about your task to a friend or family member. Encourage them to comment on your ideas and to ask you questions. The act of explaining your thoughts will force you to consider them more deeply and others' different perspectives on them may be valuable.

CRITICAL THINKING
IN PRACTICE

5

ARRIVING AT A VIEWPOINT

How to sift fact and opinion to arrive at a position on a topic

For many university assignments, you will be expected to arrive at a position on a topic, and express an opinion on it. This requires skills of research, thinking and argument, and an understanding of related concepts.

KEY TOPICS

→ Dealing with fact, opinion and truth

→ The nature of evidence and proof

→ Arriving at a position and backing it up

KEY TERMS

Evidence   Fact   Falsifiability   Hypothesis   Opinion   Proof
Scientific method   Truth

When analysing complex issues, arriving at a personal viewpoint, or position is rarely easy. It requires that you:

● read and understand sources;
● judge the arguments being put forward;
● check facts and assertions;
● arrive at a position;
● express your position clearly;
● support your view with appropriate evidence.

It is thus a multi-faceted activity, requiring elements of critical thinking (Ch 2), combined with skills of originality (Ch 4), argument (Ch 6), academic writing (Ch 15) and referencing (Ch 14). There can be no formula for arriving at a position, as each specific issue must be judged on its merits. However, understanding some concepts relevant to opinion-making should help you analyse what you read with greater clarity and thereby help you to form a view.

DEALING WITH FACT, OPINION AND TRUTH

When coming to terms with a large reading list and a wide diversity of viewpoints, you can easily become confused and lose sight of the differences between fact, opinion and truth. Being aware of this issue is fundamental to study in many subjects, particularly in the arts, social sciences and law.

A fact is a statement generally acknowledged as valid. Knowledge is built from facts. In the context of critical thinking, fact or knowledge is the basis for further theorising or discussion. Typically, you might find a fact in a textbook, encyclopaedia or website. Not all 'facts' are true – they may change with time as new information is uncovered, and some may be hotly disputed. In academic contexts, therefore, it is often important to establish the reliability of the source of a fact (Ch 10) and vital that you quote the source of your information (Ch 13).

In science, the concept of repeatability is important in relation to facts. Thus, it should be possible to repeat an observation or experiment that established a fact. This is one reason why scientists take such care to describe their materials and methods – results can sometimes depend on these factors. The unreliability of data is often acknowledged: the error associated with a value is calculated or an estimate made of the probability of a hypothesis being wrong or right (Ch 7). This information should be taken into account when using facts in a discussion.

 Should I think for myself?

You will normally be given credit for constructing your own argument, rather than simply following a 'line' expounded in lectures or a standard text but you *must* present evidence to substantiate your position. Even if your lecturer disagrees personally with your conclusions, they will mark your work according to the way you have presented it and your use of supporting evidence. However, in some subjects, such as History, Politics and Economics, it is very easy to stray into opinionated and biased conclusions (Ch 2). If your work includes these unsubstantiated viewpoints, you may be marked down.

An opinion is a view about a matter which is not wholly confirmed by the current state of knowledge or on a topic that may be regarded as a matter of judgement. Thus, in many fields, for example in arts and social sciences, there is often no 'right' or 'wrong' answer, simply a range of stances or viewpoints. It is therefore possible that your answer may differ significantly from the viewpoints of your fellow students and possibly also that of your lecturer. What you will be assessed on is your ability to argue your case and support it with evidence (Ch 6).

Truth is usually defined in relation to reality – our current state of knowledge. That is, something can be designated true if it corresponds to known facts. However, the concept of truth involves a host of philosophical concepts (including perception, for example) which may complicate the issue. In debate, something is only true when all sides of the argument accept it. For the purposes of critical thinking, if a particular line of argument can be shown to lack credibility or to be in some way unacceptable, this will add weight to the counter-argument (Ch 6).

Concepts of truth and fact involve the notions of objectivity and subjectivity. *Objective* means based on a balanced consideration of the facts; *subjective* means based on one person's opinion. Most academics aim for a detached, objective piece of writing. Nevertheless, it is important to state your own opinion at some point in the work, particularly if some of the evidence might point to a contrary view. The key is to produce valid reasons for holding your opinion.

Examples of fact, opinion and truth

The world record for the 100-metre sprint in athletics was 9.58 seconds at 16 August 2009. This is a *fact*. The record may change over time, but this statement will still be true.

Some claim that many world records are created by athletes who have taken drugs to enhance their performance. This is an *opinion*. There is evidence to back up this position, but recent controversies have highlighted the problem of proof in these cases. Claims about drug misuse are open to conjecture, claim and counter-claim, not all of which can be *true*.

Your task might be to identify the difference between fact and opinion and write with that knowledge. Do not avoid the controversy, but be clear about the facts, the truth and your opinion of the evidence.

THE NATURE OF EVIDENCE AND PROOF

The nature of evidence and proof differs according to discipline.

In the sciences, evidence will most likely be quantitative in nature, such as numerical or statistical summary data. This will be the result of an observation or experiment. The data might have been obtained with the aim of testing some hypothesis about a situation (Ch 7). If statistics are used, it may be possible to assign a probability to whether the hypothesis is true or not. Even apparently 'on or off' qualitative results, as obtained, say, in molecular genetics, rely on assumptions and are capable of multiple interpretations.

Scientific method and falsifiability

The notion of falsifiability is central to scientific method, which involves continually updating our understanding of the world through provisional notions of reality (hypotheses). Falsifiability means that, at least in theory, the evidence can be tested by observation or experiment. Thus, whether the Higgs boson exists is a falsifiable notion; however, the idea that extraterrestrial beings have visited Earth and erased all the evidence is not.

The word 'proof' often carries a connotation of certainty that is unsatisfactory in such contexts. Unsurprisingly, therefore, to most scientists, there is no such thing as proof: there is always a possibility, however remote, that an alternative explanation is true.

In the arts and humanities, evidence is more likely to be qualitative in nature; that is, a description of an event, an interpretation or an opinion. Here, proof is still very much an elusive concept, because it involves the presentation of 'convincing' evidence (a matter of degree) and notions of persuasion.

In the UK's legal systems, the notion of evidence has a special meaning regarding proof of guilt and innocence; as far as jury trials are concerned, the views of these representative members of society must be sought as to whether evidence can be established 'beyond reasonable doubt'.

ARRIVING AT A POSITION AND BACKING IT UP

When reading the literature around a topic, you should take careful notes of information and other material you might like to quote at some stage (Ch 12, Ch 14). In addition, you should also be appraising the viewpoint of the writer(s). You will find yourself naturally attracted to some positions and indifferent to others. This 'gut feeling' is a starting point for forming your own stance.

Before cementing your position, however, you should carry out an analysis of points for and against all the viewpoints you have encountered. When reviewing this, you should try to be as objective as possible. Does the evidence support your initial feelings? If not, then perhaps you should change your opinion.

Some other factors to take account of when trying to arrive at a position include:

- **The guidance that you have received from lecturers.** Of course, you don't *have* to follow this (and some staff will give great credit to those able to support a contrary view), but there is usually a very sound rationale behind their advice.

- **The writings of noted authorities in the field.** Again, you don't *have* to follow their viewpoint, but you should take account of the strong likelihood that it is likely to be considered, based on research and defensible. In many instances you will be faced with opposing sources.

- **The views of your peers.** Other students are not the most reliable of sources, but discussing the topic with your friends may assist you to form an opinion either by being swayed by an argument or by feeling the need to respond with an alternative view. In many cases this discussion will take place within a tutorial (Ch 9), but informal chats may also be valuable.

In science-related subjects, you may model scientific method by setting up an experiment specifically to test a hypothesis. The data you obtain will then lead you to a position related to the hypothesis. You must take care, however, to consider alternative explanations or reasons why your results might not be as clear-cut as they superficially appear to be. It is always valuable to support your conclusion with reference to an appropriate statistical test (Ch 7).

Your grade will frequently depend on how convincing your argument is and how well you use supporting evidence to support your position. Evidence comes in many forms, including: statistical/numeric sources, quotations, experiments, or observations. You should assess all potential evidence for relevance and value, and you must make sure you cite the source of the information in your own text, otherwise the evidence may be invalidated by the marker and you may be accused of plagiarism (Chs 13 and 14).

Above all, you should try to produce a *balanced* conclusion. This is one where you are open about counter-arguments and counter-evidence that does not, at least on the face of it, support your case. You must explain what others think or might think, then explain why you have arrived at the conclusion you personally have made.

Table 5.1 provides two examples of students trying to arrive at a viewpoint.

Taking care with concepts of evidence and proof

- Present evidence to support an assertion or statement of fact
- Account for the nature and reliability of all evidence
- Cite references to back up an assertion or statement of fact (Ch 14)
- Be clear when something is an opinion rather than a fact
- Take care when using the noun 'proof' or the verb 'proves'
- Use hedging language (Table 16.2, p. 205) to avoid implying certainty

Table 5.1 Two scenarios concerning evidence and viewpoints

1 Amy's assignment

Amy has been struggling with an assignment where she is expected to examine human rights practices in the context of education of women and girls in less-developed countries and produce her own conclusions about these. She is very committed to her own voluntary work with Save the Children and so already has a view on the topic. So far, she has done some internet searching and has found several blogs run by human rights groups; she has looked at UNICEF material and a colour supplement that came with one of the Sunday papers. She has also looked online and has found some *YouTube* footage which confirms her view that human rights are violated in many countries. At the last tutorial, other students seemed to belittle her views and even suggested that she'd not researched the topic properly. Her tutor did not disagree with them.

Analysis

Amy's tutorial colleagues are probably correct in their assessment. The material she has sourced could be regarded as biased since the material represents the views of pressure or interest groups whose analysis is probably one-sided. Similarly, the material from the colour supplement has been produced by a journalist based on anecdote rather than research. Without reliable factual information and data, Amy has little substantive information on which to base her views. Perhaps the UNICEF material could provide her with something more authoritative and backed by figures. She does not seem to have sought a clearer understanding on human rights law nor on international organisations active in this area. She needs to search the literature for academic analysis of her topic and create a plan for her essay which presents a more balanced argument before she can confirm her original view or construct a challenge to that view.

2 Ajit's project results

Ajit has been carrying out a project in life sciences, where, as a prelude to the investigation, he has been asked to repeat an important experiment originally done by his supervisor. As far as possible, he has used the same cell line (a culture of isolated cells) and methods. The cell line is exactly the same, but because the original experiment was carried out some time ago, he has sourced fresh chemicals. With as much care as possible, he makes up the requisite solutions, sets up the incubations and measures the results. The only problem is, the results are not the same as his supervisor's. He frets about this and cannot summon the courage to tell his supervisor, fearing that something has gone wrong. Two worrying weeks later, he decides to repeat the experiment using the remainder of his original solutions – and it 'works' this time. However, Ajit is suspicious, because there is a slight colour taint to the solutions, so he makes up a fresh set and goes through the procedures once more. This time the results are the same as his first attempt. Ajit goes to the library and searches for information on the chemical in the solutions – apparently it is unstable and is oxidised to a different form when in solution. When this degraded compound is sourced and used it has the original effect. He has now run out of time for the project and is left with no option but to write up exactly what he has done, taking the stance that the original published results occurred because the chemical had degraded. He fears that he will receive an extremely poor mark for his work.

continued overleaf

Table 5.1 *continued*

 PRACTICAL TIPS FOR ARRIVING AT A POSITION

Assess substance over presentation. Just because information is presented well, for instance in a glossy magazine or a particularly well-constructed website, this does not necessarily tell you much about the quality of its content. Try to look beyond the surface.

Try to maintain a healthy, detached scepticism. However reliable a source of a piece of information seems to be, it is probably a good idea to retain a degree of scepticism about the facts or ideas involved and to question the logic of arguments. Even information from primary sources may be imperfect – different approaches can give different outcomes, for reasons not necessarily understood at the time of writing. Also, try not to identify too strongly with a viewpoint, so you can be detached when assessing its merits and failings.

Look at an issue from all possible angles. This means being aware that one's own initial stance may be the result of unwitting bias (Ch 2) and therefore that you should consciously try to see things in different ways. One way of doing this would be to imagine what the different 'stakeholders' in an issue would think or say. Even the act of thinking who these groups could be might open up possible new 'takes' on the topic.

Don't be afraid to be different in your views. Many advances have come because people dared to put forward radical ideas. However, always make sure you can support your stance with valid evidence.

5.1 Think about the nature of evidence in your own subject. Go back to your notes for a recent lecture course and review the way in which the lecturer presented his or her points. Is it clear where the supporting information came from? What can this tell you about the origins of facts in your discipline?

5.2 Reflect on the origin of your position on a specific issue. Think of a situation where you have had little problem in deciding where you stand. This could be a moral issue, a political issue or an academic debate. Why do you think the way you do? Think back to influences such as people, events or books. Why were you persuaded to have a particular viewpoint? How much is this supported by evidence, or is it, at least in part, intuitive? Would you have a problem in defending it in an academic scenario? What does this tell you about the way you should handle such assignments?

5.3 Analyse politicians' or pundits' assertions. Next time you watch a televised debate, news report or sports programme, listen carefully for the way in which evidence is used. Is it unbiased (Ch 2)? Are the sources reliable? Are they even quoted? How are the assertions questioned by interviewers, commentators or opponents? Does this involve quibbles over matters of fact? Practising the analysis of positions in this way should help you consider your own and others' viewpoints with greater rigour.

6

SUPPORTING OR OPPOSING AN ARGUMENT

How to express your point of view through discussion and debate

Once you have formed a view on a topic, you need to be able state your view clearly, provide evidence to support it and argue convincingly that it is valid. This chapter explains how best to express a view in academic contexts.

KEY TOPICS

→ Putting forward your views

→ Supporting your views in writing

→ Pointers for verbal discussion

→ Recognising fallacies in arguments

KEY TERMS

Analogy Argument Debate Fallacy Jargon Metaphor Moot
Propaganda Rhetoric Simile

There are several possible interpretations of the word 'argument'. In common speaking, it refers to 'a discussion centred on a disagreement'. This may indeed be an accurate description of some academic debates, but the more usual definition in this area is 'a course of reasoning aimed at demonstrating truth or untruth'. Inherent in this definition is the notion of a logical sequence of statements which follow from each other. Your task may be to make a case either for or against a particular line of reasoning.

Skills required for putting your views forward

Discussion and debate require finely tuned critical thinking skills. You must be able to analyse and understand an argument in order to be able to reconstruct it in your own words, or to attack or defend it, according to the instruction for your assignment.

PUTTING FORWARD YOUR VIEWS

Argument through discussion, and its more formal partner, debate, is a vital part of academic studies. A valid position on any subject should be capable of being defended. Similarly, you should feel able to attack a position with which you disagree. In some cases, the acts of defence and attack are artificial devices to explore a position. In many subjects, you are expected to model such discussion in essays and tutorials.

The ground rules for this are as follows:

1 **State your viewpoint** – of course, this requires that you have first arrived at a position on the topic (Ch 5). This view should be explained clearly, demonstrating, where necessary, the steps in logic you have taken to arrive at your view. A certain amount of background information may be important here.

2 **Provide reasoning and evidence** – as part of arriving at a view, you should have researched the topic (Ch 5, Ch 10) and this is your opportunity to summarise the key evidence. It is vital not to get bogged down in detail here otherwise you risk losing the attention of your readers or listeners.

Keeping up attention and focus in your argument

When dealing with a complex issue, it is easy to become mired in detail. Avoid this by returning to your key theme from time to time. You can use 'reminding' wordings such as 'in relation to the theme of...' or 'this shows that...' which give you the excuse to repeat or summarise your position from time to time. Another approach is to 'number' your points (Firstly...; then secondly...; and finally...) so listeners/readers know where they are in the presentation of your ideas.

3 **State the counter-arguments and your points against them** – this forces you to identify and confront the potential weaknesses in your position, and is an essential part of arriving at a coherent viewpoint (Ch 5). If you have thought things through carefully, it should not be difficult to point out the flaws in other arguments, but remember again to use evidence to support this side of your case.

4 **Conclude** – this is where you summarise the key evidence for and against your position, the implications or consequences of taking this line of thought and ending perhaps with a final restatement of your case and why you feel it is valid.

Especially when the medium for discussion is in writing, you may need to provide references regarding the sources of evidence you have cited (Ch 14).

SUPPORTING YOUR VIEWS IN WRITING

As you consider discussions on academic subjects, you will notice that various linguistic devices are used to promote particular points of view. General guidance on the structure, language and presentation of academic writing is provided in Chapters 15–18. Here, the focus is on persuasive writing technique, sometimes called rhetoric. These methods are important because a poorly scripted argument will fail to convince and may lead to lower marks.

 What's the value of understanding techniques for persuasion?

This will help you to think about the way others' points are being made – particularly useful if you wish to counter their argument.

Table 6.1 outlines ten methods commonly used to persuade, all of which may be valid in academic contexts when used with sensitivity. However, it is easy to overdo some forms of persuasion and if used wrongly they may even be the source of fallacies (see section below). Moreover, certain methods commonly found in politics, advertising and bar-room arguments are regarded as unacceptable in scholarly work. These include:

● use of emotive or pejorative (derogatory) wording;
● implication of certainty when this is unjustified;

Table 6.1 Ten techniques for persuasion. These can be used for both written and oral argument – the word 'audience' here could apply to both readers and listeners.

1 Create a problem – and help solve it	Convince your audience that there is an issue at stake and that your preferred solution is the best available. The more they identify with the problem or its consequences, the more they will be inclined to connect with your argument, and, potentially, to accept your answer. This method is much used in advertising.
2 Create a consistent and logical route to your answer	Start with an initial point that is easy for the audience to agree with, then move step-by-step towards your conclusion, with each element moving on from the previous. Make the connections clear. The audience will find it difficult to escape from your logic.
3 Give reasons for agreeing	Explain the advantages of agreement with your line of reasoning and the disadvantages of disagreement. This will reinforce your position in the mind of the audience. Help the audience imagine the consequences under different scenarios. Explain why things are likely to turn out as you predict.
4 Provide evidence	Back up your argument with relevant information that supports your case. Query the status of evidence that is used by those who oppose your view.
5 Repeat your case in different words	Restate your argument several times in the hope that it hits home. Use different methods, such as direct statement, metaphor (see point 9) or anecdote (see point 10), or the repetition might antagonise the audience.
6 Get your audience thinking	Why not use rhetorical questions to do this? These are queries that you go on to answer for the reader/listener. They are a good way to engage an audience and can be used to guide them to your preferred answer.
7 Deal with potential objections	Lead the audience through any objections or counter-arguments that they might come up with, then counter each of the objections. The audience will have only one path remaining: to agree with you.
8 Help the audience identify with your argument	There are several methods for this. You could establish common ground and, by extension, a common goal; let the audience feel they are in on a secret; use humour; personalise the issue and its solution.
9 Mix up the way you express your argument	Employ metaphor, simile and analogy to restate your points in ways that will engage different sorts of audience members.
10 Illustrate your argument	Tell a story. Lead the audience via an interesting anecdote. This will help them imagine the issue and the solution. Use visual images, if this suits the situation.

- making opinion sound like fact;
- selective use of information;
- unjustified simplification and generalisation;
- use of exaggeration and melodrama;
- unsubstantiated anecdote or invented examples.

Some of these approaches may be classed as propaganda, that is, providing strongly biased or partial information. Use of any of these methods will almost certainly lead to your work being marked down.

POINTERS FOR VERBAL DISCUSSION

The main academic situations in which verbal discussion occurs are tutorials and in working groups such as committees and project teams. A discussion of the behaviour and operation of these groups is provided in Chapter 9. In particular, Table 9.3 suggests ways of interacting with some of the 'characters' you might meet in these situations, including some tips for promoting a balanced interchange of views between all members present.

Debates are rather more formal occasions for discussion, often between teams. A number of formats are adopted, each with its own set of rules. Moots are specialised debates used in law. If asked to participate in a debate or moot, you should prepare carefully with your fellow team member(s). These types of presentations require a flexible approach to scripting, because you will be penalised by the audience or judges if you fail to respond to your opponents' points – and you can't easily do this until you have heard them.

 Definition: metaphor, simile and analogy

All three involve comparisons, but they differ subtly:

A metaphor is where one term is used seemingly out of context to represent another real one (for example: *'Critical thinking can be the engine for achieving better marks'*)

A simile is a type of metaphor where two things are directly compared using 'like' or 'as' (for example: *'Critical thinking is like a sat-nav for finding your way to the answer'*)

An analogy is where two things are compared by pointing out their shared characteristics (for example: *'Thinking critically and detective work are both means of arriving at an answer'*)

An interesting feature of debates is the turn-taking aspect, so that each side gets equal chance to put its points forward. When involved in less formal discussions, you should adopt this principle by listening politely to other people's points before giving your own. Many of the persuasive techniques listed in Table 6.1 are employed in debate; understanding these methods may help you counter them.

Examples of formal argument processes

Debate

One of the most common formats, the 'Oxford-style' debate, involving four speakers, works as follows:

- The teams each consist of a proposer and a seconder.
- Each team either proposes or opposes a motion, framed in a statement such as 'this house believes that...'
- The team members take it in turn to talk:
  1. The first proposer speaks for the motion
  2. The first opposer speaks against the motion
  3. The second proposer speaks for the motion, usually countering the opposition's initial points
  4. The second opposer speaks against the motion, usually countering the proposition team's initial points
  5. Questions are sought from the audience ('the floor')
  6. The first proposer summarises the proposition key points
  7. The first opposer summarises the opposition key points
- During the debate, the other side may raise 'points of information' (perhaps disputing information that has been presented) or 'points of order' (disputing an aspect of procedure).
- A vote is taken or the judge announces a winning team.

Moot

A 'moot' is designed to discuss a question or questions of law and often centres on a mock case. The teams each consist of a senior and junior counsel, acting for the appellant and respondent respectively. Exact rules differ according to the legal system being modelled. The judge in a moot may ask the participants questions on legal points.

Many students find occasions when they are asked to speak in public rather daunting. The skill of public speaking becomes more straightforward the more it is practised, and the opportunities you have to address others at university can be valuable preparation for work, where presentations may be commonplace. Table 6.2 provides relevant guidance, including tips for answering questions during or after the event.

Table 6.2 **Practical tips for speaking in public.** The word 'audience' here means 'those to whom you are speaking' whether this be in a more formal presentation (for example, giving a seminar about project work), or a less formal occasion (such as a tutorial discussion or when defending a poster).

General tips
These apply to all forms of delivery. Even for relatively casual situations you should ensure that the basic rules of communication are followed. • **Prepare well.** It will rapidly become obvious if you don't know your subject. • **Engage the audience.** Speak directly to them, not to the floor, your notes, the screen, or a distant wall. Make eye contact. • **Take cues from audience reactions.** Look at their faces; if they don't seem to understand what you've said, repeat it in a different way. If they look bored, speed up, or ask a rhetorical question to engage their thoughts. • **Imagine the audience are your friends.** Speak to them with enthusiasm, warmth and genuine feeling. They will respond in kind. • **Ensure you can be heard.** At the start of your talk, ask the audience if they can hear at the back. • **Don't speak too quickly.** This is a common response to nerves. Make a determined effort to slow yourself down and speak clearly.
Tips especially for formal presentations
These are often stressful due to the larger audience and the fact that the presentation may be assessed. Technology is more likely to be used, carrying its own challenges. • **Dress appropriately for the occasion.** You should look smart, but should feel comfortable in what you wear. • **Check out the venue.** This will make you feel more at home when speaking and ensure you are familiar with, for example, lighting and IT systems. • **Don't read from a script.** This can seem stilted. Instead use cue phrases (such as the bullet points on a PowerPoint slide) to give structure to your points. • **Make sure your audio-visual aids can be seen.** If you are using some kind of projection system, make sure that you – or your shadow – don't block out the projected image. • **To reduce tension, take deep breaths.** This can be done both before you address the audience and during pauses in your presentation. • **Relax, and try to enjoy the occasion.** If you seem to be taking pleasure from speaking, your audience will also enjoy the session.

continued next page

This often causes worry due to feelings of lack of control over what may be asked, and the potential to look stupid if you don't know an answer.

- **Prepare for likely questions.** Think through what people might ask and have an answer ready. Ask a friend or family member to question you in preparation.

- **Ask for clarification if you don't understand a question fully.** You could also ask the questioner or chair to repeat the question if a part of it was indistinct or didn't seem to make sense to you.

- **Repeat the question for the benefit of those who might not have heard it.** The questioner will be facing you, not the audience, and their voice may be indistinct. This will also buy you some time for thinking through the question and composing an answer.

- **Think before you answer.** Rather than blurting out the first thing that comes to mind, take time to weigh up the different aspects. You may feel the necessary pause is long, but this will not be how the audience perceives it.

- **If you don't know an answer, say so.** Everyone recognises when a speaker is waffling. Try saying '*I don't know the answer at the moment, but I'll find out and get back to you ...*' if you want to say something rather than leaving a pause.

RECOGNISING FALLACIES IN ARGUMENTS

The ability to dissect arguments is a key aspect of critical thinking. In some cases you will be trying to understand and counter a viewpoint while in others you will be constructing a coherent view of your own. In both instances, you need to assess whether the argument is logical or whether it involves a fallacy – a breakdown in reasoning. A fallacy occurs where an argument superficially appears to be valid, but is logically flawed, or is based on assumptions that may be untrue.

Try not to be bamboozled when presented with a multitude of facts, complex arguments or strong rhetoric. Look beyond the superficial and analyse the basic line of reasoning that is being used. Sometimes you will sense something is wrong and spot it immediately; at other times an error will only become apparent after close scrutiny. A good way to detect fallacies is to study the basic types of fallacy, and then, by analogy, extend this understanding to the argument with which you are faced.

Unfortunately, there are many different types of logical fallacies – one web source recognises over 70. Here we focus on some of those you are most likely to encounter (Table 6.3). Once tuned in to this way of thinking, you should observe that faulty logic and debating tricks are frequently used in areas such as advertising, politics and newspaper opinion columns. Analysing the methods being used in these presentations can be a useful way of practising your critical thinking skills.

Table 6.3 Some common examples of logical fallacies, bias and propaganda techniques found in arguments

Type of fallacy or propaganda	Description	Example	How to counteract this approach
Ad hominem (Latin for 'to the man')	An attack is made on the character of the person putting forward an argument, rather than on the argument itself. This is particularly common in the media and politics.	*The President's moral behaviour is suspect, so his financial policies must also be dubious.*	Suggest that the person's character or circumstances are irrelevant.
Ad populum (Latin for 'to the people')	The argument is supported on the basis that it is a popular viewpoint. Of course, this does not make it correct in itself.	*The majority of people support corporal punishment for vandals, so we should introduce boot camps.*	Watch out for bandwagon and peer pressure effects and ignore them when considering rights and wrongs.
Appeal to authority	An argument is supported on the basis that an expert or authority agrees with the conclusion. Used in ads, where celebrity endorsement and testimonials are frequent.	*My professor, who I admire greatly, believes in Smith's theory, so it must be right.*	Point out that the experts disagree and explain how and why. Focus on the key qualities of the item or argument.
Appeal to ignorance	Because there's no evidence for (or against) a case, it means the case must be false (or true).	*You haven't an alibi, therefore you must be guilty.*	Point out that a conclusion either way may not be possible in the absence of evidence.
Biased evidence	Selection of examples or evidence for or against a case.	*A writer who quotes those who support his/her view, but not those against.*	Read around the subject, including those with a different view and try to arrive at a balance.
Euphemisms and jargon	Use of phrasing to hide the true position or exaggerate an opponent's – stating things in mild or emotive language for effect. Use of technical words to sound authoritative.	*My job as vertical transportation operative means I am used to being in a responsible position.*	Watch for (unnecessary) adjectives and adverbs that may affect the way you consider the evidence.

Repetition	Saying the same thing over and over again until people believe it.	*Common in politics, war propaganda and advertising – e.g. 'Beans means Heinz'.*	Look out for repeated catch-phrases and lack of substantive argument.
False dilemma	Offering a choice of alternatives when other options may be available.	*The patient can be treated with Drug A or Drug B. Drug B has side effects, so we should choose A.*	Demonstrate that there are other options.
Slippery slope	The notion that a step in a particular direction will start a chain of events leading to an undesirable outcome.	*If we let one property become a house of multiple occupancy, soon the whole street will be full of them.*	Point out that progress along the chain of events is not a foregone conclusion.
Correlation used to imply cause	A correlation between two events (that is, they appear or disappear or rise and fall together) is taken to imply that one causes the other.	*Whenever I wear this lucky jacket my football team wins.*	Point out that the two things are in no way connected or that there may be other factors causing the event.
Straw man	A position is misrepresented in order to create a debating point that is easily accepted or rejected, when in fact the core issue has not been addressed.	*Asylum seekers all want to milk the benefits system, so we should turn them all away.*	Point out the fallacy and focus on the core issue.
Anecdotal evidence	Use of unrepresentative exceptions to contradict an argument based on statistical evidence.	*My Nan was a heavy smoker and she lived to be 95, so smoking won't harm me.*	Consider the overall weight of evidence rather than isolated examples.

Keep things simple without being simplistic. Your argument should be easy to follow and not overburdened with examples or evidence. However, it should acknowledge the complexity in the real-life situations that are encountered.

Always be polite. It is easy to get attached to a point of view and to become angered with those who oppose it. For academic purposes, you should always respect your 'opponent' and counteract their points with courtesy and good grace. *Never* raise your voice or insult an opponent.

If speaking formally, respect the time limits. It is very bad form to over-run and may deny others the chance to comment or make their own presentations. To avoid this, practice your talk and adjust its length as necessary. Allow about 10% of spare time for slow starting, unexpected interruptions and the fact that you may speak more slowly or say more on the day.

State your 'take-home message' clearly. This is the point you most want your audience to remember after reading your work or listening to you speak. It is often a good idea to finish your presentation by making this position abundantly clear.

 AND NOW ...

6.1 Look back at a piece of your own writing (or material from lectures or a reading list) and examine how methods of persuasion have been used. See how many of the methods covered in Table 6.1 you can spot. Which other techniques might have been successfully employed?

6.2 Take small opportunities to practise so you can build up confidence. These might include making a comment at a meeting or asking questions at other talks – anything that reduces shyness and gets you used to hearing your own voice speaking.

6.3 Look further into the murky world of fallacies and biased arguments. There are some very good websites that provide lists of different types of these with examples. Investigate these using 'fallacy' or 'logical fallacies' in a search engine. Not only are the results quite entertaining at times, but you will also find that your increased understanding improves your analytical and debating skills.

7

INTERPRETING AND MANIPULATING DATA

How to approach graphs, tables, formulae and basic statistics

You will come across data in many forms during your studies, including graphs, tables and statistics. Understanding what they mean calls for knowledge of the formats used in data presentation, combined with skills of interpretation and numerical analysis.

KEY TOPICS

→ How to 'read' a graph

→ How to 'read' a table

→ Using formulae in numerical problems

→ Making sense of descriptive statistics

→ Understanding hypothesis-testing statistics

KEY TERMS

Descriptive statistics   Dispersion   Error bars   Extrapolation
Frequency distribution   Hypothesis testing   Interpolation   Location
Outlier   Parametric   Qualitative   Quantitative

In many disciplines, being able to interpret data is an important thinking skill. It helps you to decipher complex results and understand more fully what they mean. There are many ways of presenting data sets, and the method chosen might affect your analysis:

● data are presented in graphs when it is thought a visual presentation will assist interpretation, but despite this, it is very easy for results in this format to be misconstrued;

● tables offer detailed data values in a condensed form, but it is possible to become bewildered by the proliferation of numbers and confused about what they mean;

- statistics are used to indicate the size of errors or the likelihood of a particular hypothesis being correct or incorrect, but they can involve difficult concepts and can only be interpreted with specialist knowledge about their precise meaning.

In some cases, the presentation of data can be manipulated to alter the appearance of a result. A healthily critical approach is therefore essential when you are interpreting graphs, tables and statistics.

HOW TO 'READ' A GRAPH

The following elements are present in most graphs and charts (collectively known as 'figures'), but not all. They are illustrated in Figure 7.1 for a standard plotted curve. Analysis of these features will help you work out what a specific graph means.

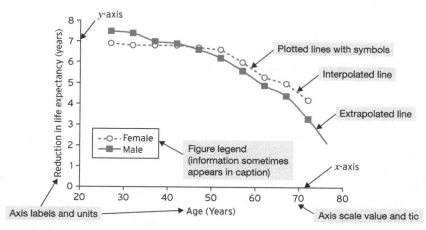

Figure 89 **A standard plotted curve.** This figure type uses x-y axes and points and lines to illustrate the relationship between two variables. *Source*: Data modified from Rogers, R.G. and Powell-Griner E., 1991. Life expectancies of cigarette smokers and non-smokers in the United States. *Soc. Sci. Med.*, 32, 1151-9.

Figure 7.1 **The basic components of a standard plotted curve**

- **The figure title and its caption.** These should appear below the graph. Read them first to determine the overall context and gain information about what the graph shows. If the caption is detailed, you may need to revisit it later to aid your interpretation.

- **The type of graph.** With experience, you will come to recognise the basic chart types (Figure 7.2) and others common in your discipline. This will help you to orientate yourself. For example, a pie chart is normally used to show proportions of a total amount.

- **The axes.** Many forms of chart represent the relationship between two variables, called *x* and *y* for convenience. These are often presented between a pair of axes at right angles, with the horizontal *x*-axis often relating to the 'controlled' variable (for example, concentration or time) and the vertical *y*-axis often relating to the 'measured' variable (for example, income, weight (mass), or response). More than one measured variable may be plotted on the same graph, either using the same *y*-axis, or a second one (see Figure 7.3b). Some types of graph don't follow this pattern and if you are unfamiliar with the form being used, you may need to investigate further.

Plural terms

The following plurals are often misused or misunderstood:

Singular	Plural
axis	axes
datum	data
formula	formulae
maximum	maxima
Minimum	minima

(Hence, for example, 'these data *are* presented in Fig. 4')

(a)

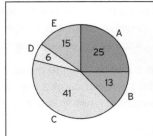

(b)

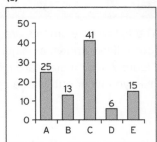

(c)

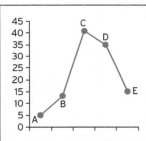

Figure 7.2 Common forms of graph. These are in addition to the standard plotted curve shown in Figure 7.1. **(a)** *Pie chart*, showing % proportions of a total. **(b)** *Histogram*, showing amounts in different categories. **(c)** *Frequency polygon*, showing distribution of counted data across a continuous range.

- **The axis scale and units.** An axis label should state what the axis means and the units being used. Each axis should show clearly the range of values it covers through a series of cross-marks ('tics') with associated numbers to indicate the scale. To interpret these, you will also need to know the units. Some axes do not start from zero, or incorporate a break in the scale; others may be non-linear (for example, a logarithmic axis is sometimes used to cover particularly wide ranges of numbers). Pay attention in these cases, because this could mean that the graph exaggerates or emphasises differences between values (compare Figures 7.3a and b, for example).

- **The symbols and plotted curves.** These help you identify the different data sets being shown and the relationship between the points in each set. A legend or key is sometimes included to make this clearer. Your interpretation may focus on differences in the relationships, and inevitably, on the plotted curves (also known as 'trend lines'). However, it is important to realise that the curves are merely hypothetical interpolations between measured values or, worse, extrapolations beyond them; and, because they may involve assumptions about trends in the data, they should be examined with care. Symbols may also include information about variability in the data collected (for example, error bars), which provide useful clues about the reliability of data and assumed trends.

Definitions: trend lines on graphs

Interpolation – an assumed trend or relationship *between* available data points

Extrapolation – an assumed trend or relationship before or after (below or above) available data points. Extrapolation is risky because the assumption may be made that a trend will continue when there may be little supporting evidence that this will happen

---

The checklist overleaf provides a generalised sequence you should follow when looking at a graph for the first time.

Checklist for interpreting a graph

- Consider the context by reading the title, legend and main text
- Recognise the type of graph
- Examine what the axes show
- Inspect the scale of the axes
- Study the symbols and plotted curves
- Evaluate what any error bars or statistics mean
- From the trends in the lines, their maxima/minima or convergence/ divergence, etc., work out what the results appear to show

HOW GRAPHS CAN MISLEAD

You can learn a lot about data presentation by studying misleading graphs and learning why they might lead to incorrect interpretations. A selection of examples is shown in Figure 7.3.

Some of the graphs you will see may use these 'tricks' to emphasise differences and trends. This isn't always a bad thing, but it is essential to be aware of the fact that the visual representation may bias your interpretation. If in doubt, it is often a good idea to convert a selection of the data to numbers and look at them afresh in this 'raw' state.

HOW TO 'READ' A TABLE

A good table presents data in a compact, readily assimilated format. In general, tables are used when:

- a graphic presentation is not suitable for some or all of the data (for instance, when some are qualitative);
- there are too many data sets or variables to include in a chart;
- the audience might be interested in the precise values of some of the data;
- large amounts of original data need to be placed on record.

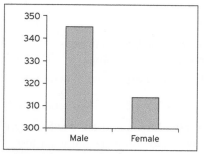 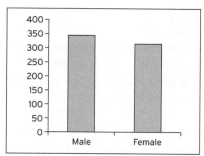

(a) Use of non-zero axis. In the chart on the left, it looks as if the differences between males and females are large; however, when the y-axis is zeroed, as on the right, the differences are much less noticeable.

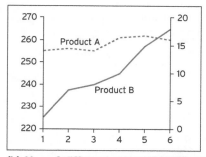 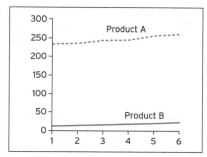

(b) Use of different y-axes for different curves. In the chart on the left it looks as if sales of product B are catching up with those of product A; however, when the same axis is used for both curves, then it can be seen that product A vastly outsells product B.

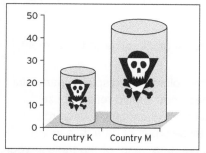 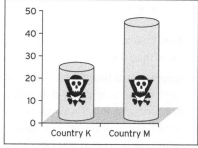

(c) Use of a 2-D or 3-D object to represent a linear scale. In the chart on the left, the barrel retains its shape in relation to the y-axis scale, so it makes it look as if country M produces much more toxic waste than country K. On the right, a truly linear representation is shown.

Figure 7.3 **Three common examples of misleading graphs**

i **Definition: data types**

Qualitative data – these are data that are descriptive and non-numerical, such as colour, place of manufacture, or name

Quantitative data – these are data that can be expressed in numbers, such as length, height or price

The following elements are present in most tables and are illustrated in Figure 7.4. Analysis of these features will help you work out what the data in a specific table mean.

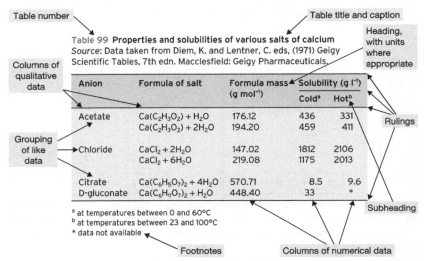

Table number

Table title and caption

Heading, with units where appropriate

Columns of qualitative data

Grouping of like data

Table 99 **Properties and solubilities of various salts of calcium**
Source: Data taken from Diem, K. and Lentner, C. eds, (1971) Geigy Scientific Tables, 7th edn. Macclesfield: Geigy Pharmaceuticals.

Anion	Formula of salt	Formula mass (g mol⁻¹)	Solubility (g l⁻¹)	
			Cold[a]	Hot[b]
Acetate	$Ca(C_2H_3O_2) + H_2O$	176.12	436	331
	$Ca(C_2H_3O_2) + 2H_2O$	194.20	459	411
Chloride	$CaCl_2 + 2H_2O$	147.02	1812	2106
	$CaCl_2 + 6H_2O$	219.08	1175	2013
Citrate	$Ca(C_6H_5O_7)_2 + 4H_2O$	570.71	8.5	9.6
D-gluconate	$Ca(C_6H_{11}O_7)_2 + H_2O$	448.40	33	*

[a] at temperatures between 0 and 60°C
[b] at temperatures between 23 and 100°C
* data not available

Rulings

Subheading

Footnotes

Columns of numerical data

Figure 7.4 The basic components of a table. Note that shading is included here to emphasise the heading and data sections and would not usually be present in formal academic tables.

- **The title and caption.** These provide a quick guide to the content, as with a figure.

- **Layout and headings.** Each vertical column will display a particular type of data, and the descriptive headings should reflect these contents, giving the units where data are quantitative. Each row might show different instances of these types of data. It is worth taking time to use the headings to create a 'map' of the table in your mind.

- **Rulings.** In some cases these can help you to group types of data; however, the modern style tends to restrict their use to horizontal lines, as in Figure 7.4. You will then have to rely on the spacing of columns and rows to differentiate data types – for large tables, it may be worth using a highlighter to mark out key information on a copy.

- **Data values.** These will be presented to an appropriate number of significant figures, which should be noted. Any error values should be used to give an indication of the reliability of the data.

- **Footnotes.** These can be used to explain abbreviations or give details of specific cases. It is important to study these carefully as they may provide essential indications about meaning or highlight exceptional data.

When interpreting a table, you are often only interested in a selection of the data and is it easy to be 'swamped' by the remainder. It may help you to interpret these results if you isolate the information of relevance and create a new 'mini' table or chart for your own use, or carry out further calculations (for example expressing one value as a percentage of another).

How is this information relevant to my own figures and tables?

The tips presented here for interpreting figures and tables should help you when you are constructing your own data presentations. Your aim should always be to allow your audience to assimilate the meaning behind the data as easily as possible. In particular, you should try to avoid any of the forms of misrepresentation shown in Figure 7.3 when constructing your own figures.

USING FORMULAE IN NUMERICAL PROBLEMS

Many university subjects include topics that require skills of numeracy, especially in the later stages of study. Examples include biology, economics, geography and psychology. In many situations, the mathematics involved is not particularly advanced and a logical approach combined with basic elementary principles of algebra and geometry will suffice.

Equations (formulae) are often used to model phenomena using variables, constants and mathematical operations. Associated problems often require you to rearrange equations. For example, if you wish to find a particular variable or constant in a formula, you may wish to express it in terms of other variables and constants, whose values you already know. This key mathematical skill usually involves carrying out an operation on both sides of the equation so that a particular term 'disappears' from one side and reappears on the other. You may need to simplify some of the terms before doing this or express them in a different mathematical way.

 Create a personalised list of formulae

These might be ones covered in lectures, or those that appear frequently in the problems you are given. During revision, test whether you can recall them and can remember the conditions or assumptions that may apply to their use. This is probably a good idea even if you will be given a sheet of formulae to use in exams.

The following is a potential approach to numerical problems.

1 **Where relevant, try to work out which formula applies** – if you do not instantly recognise which equation applies to the problem you have been given, think through the values and dimensions you have been given and work out which of these appear in the 'candidate' formulae you are considering.

2 **State your assumptions** – if modelling using a 'perfect' shape or object, you should state the assumptions you are making (for example, 'the organelle was assumed to be spherical...'). When discussing your result, you may also wish to state why these might not be valid in practice.

3 **Show intermediate calculations and express your answers neatly** – if you work through the problem step-by-step in your answer, you can be given part-marks even if you get a simple numerical calculation wrong. Show your answer by repeating what you have been asked to show and its value (including the number of significant figures, where relevant) and underlining it using a ruler, thus:

The total mass of the patient's brain is 1.34 kg (to three significant figures)

4 **Check the units and scale of your answers** – firstly, make sure that you have converted any answer into the units requested in the question, and with the appropriate number of significant figures, either as specified or as seems sensible to you. Secondly, make sure that your answer is not absurdly high or low. Areas and volumes are particularly difficult to visualise. Try to relate these to

'real life' objects if you can – for example, imagine what the value you obtain might look like in relation to something you are familiar with, like a stamp, piece of paper, glass of beer, and so on.

When working with formulae, express all values in terms of base units

Nearly all scientific and engineering formulae are expressed in terms of SI base units (i.e. metres, seconds, grams), so if you are given a length as 10 mm, do not enter 10 into a formula, enter 10×10^{-3}, thereby expressing the length in metres.

MAKING SENSE OF DESCRIPTIVE STATISTICS

Descriptive statistics are used to simplify a complex data set, to summarise the distribution of data within the data set and to provide estimates of values of the population frequency distribution. The latter is a representation of the way the data are spread out along the 'controlled' or x-axis, and often involves placing the data into classes.

Two types of descriptive statistics that are often quoted are:

- measures of location – these estimate the 'centre' of the frequency distribution;
- measures of dispersion – these estimate the spread of data within the frequency distribution.

Definition: frequency distribution

This is a description of the frequency of occurrence of values of a variable. You may be interested in the actual distribution in the sample you have taken, and you might use a frequency polygon (Figure 7.2c) to represent this. You might also be interested in the underlying population frequency distribution. This is often theoretical in nature and a smooth curve representing a model function might be used to represent it.

Different measures of location and dispersion are outlined in Table 7.1. Each is appropriate in specific circumstances and when interpreting data you should take account of the advantages and disadvantages noted in column 4 of this table. For example, while a mean is

Table 7.1 Descriptive statistics and their uses

Measure	Statistic	How calculated*	Uses, advantages and disadvantages
Location	Mean	The sum of all the data values divided by the number of values, n.	This is the most commonly used measure. It takes account of all the values in the data set, but can be influenced by the presence of outliers and is not representative of the whole body of data if this is asymmetric. Units same as the data.
	Median	The mid-point of the data values when they are ranked in numerical order. For odd-sized data sets, it is the value of the middle datum, while for even-sized data sets, it is the mean of the two central values.	This may represent the location of the majority of the data better than the mean if the data set is asymmetric or there are outliers. Units same as the data.
	Mode	The most common value in the data set.	Easily found and unaffected by outliers; however, especially when the data set is small, it may be susceptible to 'random' variation in the distribution of values. Units same as the data.
Dispersion	Range	The difference between the largest and the smallest values in the data set.	Easy to determine, but its value is greatly affected by outliers and the size of the data set. Units the same as the data.
	Semi-interquartile range	The difference between the first and third quartiles, which are the median values for the data ranked below and above the median value of the whole data set.	Less easy to calculate than the range, but less affected by outliers and the size of the data set. Suitable to match with the median as a measure of location. Units same as the data.
	Variance	The sum of the squares of the difference between each data value and the mean, divided by $n - 1$.	Measures the average difference from the mean for all the data values. Good for data sets that are symmetrical about the mean. Units are the square of those of the data.
	Standard deviation	The positive square root of the variance.	A measure of the average difference from the mean for all the data values. Good for data sets symmetrical about the mean Units are same as the data, so preferable to the variance.
	Coefficient of variation	The standard deviation multiplied by 100 and divided by the mean.	A dimensionless (%) measure of variability relative to location. Allows the relative dispersion of data sets to be compared.

* Note that each method is usually expressed in the symbols of the equivalent mathematical formula.

commonly used to summarise the central location of a data set, it may be sensitive to outliers (defined as individual data distant from the remainder of values). This can be especially important for small data sets.

Dispersion values are particularly important to assess as these evaluate the error present in the data. They provide an indication of the reliability of a particular statistic and also whether data that differ numerically can be considered to be 'significantly different' (see below). Error in data comes from several sources, so consideration of likely types of error may aid interpretation of the result and of the methods used to obtain it. In many cases, the way in which specimens or data were sampled and measured is a crucial part of the 'materials and methods' section and this should be scrutinised in detail.

More complex descriptive statistics are sometimes used, such as standard error (describing the precision of a mean), or values quantifying the shape of frequency distributions. However, details of these are outwith the scope of this book and a specialist text should be consulted.

Sources of random error and variability

The following are reasons why the values and hence the descriptive statistics of samples of data may vary:

- **sampling error** – due to the selection of a small number of individuals from a larger, variable population

- **measurement error** – due to the method of measurement of the variable

- **rounding error** – due to an attempt to use an appropriate number of significant figures, but often compounded in calculations

- **human error** – due to inaccurate writing or copying of data, mixing up of samples, and so on

- **error from unknown sources** – or unappreciated effects of sampling

---

UNDERSTANDING HYPOTHESIS-TESTING STATISTICS

Hypothesis-testing in a statistical context is used to compare the properties of a data set with other samples or to compare the data set with some theory about it.

Error and variability exist in all data sets, which means that it is impossible to be 100% certain about differences between values. The question you should ask is: 'are the differences "genuine" and due to a true dissimilarity between the samples, perhaps because of a treatment administered to one of them, or are the differences you observe just the result of random errors?' Hypothesis-testing works by trying to put a probability on these alternatives.

The norm is to set up a 'Null hypothesis' (NH) that says that the samples are the same or that they conform to some theoretical description. By making certain assumptions about the data, calculating a hypothesis-testing statistic, and looking up tables of probability (or calculating), it is possible to estimate the probability P of the NH being true. The lower P, the less likely you are to accept it in favour of the hypothesis that the differences were 'real' and due to the genuine difference between the samples (caused by a treatment to one set, for example). Conventionally, if P is < 0.05, then the NH is rejected, and the difference is said to be 'statistically significant'. If P is > 0.05, then the convention is to assume that the difference observed could be due to random sampling from a variable population.

Hypothesis-testing statistics differ in their assumptions about the data and what they set out to test. Some common ones and their uses are:

- **t-test** – used for comparing two means;
- **x^2 (Chi squared) test** – used for comparing observed against expected values;
- **analysis of variance (ANOVA)** – used for comparing several means.

Precise details can be found in specialist texts.

Parametric and non-parametric statistical tests

The former make the assumption that the data are distributed according to a particular mathematical function, usually the so-called 'Normal' function; the latter make no assumptions of this kind, but are less powerful in distinguishing between samples which differ marginally.

PRACTICAL TIPS FOR PRODUCING GRAPHS, TABLES AND BASIC STATISTICS

Find out more about different graph types. Some common forms of graphs are illustrated in this chapter, but a quick way of finding out about different options is to explore the 'chart' forms available in a spreadsheet like Microsoft Excel: the *Insert > Charts* menu illustrates sub-types and provides brief descriptions. This is also a good way of exploring ways of presenting your own data.

When looking at a complex graph or table for the first time, make notes. This can help you to focus your interpretation. Using the checklist on p. 80 might help your analysis (this can also be adapted for tables) and you may need to refer to the materials and methods section of the original source to understand in full how the data were obtained and by extension, what exactly they represent.

AND NOW . . .

7.1 Examine all graphs critically. You will see, for example, how those in newspapers are often presented in a way that supports the journalist's viewpoint, while presentations in academic articles tend to be less prone to bias. In all cases, you should think about why a particular graph format was chosen, whether the presentation is an aid to your understanding and how it might be improved, as this will help you to analyse and present your own data.

7.2 Focus on the caption of figures. Ideally this should contain much of the information required to interpret the data. In particular:

* the title might indicate what the author(s) think the data show;
* the meaning of the symbols and error bars will let you know which line shows what;
* statistical data will help you judge the significance of any differences shown;
* the way the plotted curve was chosen can help you consider what might have happened between the data values shown or beyond and below them.

For tables, the caption information may also help you to interpret the columns and rows.

7.3 Learn more about the statistical tests used in your discipline. As noted above, this topic is too wide to cover in a book of this type, but it could be vital for interpreting results you come across. Because statistics can be chosen and applied in different ways, knowing when and where this is valid will assist your interpretation. It is surprisingly common for statistics to be used incorrectly and you may be able to spot this. If you lack confidence in your statistical abilities, you may wish to enrol on a supplementary module or buy additional texts to help you to improve.

8

DECISION-MAKING AND WORK-PLANNING

How to make choices, plan ahead and prioritise

Making a choice or decision is often a key outcome of the thinking process. Getting to this stage is hard enough sometimes, but to make something of your efforts, you must also consider the actions required to achieve your chosen goal. This involves effective planning, time management and prioritisation – important skills for both university and workplace.

KEY TOPICS

→ Weighing up your options

→ Planning ahead and managing time

→ Prioritisation

KEY TERMS

Gantt chart   Opportunity cost   Perfectionism   Priority   Procrastination

One of the important 'rites of passage' that occurs while you are at university is a progressive increase in responsibility for making your own decisions. This is good preparation for later life and employment, and decision-making is regarded as an important graduate skill. However, decisiveness on its own is not sufficient to obtain results. For this, the allied skills of planning, time management and prioritisation are also important. Moreover, your decisions should be competent and thought-through, rather than irrational, spontaneous or intuitive. This implies that you can trace the decision-making process and are able to justify your choices.

Examples of decision-making

Typical areas of your personal life requiring decisions and follow-up action include:

- deciding on a high-value purchase (for example, a car)
- choosing a holiday destination
- voting in an election

In the academic area, examples might include:

- selecting which modules to study
- deciding which exam question to answer
- choosing a project topic

WEIGHING UP YOUR OPTIONS

An uninformed decision is essentially a guess, so the first stage in decision-making is reviewing your options to find out exactly what they are. Where appropriate, you should research the consequences of taking each path of action. As part of this process you should create a list of 'aspects' which appear to be important in making your choice.

A relevant example could be selecting from options for experimental project work where the initial information you might be provided with would be a list of project titles and supervisors. Aspects that could prove relevant to your choice include:

- personal interest in area of study;
- availability of resources and/or experimental material;
- techniques involved in obtaining data;
- likelihood of obtaining useful results;
- range of skills you will learn or develop;
- ease of data analysis;
- reputation of supervisor;
- personal rapport with supervisor;
- impact of topic on curriculum vitae and employment prospects.

You could, for example, find out about the first of these by reading the recent literature about the topic; and you could perhaps establish the track record of the supervisor by asking previous students. This phase is relatively easy – the same in principle as researching the features of a new mobile phone or laptop. Assuming there is no clear-cut favourite, the next phase is the more difficult one: comparing several possible options.

There are a number of techniques for analysing options to help arrive at a decision. Each will suit different situations and personalities. They are described below with reference to the 'project selection' example above.

Listing pros and cons

This method helps to clarify your thinking about each option by weighing up the good and bad aspects. For each, simply draw a line and write down the 'pro' (for) points on one side and the 'con' (against) points on the other. Neutral aspects are omitted. This results in a simplified 'high contrast' representation of your views that can help the selection process.

For example, in choosing a project, you might have placed several practical aspects for a given project on the 'pro' side, but placed 'personal interest' on the 'con' side. Your decision might then come down to whether you will feel more motivated by the appeal of the topic or by the utility of the choice.

Scoring

This is a means of making decisions a little more objective. For each option, you give separate scores for each aspect, and then compare the totals.

You could mark each aspect out of the same total (say 10), or you could 'weight' the aspects, by making each out of a different total. This allows you to give more credit for the aspects you consider important. It doesn't really matter what the total weighting comes to, so long as the values correspond to the relative importance you place on each aspect.

Table 8.1 shows the imaginary results of this type of an analysis for the project example; it is evident that despite a strong preference for the supervisor in option A, other factors outweigh this one and might lead the student to select option C.

Table 8.1 Example of scoring aspects when deciding on a possible project

Aspect	Personal weighting	Scores		
		Project A	Project B	Project C
1 Interest in area of study	20	13	10	15
2 Availability of resources and/or experimental material	15	12	12	14
3 Techniques involved in obtaining data	10	6	8	9
4 Likelihood of obtaining useful results	10	6	6	10
5 Range of skills you will learn or develop	10	5	7	10
6 Ease of data analysis	15	8	9	12
7 Reputation of supervisor	10	8	4	7
8 Rapport with supervisor	15	15	5	8
9 Impact of topic on curriculum vitae and employment prospects	5	2	3	5
Total	**110**	**75**	**64**	**90**

What is the best way to make decisions in exam situations when time is very limited?

The scoring method provides a 'quick and dirty' method for selecting options in an exam paper: simply go down the list of questions and give each a score out of ten according to the mark you feel you would gain for a competed answer. Select the required number of options from those with the best scores and start answering (you don't *have* to do them in sequence, but it is a valid tactic).

Last person standing

This technique focuses on negative points rather than positive, so you end with the 'least objectionable' choice rather than a true favourite. It is useful in situations where all or most options are unpleasant. The technique is simply to eliminate the least favourite choice sequentially until there is only one option remaining.

In the project choice example, you might eliminate a particular option at stage one (say because it involves a dangerous chemical, or sources mainly in a foreign language you can't easily translate); another at stage 2 (perhaps you really don't get on with the supervisor), leaving your final choice.

Finding a consensus

This approach relies on asking others about their opinion and arriving at a joint decision. It is of obvious relevance to groupwork situations (**Ch 9**) but can also be useful where solo decisions are to be made. The 'sounding board' aspect can be useful at an initial stage to gauge the aspects considered important by others, thereby helping you to clarify your own feelings. Voicing your thoughts to others can also help you to clarify your own views. A disadvantage of this tactic is that you might be overly influenced by others' views.

In the project choice example, you might choose to discuss your options with an independent third party, such as a personal tutor. They will be unlikely to express an opinion themselves as this would be unprofessional, but they might suggest useful criteria to consider, for example the employment destinations of past students, and they might ask you relevant questions to draw out your thoughts.

'Phone-a-friend' and 'ask-the-audience'

These 'lifeline' opportunities given in a popular TV quiz are examples of consensus decision-making where the number of people consulted ranges from 1 to over 100. (As an aside, the '50:50' option to remove two of the four possible answers is an example of the 'last person standing' approach to decision-making.)

Cost-based analyses

These methods are mostly suited to the business environment and involve working out the costs associated with making each decision. As well as direct costs of a particular pathway of action, an important matter to consider is the 'opportunity cost' – that is gains that you could miss out on if you make a particular decision.

This could be relevant to the project example if a particular choice meant you had to forgo a future job opportunity because you might be judged to lack suitable experience or skills to apply. Alternatively, one project option might involve working extensively at a field station or remote library, meaning you would lose the chance to see your friends and family (not all costs are valued in money terms).

Further decision-making strategies

These would not always be advised, but sometimes work out:

- *random choice:* flip a coin or draw lots to make a decision
- *gut reaction:* follow your instinctive feeling (often your first thought on a matter)
- *follow the expert:* do what someone else advises or orders

These are suitable only for certain situations:

- *negotiate:* useful when parties disagree (perhaps applicable in groupwork)
- where time is a factor, *take the best currently available option:* don't wait for a better one to come along (it might not)

PLANNING AHEAD AND MANAGING TIME

All complex and lengthy activities need to be planned. This applies equally to building a house, studying for an exam or carrying out a research project. Without adequate planning, you are more likely to: lose track of where you are and what needs to be done; fail to balance the different elements of the task; run out of time; and fail to achieve your goal.

Certain principles apply to project management in all areas. The example chosen here is again one of an undergraduate research project, but the basic approach would apply elsewhere.

1 **Start with a plan, but regard it as flexible.** The origin of your plan should be specification of the task you have been asked to carry out, such as a project proposal you may have submitted. You now need to divide the task into its constituent elements and hence phases of work. For the example of a research project, this might consist of:

   (1) reading around the subject to gain a solid understanding of concepts, methods and potential areas of investigation;

   (2) arriving at a central hypothesis or approach for your research;

   (3) creating a detailed and practical plan for your experiments or reading;

(4) carrying out the research;

(5) analysing the research results, findings or ideas;

(6) drafting the report, dissertation or thesis;

(7) completing and submitting the report.

Keeping plans flexible

One of the main reasons for having a plan is to let you know how well you are progressing with a task. Progress with your plan should therefore be reviewed frequently. If you are not meeting targets, then the plan should be adjusted for the time remaining. Expect the unexpected – adding empty slots in the initial version to allow for contingencies will help to minimise disruption.

The total length of time available for the project should be allocated into suitable periods for each of the phases. This will allow you to monitor progress and adjust your work-rate if, for example, progress is slow in one aspect. The list of phases above is presented sequentially, but you do not always have to schedule work in this way. To achieve the greatest efficiency, it is sometimes important to allow some aspects to proceed in parallel. Where the phases are complex, there may be benefits in subdividing them to make the planning process more manageable.

2 **Schedule your project.** Simple charts can be produced for relatively uncomplicated plans, such as an exam revision timetable (Figure 8.1).

Week: 12			Personal revision timetable *Sophie Pringle*		Key to subjects/topics *Geography* / *Biomes + Diversity* / *Environmental Chemistry*		
	Monday	**Tuesday**	**Wdenesday**	**Thursday**	**Friday**	**Saturday**	**Sunday**
Morning	*Geog Lectures 1 & 2*	*Env Chem Topic B*	*Biomes + Div Week 3*	*Env Chem Topic C*	*Geog Lecture 8 & 9*	*WORK*	*Lie in*
	Env Chem Topic A	*Geog Lectures 3 & 4*	*Biomes + Div Week 4*	*Env Chem Topic C*	*Study buddy meeting Geog*	*WORK*	*Laundry*
Lunch							
Afternoon	*Env Chem Topic A*	*Geog tutorial*	*Geog Lectures 5 & 6*	*Biomes + Div Practicals*	*Env Chem Topic D*	*WORK*	*Biomes + Div Practicals*
	Prep for last Geog tutorial	*Break*	*HOCKEY*	*Biomes + Div Practicals*	*SPARE*	*WORK*	*Mock exam with Hilda*
Evening meal							
Evening	*Biomes + Div Week 1*	*Env Chem Topic B*	*EVENING OFF!*	*Library – look out past papers*	*SPARE (go out to union if up to speed)*	*Phil's birthday bash*	*Sunday tea with Mum and Dad*
	Biomes + Div Week 2	*SPARE*	*EVENING OFF!*	*Geog Lecture 7 (difficult)*	*SPARE*	*Phil's birthday bash*	

Figure 8.1 Sample revision plan for a student studying environmental sciences

How to set up a revision timetable

1 Create a blank weekly table, subdividing into days and study periods

2 Fix your start and end dates and copy enough weekly tables to cover this period

3 Fill in your essential non-study commitments

4 Decide on the number of revision sessions for study in each day and week and note on the table when they should be

5 Decide subjects and topics you need to cover and allocate these to the sessions, balancing the time appropriately

6 Ensure you allocate time for some relaxation activities and include some empty slots to allow for slippage

7 If possible, do not overload yourself near to the exam so you can avoid fatigue associated with cramming

See Figure 8.2 for an example of one week of a completed timetable. Further tips for planning revision are provided in *The Study Skills Book*, McMillan and Weyers, 3rd edn, 2013a.

A standard way of presenting the timeline of a more complex project is called a Gantt chart, named after its inventor, Henry Gantt, an American management consultant. This has two axes, the horizontal one generally being time and the vertical one showing the different tasks or elements of project activity, usually in bar chart form.

Gantt charts are useful for:

– separating out the different elements required to complete a project;

– showing the interdependence of project activities;

– indicating progress on a project as it moves forward, including showing important milestones.

Relationships between sequential activities are classified as 'end to start' and between parallel elements as 'start to start'. Aspects that must finish close together are termed 'end to end'. These connections may be shown on the chart using a dashed link line. Milestones are generally shown using a lozenge (diamond) symbol. Figure 8.2 shows an example of a Gantt chart for a research project.

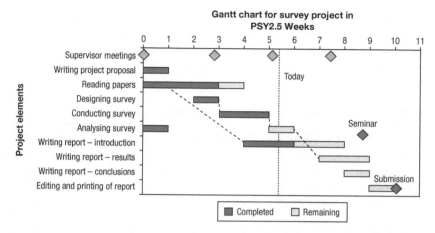

Figure 8.2 **Representative Gantt chart.** This chart was created using the 'stacked bar' type of chart in Excel and illustrates progress at the start of the 6th week of a simple project based on a survey. Note how progress in each phase is shown by shading the horizontal bar for each element: this student is shown as 'behind schedule' with their reading of the literature and analysis of the survey results, but has started to write parts of the introduction to the report, so is 'ahead of schedule' on this aspect. Connections between elements are shown with a dotted line, such as the obvious need to complete the design of the survey before conducting it. Key milestones (diamonds) shown include meetings with the student's supervisor, a seminar to be presented in week 8 and the final report to be submitted in week 10.

Creating planning charts

Specialist computer programs are available for creating Gantt charts (such as Microsoft *Project*), but a generic spreadsheet such as Microsoft *Excel* can be used to create simple versions using the 'stacked bar' type of chart (see Figure 8.2). Be aware, however, of the danger of spending too much time producing such plans at the expense of time that should be spent on achieving the goals of the project itself.

3 **Complete your project.** It is important that you recognise the need to draw your project to a close on time. For a research project, this 'closure' could involve making a decision about when you have enough material to write up a viable report. In most cases, you simply need enough data or ideas to demonstrate that you can follow the 'model' of a typical research report in your discipline, since you will be judged on this.

Time management is critical for successful project management. As a student, you will need to balance the time you devote to study, family, work and social activities. You may have more freedom to do so than many others, but it is still a challenging task. Table 8.2 provides some tips for organising your time.

Table 8.2 Tips for successful time management

1 Organise your activities more methodically
Key tools for achieving this are: • Diaries and planners. These should be used to keep track of your day-to-day schedule and to note submission deadlines. • Timetables. These are useful for lengthy tasks such as exam revision, or project work. • Wall-planners. Another way of charting out your activities with the advantage, like a timetable, that you can see everything in front of you.
2 Adopt good working habits
For example: • Get into a work routine, for example, perhaps by making specific evenings the time for library study or working on a project. • Do important work when you are at your most productive – most of us can state a time of day we work at our best. Timetable your activities to suit: academic work when you are 'most awake' and routine activities when you are less alert. • Make the most of small scraps of time – use otherwise unproductive time such as when commuting to jot down ideas, edit work or make plans. • Keep your documents organised – if your papers are well filed, then you won't waste time looking for something required for the next step. • Extend your working day – if you can deal with early rising, you may find that setting your alarm earlier than normal provides a few extra hours to help you achieve a short-term goal.
3 Avoid putting things off
One of the hardest parts of time management is getting started on tasks. Putting things off – procrastination – is all too easy. The symptoms include: talking about your work rather than doing it; excessive planning; doing other low priority work in preference; switching frequently among tasks and doing unproductive things like watching TV programmes or socialising. To avoid this, find a way to get started, possibly by carrying out a more mundane element of the task such as listing references, or writing a materials and methods section.
4 Avoid perfectionism
Delaying completion of a task because you want it to be perfect is a form of procrastination. Good time managers recognise when to finish tasks, even if they are not in a 'perfect' state. When you have multiple assignments, doing this can mean that the sum of results is better, because your attention is divided more appropriately, rather than focusing on a single task to the detriment of the others.

At times you may run into problems because you have a number of different tasks that need to be done. Deciding on their priority involves distinguishing between important and urgent activities.

● 'Importance' implies some assessment of the benefits of completing a task against the loss if the task is not finished.

● 'Urgency' relates to the length of time before the task must be completed.

For example, in normal circumstances, doing your laundry will be neither terribly important nor particularly urgent, but if you start to run out of clean underwear, you may decide otherwise. Hence, priorities are not static and need to be reassessed frequently.

It is useful to write your current tasks down in a list each day, rather than risk forgetting them. You will then have a good picture of what needs to be done and will be better able to prioritise the tasks. Once you've created a list, rank the tasks by numbering them 1, 2, 3 and so on, in order from 'important and urgent' to 'neither important nor urgent' (see Figure 8.3). Your 'important' criteria will depend on many factors: for example, your own goals; the weight of marks given to each assessment; how far away the submission date is.

High ← **Urgency** → Low

Figure 8.3 **The urgent–important approach to prioritising.** Place each activity somewhere on the above axes in relation to its importance and urgency. Do all the activities in sector 1 first, then 2 or 3, and last, 4.

Each day, you should try to complete as many of the listed tasks as you can, starting with number one. The process of striking out each task as it is completed provides a feeling of progress being made, which turns into one of satisfaction if the list has virtually disappeared by the evening. Also, you will become less stressed once high-priority tasks are tackled. Carry over any uncompleted tasks to the next day, add new ones to your list and start again – but try to complete yesterday's unfinished jobs before starting new ones of similar priority, or they will end up being delayed for too long.

Advantages of being organised

If you organise your time well, you will:

■ keep on schedule and meet deadlines

■ complete work with less pressure and fulfil your potential

■ reduce stress caused by a feeling of lack of control over your work schedule

■ build your confidence about your ability to cope

■ avoid overlapping assignments and having to juggle more than one piece of work at a time

Being organised is especially important for large or long-term tasks because it seems easier to put things off when deadlines seem distant.

 PRACTICAL TIPS FOR DECISION-MAKING, PROJECT MANAGEMENT AND PRIORITISATION

When planning, set yourself an artificial deadline a little before the true completion date. This will have several benefits: it will provide potentially valuable 'slippage time' in case things go wrong; it will give you more time to think about your work (especially writing); and it will help you to avoid any problems with producing and delivering any outcome (such as a report).

Improve your work environment. Your focus and concentration will depend on this. Create a tidy workplace; gather all the materials you need in one place; file away everything else tidily (including computer folders and files); reduce external noise. If necessary, escape from distractions by working somewhere else.

Analyse your time management personality. Can you recognise any character traits that are preventing you from organising your time effectively? Might any of the tips in Table 8.2 help you to become better at time management? How could you adapt them to your own situation?

Invest in tools to support your time management. Helpful items could include a diary/planner; wall-planner; mobile phone with diary facility or app; or alarm clock ... then use them!

Try not to be a perfectionist. Many projects never get started, stall or fail to be completed because the people involved are aiming for perfection, when this is either impossible or impractical. Often, achieving perfection would be a waste of resources. If you identify this as a potential characteristic in yourself, try to accept that fact, and focus on minimising the larger flaws in your work and on completing the task despite any minor faults you believe are present.

 AND NOW ...

8.1 Reflect on past examples of your decision-making. Thinking about a specific difficult decision you have faced in the recent past, what method(s) did you use to evaluate your options and choose one of them? Was it effective? How well did you plan the consequent actions? Did you achieve your goal on time? How might you improve these skills?

8.2 Investigate how you really use your time. Time management experts often ask clients to write down what they do for every minute of several days and thereby work out how to maximise their productive time. Use a timesheet to keep a detailed record of your activities for a short period, using a suitable coding for your activities. Now, analyse the data to see whether you spend excessive amounts of time on any one activity or have an incorrect balance of activities.

8.3 Experiment with listing and prioritising. If you haven't used this method before, test it out for a week or so. After your trial period, decide how effective the method was in organising your activities and helping you to ensure that tasks were done on time.

9

GROUP EFFORT AND COLLABORATION

How to enhance your contribution to teamwork

At university, you will find teamwork involved in tutorials, project work, role-play exercises and some extra-curricular activities. Understanding groupwork psychology and interactions can help you gain more from these activities. 'Team thinking' requires a collective awareness of others and shared skills.

KEY TOPICS

→ Principles of team membership

→ Working in a group

→ Participating in tutorials

→ Taking part in committees and meetings

KEY TERMS

Devil's advocate   Study group   Team role   Tutorial

Contributing as a team member requires different thought patterns compared to solo activities. Your thinking must be in tune with the group's common aim, rather than your personal agenda. You will benefit from an understanding of team interactions and the team ethic. Collectively, the group's 'team thinking' requires shared skills and qualities, including those of communication and negotiation.

Research suggests that there are many distinct team personalities and that each of us has a 'natural' team role. Groupwork exercises at university can help you discover which role suits you best. Reflecting on these group activities will help you develop as a team member. What you find out about yourself may even influence your eventual choice of career and job.

Examples of teamwork at university

- Preparing a group poster
- Writing a joint report
- Some types of problem-based learning
- Practical and project work
- Running a society or sports club

PRINCIPLES OF TEAM MEMBERSHIP

Table 9.1, which is based on the work of Meredith Belbin, gives a breakdown of team roles and the personality features associated with them. His analysis recognises that there are both 'good' character traits and 'allowable weaknesses' for each role. This notion is valuable, because it reduces the feeling that any one role is superior. For example, you may have the impression that 'team leader' is the star role in any group. However, leader types are generally poor at coming up with ideas and can be weak at putting them into practice (Table 9.1); these are functions vital to the success of any group and they may well be your strength.

Effective teamwork requires an insight into these roles and the ways in which teams operate. Collectively, your team will need to demonstrate certain key features:

- **Ability to communicate** – group members need to understand what is expected of them; time frames have to be defined; arrangements for meetings made; information or files exchanged. The larger the group, the more important this becomes.
- **Time management** – there will always be a deadline for your team's work and this implies that planning will be required to meet your goal (Ch 8).
- **Compromise** – give-and-take is essential to team function at many levels. To succeed as a group you will have to get along together. This may require diplomacy, tact and a willingness to give and receive criticism constructively.
- **Focus and commitment** – teamwork exercises are often demanding in time and effort; everyone needs to take responsibility and work hard if high standards are to be achieved. Your group must keep its collective eye on its goals and targets.

Table 9.1 The nine team roles identified by Meredith Belbin. Use this table to identify the role(s) suited to you and their key features. Some authorities prefer to simplify this analysis. One grouping of roles, using the role numbering of the table, is: 'Leader type': A+ B; 'Creative person': C + E; 'Critic': D; 'Organiser': F + G; 'Worker': H + I.

Team role	Key attributes and beneficial functions in a team	Allowable weaknesses
A The coordinator	A 'caring' leader type who is calm and authoritative. Takes a balanced view and displays sound judgement. Makes the team work towards its shared goal. Good at spotting others' talents and delegation.	May be less creative or intelligent than others and have no special expertise.
B The shaper	A 'manipulative' leader type who is a dynamic go-getter but impatient for results. Good at generating action, trouble-shooting and imposing a pattern. Provides drive and realism to team activities.	Can be headstrong, emotional and impatient with others.
C The innovator	An intelligent, creative, ideas person, who generates solutions to problems and often uses unusual approaches. A source of originality for the group's activities.	May work in isolation and ideas may be impractical. May not communicate well.
D The monitor–evaluator	The 'critic' who analyses what the team is doing in a detached and unemotional way. Good at evaluating the group's ideas and making sure they are appropriate.	May lack drive and have a low work rate. Critical comments may act to de-motivate others.
E The resource investigator	An extrovert, communicative sort, who enthusiastically investigates new information and ideas. Good at exploiting resources and developing external relations.	Can be over-optimistic and may have a short attention span.
F The implementer	A hard worker who uses energy, discipline and common-sense to solve problems. Turns ideas into actions. Good at making sure things get done.	May lack flexibility and resist new ideas.
G The completer-finisher	A conscientious individual who is anxious that tasks are completed to a high standard. Painstaking, orderly and well-organised. Good focus on fulfilling objectives.	Obsessive about details and may wish to do too much of the work to control quality and outcome.
H The teamworker	A social type whose aim is to support others and provide cohesion to the team. Perceptive of others' feelings – helpful and diplomatic in approach. Promotes team spirit.	Doesn't like to lead or make decisions.
I The specialist	The kind of person who provides essential expertise and skills to the group. Adds a professional dimension but can be single-minded and may not suffer fools gladly.	Narrow outlook. Can be obsessed by technical detail and not see the big picture.

Which team role suits you best?

To help decide which role might suit you, think whether you would describe yourself as action-orientated, people-orientated, or as a thinker. Belbin classified his nine team roles in this way and, by narrowing the options, this approach may help you to decide which fits you best:

- **Action-oriented** members should be a shaper, implementer or a completer–finisher (types B, F or G in Table 9.1)
- **People-orientated** members should be a coordinator, a resource investigator or a teamworker (types A, E or H)
- **Thinkers** should be an innovator, a monitor–evaluator or a specialist (types C, D or I)

Any difficulties in groupwork are best treated by discussing them as soon as they become apparent, either within the team or with mediation by the staff supervising the task.

- Where possible, try to ensure that people are assigned roles that best fit with their personality. Otherwise, they may feel uncomfortable. Be aware that difficulties also occur when someone tries to assume a different role from the one they have been assigned.

- When you work in a small team, members may be asked to play multiple roles or to switch between roles at different times as the project progresses.

- If some members do not feel sufficiently motivated, then the group as a whole may lack drive. One of the leader's roles is to stimulate the group, and this might be done by emphasising the relevance of the task and the rewards for doing it well.

- For perfectionists, teamwork can be taxing because they may need to accept that some aspects of the group's activities will be below their normal standards – but this could be essential to ensure that the team as a whole fulfils its remit. Likewise, for those who like to be 'in control', giving over tasks to others can be stressful. In teamwork, everyone needs to accept that others may take a different approach to themselves.

- Sometimes, personalities clash when it is felt that someone is not pulling their weight, or when someone acts as an outsider (or is treated as one). If this is suspected, early and frank discussion is essential.

- If the team's progress falters, you may need to consider how you modify the task or the method you have agreed upon. This may result in an outcome less ambitious, but still of a high standard.

WORKING IN A GROUP

Studying formally as a group normally means that you are participating in a learning activity that has been initiated by an academic staff member. This could be a project, lab activity or practical facilitated by a lecturer, or it may be an exercise that is conducted independently of the staff member.

Groupwork pointers

Important rules for working effectively in a group, whether in a formal or informal setting:
- learn to listen as well as speak
- respect the views of others
- understand that criticism of your views is not a personal slight
- prevent anyone from dominating the discussion or activity
- ensure that everyone is given space to give their views

In staff-led study groups, you should:

- ensure that you are prepared adequately for the group activity;
- participate in the discussion and do not leave one or two people to do all the talking;
- have the confidence to express your views even if these seem to be at variance with those of others;
- be prepared to defend your views or suggestions with reasoned argument supported by well-considered evidence;
- use the group learning experience as an opportunity to explore issues or ideas in greater depth with an expert to guide you;
- recognise that a tutor may act as 'Devil's advocate' to push you into exploring alternative scenarios, options or strategies.

Tutorials are an example of this kind of study group, discussed further below.

In unsupervised student study groups, you should:

- work out and agree some ground rules, such as setting goals, responsibilities and deadlines;

- ensure that the work allocation is evenly distributed across the group;

- create a positive learning environment by addressing the task in hand and ensuring that people do not feel constrained in presenting their ideas;

- engage in analytical thinking to tackle the task in hand;

- encourage everyone to contribute ideas and explore their implications and also counter-arguments.

Typically, these sorts of groups will work on a presentation such as a poster or brief talk.

Set up an informal study group

Sometimes a self-selected group of students decides to tackle a particular issue or topic independently, perhaps as part of revision for exams. It is a fun and sociable way to learn. To set up such a group:

- speak to your lab partners or fellow members of formal groups

- speak to people before or after lectures, or as you walk between lecture theatres

- place a message on a discussion board on your virtual learning environment

- email fellow class members

- ask your class rep or the lecturer to make an announcement ('anyone interested in setting up a study group, meet after the lecture...')

Next, agree on a specific time and place to meet – for example, in the open discourse area of the library rather than in the union bar where other distractions could interfere with the purpose of the group. Agree targets and work towards fulfilling these within a certain time span: the group might share resources; debate issues from lectures; discuss learning approaches. Not everything you may wish to tackle can be solved within the group and it is sometimes appropriate to seek help from a staff member.

Finding the right person for the job

At different times, your team will need someone to coordinate the task; someone to come up with bright, inventive ideas; someone to keep everyone else on target; someone who can find useful facts; someone who is good at design; someone who can organise materials; and someone to act as a spokesperson. By sharing these tasks appropriately, the overall output from the team will be improved.

PARTICIPATING IN TUTORIALS

Tutorials are a method of gathering a small group of students together to discuss a topic or tackle problems related to a particular aspect of their course. Among other things, they require you to think on your feet, create logical arguments, recognise flaws in others' positions and problem-solve.

There are essentially three types of university tutorial. One is common in subjects related to the Arts, Social Sciences, Law and Social Work, for example. In this kind of tutorial a pre-set topic is considered in a discussion format.

Tips for tutorial preparation

For discussion-style tutorials in non-scientific subjects, you should have:
■ done the required reading
■ identified and analysed the topic or theme
■ reflected on the key issues that arise
■ considered the topic from different angles, e.g. arguments for and against a particular set of ideas or proposals

For tutorials in practical or numerical subjects, you should have:
■ tackled the full set of problems or done the prescribed reading
■ where required, to have submitted answers on time
■ thought about difficulties that you may have found with the tutorial problems or about possible issues that might arise in the discussion
■ reflected on how this topic or set of problems fits into the wider course structure and learning process

A second type is more common in scientific, engineering and business-related disciplines; here, students discuss answers to a series of problems or calculations under the guidance of a tutor.

A third type is the personal tutorial where a student meets with a tutor (sometimes called an adviser of studies) to discuss your academic progress and curriculum options.

The tutor's role is to facilitate discussion or, for problem-solving tutorials, to assist students encountering difficulties. In addition, he or she may be required to make an assessment of your participation and performance. Regardless of your discipline, your role in these tutorial situations requires preparation and participation.

TAKING PART IN COMMITTEES AND MEETINGS

Committees and their meetings are important for the operation of large organisations like universities. As a student, you might contribute as a student representative to formal university meetings or organise your own as part of the students' association. Such meetings have a format and a set of implicit rules that can seem intimidating to the uninitiated. Table 9.2 provides definitions of some of the terms and procedures that are used.

The thinking skills required for committee work involve such matters as:

● evaluating papers on complex topics;
● critically analysing issues and arriving at a point of view;
● persuading other members that your stance is appropriate;
● responding to the points of others in discussion.

The formality of the meeting and the impact of any decisions made may add a dimension of difficulty to your input.

To be an effective committee member, you should be well-prepared. You will be expected to read the relevant paperwork, contribute to the discussion when appropriate and sometimes be part of a sub-committee or working group. If you are a member because of a specific role, you may be expected to contribute reports and other agenda items. If you are the chair (or convenor) of a committee, you will help organise the agenda, conduct the meeting and either write or approve the draft minutes.

Table 9.2 Membership, key terms and rules of conduct for committee meetings. A university committee is usually a subordinate group to a larger body (such as a university senate) that has been given powers to make decisions or recommendations and suggest actions.

1 Membership

- **A chair** (or convenor), whose role is to organise the agenda, sometimes in partnership with the secretary; conduct the meeting by selecting speakers, summarising discussion and helping the group to arrive at decisions; approve the draft minutes.
- **The minute secretary** takes notes at the meeting and writes the draft minute.
- **Ordinary members** may be elected or appointed according to the rules of membership of the committee.
- **Ex-officio members** are those who are present because they hold a particular office.
- **Coopted members** may be appointed to bring specialised knowledge or experience to the committee.
- **Invited participants** may make presentations or act as observers, usually for a single meeting, but are not otherwise involved in decision-making.

2 Key terms

- **The remit** gives the terms of reference of the committee; it defines the limits of what should be discussed and where it reports to. An appendix usually outlines what the membership is.
- **The agenda** gives the order of discussion at the meeting and usually has the following elements:
  (1) minute of previous meeting
  (2) matters arising – points from the minute, possibly with reports from those delegated with tasks at the previous meeting
  (3) items for discussion (sometimes only 'starred' items are discussed)
  (4) any other business
  (5) date of next meeting.
  Discussion papers and policy proposals may accompany agenda items. Together with the agenda and minute of the previous meeting, these are usually circulated beforehand.
- **The minute** is an abbreviated record of what was said at the meeting. It indicates who was present and what actions were agreed. After approval, these may be circulated to other groups or published on an internal website.

3 Rules of conduct

- The chair leads the meeting and introduces agenda items or asks others to do so.
- Members of the committee should ask to speak by gaining the chair's attention, perhaps by part-raising a hand.
- The minute of the previous meeting is usually corrected and formally approved as an initial part of the agenda.
- If the committee reports to another group, its observations may be reported back to the original committee.
- After discussion of each agenda item, any observations or actions are agreed by consensus or formal vote. The chair usually summarises these decisions before moving on.
- The secretary rarely contributes, but should inform the committee about matters of procedure and assist the chair regarding points of information and the committee's remit.
- If discussion does not fall within the remit of the committee, the chair may state this, sometimes using the Latin term *ultra vires* ('beyond strength').
- 'Any other business' includes items not on the agenda that the members wish to raise. Normally the chair should be given warning that a member wishes to raise an issue.
- A 'point of order' is a quibble about the relevance of an item or point of procedure.

In all group meetings, the members will have views of their own and something to say, if given the opportunity. Sometimes one person dominates the discussion, so you will need to develop some skills in interpersonal communication to ensure that you have the chance to be both a speaker and a listener (Ch 6). Table 9.3 introduces some of the 'characters' you may encounter in meetings and suggests some conversational strategies that can help to promote turn-taking in group dialogue.

 PRACTICAL TIPS FOR PARTICIPATING IN GROUPWORK

Think ahead. One of the secrets of successful participation in tutorials and committees is to have thought through your position carefully in advance. This may involve thinking one or more steps beyond your own position, so that you are able to counter any immediate arguments against it.

In problem-solving tutorials, make sure that you have done the full set of examples beforehand. Identify those which have caused difficulty or raised questions in your mind so that you can discuss these points with the tutor. Think about the underlying principles involved in the exercises and how the examples fit into the wider scheme of things, especially your lectures.

In tutorials based on discussion, make sure that you contribute. Make your points clearly and objectively – while you may hold strong views on a topic, you will be expected to explain these on the basis of supporting evidence and argument, not on emotion. Don't take criticism of your points personally – this is an objective academic exercise and the tutorial would be dull and possibly pointless if everyone agreed.

Learn to listen as well as to speak. The convention in meetings is that everyone has space to speak and be heard. Although you may not agree with the views of others, at least listen to what they have to say and consider their argument for its merits as well as its flaws.

Believe in yourself and your ideas. Your thoughts are probably as valid as anyone else's; do not be put off by those who sound extremely eloquent and well-read – sometimes there is little substance behind what they say.

Table 9.3 **Typical personalities found in meetings.** Groups like tutorials and committees comprise people with different personalities, views and experience. Learning to interact with these individuals can be challenging. The rightmost column suggests some approaches that might be useful to stimulate an even balance of discussion.

Character	Characteristic behaviour	Typical oral strategies	Oral strategies in response
The quiet one	Shy and retiring. Never, or rarely, offers an opinion on topic. Takes lots of notes. Avoids eye contact with others. Speaks only when spoken to.	• *I don't know.* • *Says nothing.*	• *What do you think about this?* • *What do you think about X's work?*
The know-it-all	Has an opinion on almost everything. May have done reading but no reflection on deeper meaning; or has done problems but omits key steps.	• *In my opinion...* • *I think...* • *It's my view that...* • *If you ask me...*	• *I think you're taking rather a narrow view on this. What about...?*
The centre-stager	Likes to be the centre of attention. Attempts to monopolise the attention of the group and prevents others from asking questions or from contributing.	• *I see this breaking down into 10 areas. The first one is...; the second one is...; the tenth one is...*	• *Could I come in here?* • *Actually, I have a related point...* • *I'd like to come in here.*
The conversation monopoliser	Is bright, has a lot to say but goes on and on. Rarely gives way to others.	• *My understanding of X is that... furthermore... on the other hand... I'd also like to say that...*	• *Could we hear other views?* • *Let's summarise what you've said so that I can make sure I understand your point.*
The interrupter	Not a good listener. Keeps talking over others or interrupting when others are speaking.	• *If I could come in here...* • *I can't let that point go unchallenged...*	• *Could I just finish my point?* • *That's really a digression.*
The uncertain one	Not very confident of own understanding or abilities – usually unfairly. Doesn't ask questions to confirm understanding. Rarely offers opinion except when asked directly.	• *I'm not sure.* • *I don't think I know.*	• *How would you tackle this?* • *That's a really good point. I quite agree with you.*
The uninterested one	Appears to be unsure why he or she is present. Gazes out of the window, plays with mobile device.	• *Don't know. I'm only here until the pub opens.* • *This is really boring, isn't it?*	• Ignore.
The active member	Contributes and listens. Has done the preparation; sorted out some of the ideas; not too sure about some points. Asks for clarification.	• *Could you explain...?* • *There are three points to make.* • *What do other people think?*	• *I think that's a well-considered point. Could you expand?* • *That's an interesting observation. What do others think?*

GO AND NOW ...

9.1 Establish your 'ideal' team role. Categorise yourself as action-oriented, people-oriented or a thinker (see p. 107), then decide which of Belbin's categories best fits you (Table 9.1). It may be helpful to ask a friend or past teamwork colleague what they think, although be prepared for a different answer to the one you were expecting.

9.2 Reflect on your last teamwork activity. What were your major contributions to the overall team activity? Looking at Table 9.1, what role or roles did you adopt? How did the team work to achieve the target? What were its strengths? What were its weaknesses? How might you use this experience to modify your approach to your next team exercise?

9.3 Identify 'characters' in groups and meetings. Read through Tables 9.1 and 9.3 and see if any of the personalities outlined there are present in your group(s). Think about how these characters interacted in previous meetings. Might some of the strategies noted in Table 9.3 have assisted in creating a more balanced discussion? What kind of a character are you? Would it be helpful to your learning, and that of others, if you modified your behaviour?

EVALUATING THE
IDEAS OF OTHERS

10

EVALUATING INFORMATION SOURCES

How to filter and select reliable material

So much information is available nowadays, and through such a wide range of media, that the evaluation of sources has become a core skill. This chapter will help you understand the origin of information and ideas and judge the reliability of sources.

KEY TOPICS

→ The origin of information and ideas

→ Assessing sources of facts

→ Checking the reliability of fact and opinion

KEY TERMS

Jargon   Peer review   Primary source   Provenance   Secondary source

Whatever subject you are studying at university, the ability to evaluate information and ideas is essential. This is a key aspect of 'information literacy', involving multi-faceted skills that will differ according to the task in hand.

Your analysis may centre on the accuracy or truth of the information itself, the reliability or potential bias of the source of the information, or the value of information in relation to some argument or case. You may also come across contradictory sources of evidence or conflicting arguments based on the same information. You will need to assess their relative merits. To do any or all of these tasks, you will need to understand more about the origin and nature of information.

Information literacy and critical thinking

Information literacy has been defined as: *'knowing when and why you need information, where to find it, and how to evaluate, use and communicate it in an ethical manner'* (CILIP, 2012). Seven key thinking skills are associated with information literacy (adapted from SCONUL, 2012):

1 the ability to identify a personal need for information ('identify' information)

2 the ability to assess current knowledge and identify gaps ('scope' information)

3 the ability to construct strategies for locating information and data ('plan' information)

4 the ability to locate and access the information and data needed ('gather' information)

5 the ability to review the research process and compare and evaluate information and data ('evaluate')

6 the ability to organise information professionally and ethically ('manage' information)

7 the ability to apply the knowledge gained: present the results of personal research, synthesise new and old information and data to create new knowledge and disseminate it in a variety of ways ('present' information)

You should assess how well you can carry out each of these skills. Consult library staff for assistance if necessary.

THE ORIGIN OF INFORMATION AND IDEAS

Essentially, facts and ideas originate from someone's research or scholarship. These can be descriptions, concepts, interpretations, or numerical data. At some point, information or ideas must be communicated or published, otherwise no-one would know about them. The medium of publication can vary depending on discipline. Advancing research is often published in academic journals, but particularly in the arts and humanities, books may contain new information and ideas. Table 10.1 provides a list of information sources, with an indication of typical content.

Table 10.1 Some of the types of content that can be obtained from library resources. These may be available in hard copy or online.

Type of resource	Examples	Indication of content
Books	• Prescribed texts	Provide clear linkage with the course content
	• General textbooks	Give an overview of the subject
	• Supplementary texts	Discuss subject in greater depth
Reference books	• Standard dictionaries	Provide spelling, pronunciation and meaning
	• Bilingual dictionaries	Provide translation of words and expressions in two languages
	• Subject-specific dictionaries	Define key specialist terms
	• General encyclopaedias	Provide a quick overview of a new topic
	• Discipline-specific encyclopaedias	Focus on in-depth coverage of discipline-specific topics
	• Biographical dictionaries or encyclopedias	Source of information on key figures both contemporary and from the past
	• Yearbooks	Provide up-to-date information on organisations
	• Atlases	Provide geographical information
	• Directories	Provide up-to-date access information on organisations
Newspapers	• Daily or weekly newspapers	Provide coverage of contemporary issues
Periodical and academic journals	• Discipline- or subject-specific publications produced three or four times per year	Provide recent ideas, reports and comment on current research issues
Popular periodicals	• *New Scientist, The Economist*	Provide coverage of emerging themes within broad field such as their titles suggest

One way of categorising the literature in any subject is as a 'primary' or 'secondary' source. Information and ideas usually appear first in the primary literature and may be modified later in the secondary literature (Table 10.2). Understanding this process is important when analysing and evaluating information and when deciding how to cite evidence or references within the text of your own assignments. Logically, the closer you can get to the primary source, the more consistent the information is likely to be with the original.

Table 10.2 Characteristics and examples of primary and secondary sources of information

Primary sources – those in which ideas and data are first communicated or found	• The primary literature in your subject may be published in the form of papers (articles) in journals. • The primary literature is usually refereed by experts in the authors' academic peer group, who check the accuracy and originality of the work and report their opinions back to the journal editors. This system helps to maintain reliability, but it is not perfect. • Books (and, more rarely, articles in magazines and newspapers) can also be primary sources but this depends on the nature of the information published rather than the medium. These sources are not formally refereed, although they may be read by editors and lawyers to check for errors and unsubstantiated or libellous allegations. • In some subjects, sources may be 'unofficial' documents such as letters or diaries or other types of 'official' documents such as company or commission reports, Acts of Parliament or legal judgments.
Secondary sources – those which quote, adapt, interpret, translate, develop or otherwise use information drawn from primary sources	• It is the act of recycling that makes the source secondary, rather than the medium. Reviews are examples of secondary sources in the academic world, and textbooks and magazine articles are often of this type. • As people adopt, modify, translate and develop information and ideas, alterations are likely to occur, whether intentional or unintentional. Most authors of secondary sources do not deliberately set out to change the meaning of the primary source, but they may unwittingly do so. Others may consciously or unconsciously exert bias in their reporting by quoting evidence only on one side of a debate. • Modifications while creating a secondary source could involve adding valuable new ideas and content or correcting errors.

 Who should you quote?

Always try to read and cite the primary source if you can. Do not rely on a secondary source to do this for you as you may find the author uses information selectively to support his or her case, or interprets it in a different way than you might.

ASSESSING SOURCES OF FACTS

Being able to assess sources is a key thinking skill. To do this, you will need to:

- gauge the reliability of the source or its author(s);
- understand the material within and filter out relevant facts and ideas;
- evaluate the reliability of any information or data presented;
- summarise the meaning of the source in relation to your own work.

Some sources and facts can be considered very reliable. In the sciences, one interpretation of reliability is that the observation or experiment can be repeated by a competent peer – well-established 'textbook' knowledge usually falls into this category. In other areas, reliability may be bound up with the track record and authority of the person making the assertion, or in the nature of the evidence which is cited to support a case.

One important method of establishing reliability is whether the original source has been 'peer reviewed'. This is where the material is reviewed by one or more academics ('referees') working in the same field, prior to being accepted for publication. This helps to ensure:

- the material is original;
- all relevant past work is quoted;
- conflicting theories and opinions are mentioned;
- any data and calculations are checked;
- interpretations of information and data are valid.

Such reviews cannot guarantee reliability, and it can be argued that they may act to entrench 'established' viewpoints: radical new ideas often encounter extreme resistance when they are first put forward. It is the journal editor's task to ensure that a balance between freedom of speech and satisfactory reasoning is maintained.

Other sources are a lot less reliable. They may not cite evidence, or this may not be available for examination by others. In the worst cases, evidence may be fabricated or impossible to assess or test. What you read could be misquoted, misrepresented, erroneous, or based on a faulty premise. The data presented may carry no indication of error levels. These risks are particularly important for web-based information as this is less likely to be refereed or edited.

Clearly, a lot depends on who wrote the source and under what patronage (that is, who paid them?). Hence, another important way of assessing sources is to investigate the ownership and 'provenance' of the work (who and where it originated from, and why).

- **Authorship.** Can you identify who wrote the piece? If it is signed or there is a 'by-line' showing who wrote it, you might be able to judge the quality of what you are reading. This may be a simple decision, if you know or can assume the author is an authority in the area; otherwise a little research (for example, by putting the name into a search engine) might help.

  Of course, just because Professor X thinks something, this does not make it true. However, if you know that his or her opinion is backed by years of research and experience, then you might take it a little more seriously than the thoughts of an unknown web author. If no author is cited, this may mean that no one is willing to take responsibility for the content. Could there be a reason for this?

- **Provenance.** Is the author's place of work mentioned? This might tell you whether there is likely to have been an academic study behind the facts or opinions given. If the author works for a public body, there may be publication rules to follow and they may even have to submit their work to a publications committee before it is disseminated. They are certainly more likely to get into trouble if they include scurrilous or incorrect material. Another question to ask is whether a company may have a vested interest behind the content.

Table 10.3 is a checklist for assessing the reliability of information you may read.

 Determining authorship and provenance

This information is easy to find in most published academic sources, and may even be presented just below the title for convenience. In the case of the World Wide Web, it may not be so easy to find what you want. Often relevant clues can be obtained from the header, body and footer information.

Table 10.3 A checklist for assessing the reliability of information. These questions are based on commonly adopted criteria; the more 'yes' answers you can give, the more trustworthy you can assume your source to be.

Assessing authorship and the nature of the source	Evaluating the information and its analysis
• Can you identify the author by name? • Can you determine what relevant qualifications he/she holds? • Can you say who employs the author? • Do you know who paid for the work to be done? • Is this a primary source rather than a secondary one? • Has the source been refereed or edited? • Is the content original or derived? • Does the source cite relevant literature? • Have you checked a range of sources?	• Is the source cited by others? • Is the date of the source likely to be important regarding the accuracy of the information? For example, is it contemporary to events, or is it written with the benefit of hindsight? • Have you focused on the substance of the information presented rather than its packaging? • Is the information fact or opinion? • Have you checked for any logical fallacies in the arguments? • Does the language used reveal the status of the information? • Have the errors associated with any numbers been taken into account? • Have the data been analysed using appropriate statistics? • Are any graphs constructed fairly?

CHECKING THE RELIABILITY OF FACT AND OPINION

The most obvious way to check reliability is to make cross-referencing checks. 'Triangulating' in this way involves looking at more than one source and comparing what is said in each. The sources should be as independent as possible (for example, do not compare an original source with one that is directly based on it). If you find the sources agree, you may become more certain of your position. If two sources differ, you may need to decide which is better.

Reliability of wikis and other web resources

The temporary nature of much of the material on the Web is a disadvantage for academic purposes because it may change or even disappear after you have cited it. It may be difficult or impossible to find out who authored the material. Wikis such as *Wikipedia* fall into this category.

One important focus should be distinguishing fact from opinion. To do this, you may need to answer the following questions. To what extent has the author supported a given viewpoint? Has relevant supporting information been quoted, via literature citations or the author's own researches? Are numerical data used to substantiate the points used? Are these data reliable and can you verify the information, for example, by looking at a source that was cited? Might the author have a hidden reason for putting forward biased evidence to support an opinion?

The task of evaluation

In 'scientific' subjects, you will need to interpret and check the reliability of data. This is essential for setting up and testing meaningful hypotheses, and therefore at the core of the scientific approach.

In 'non-scientific' subjects, ideas and concepts are important, and you may need to carry out an objective analysis of information and arguments so you can construct your own position, backed up with evidence.

At some point, you should concentrate on analysing the method being used to put the points over, rather than the facts themselves. This will help you detect fallacious arguments and logical flaws (Ch 6).

You should look closely at any data and graphs that are presented and the way they have been analysed. If the information you are looking at is numerical in form, have the errors of any data been taken into consideration, and, where appropriate, quantified? If so, does this help you arrive at a conclusion about how genuine the differences are between important values? Have the appropriate statistical methods been used to analyse the data? Are the underlying hypotheses the right ones? Have the results of any tests been interpreted correctly in arriving at the conclusion? Look closely at any graphs. These may have been constructed in such a way as to emphasise a particular viewpoint, for example by careful selection of axis starting points (Ch 7).

Don't be blinded by statistics. Leaving aside the issue that statistical methods don't actually deal with proof, only probability (p. 88), it is generally possible to analyse and present data in such a way that they support one chosen argument or hypothesis rather than another ('you can prove anything with statistics'). To deal with these matters, you will need at least a basic understanding of the 'statistical approach' and of the techniques in common use (Ch 7).

Consider the age of the source. 'Old' does not necessarily mean 'wrong', but ideas and facts may have altered between then and now. Can you trace changes through time in the sources available to you? What key events, works or changes in methods have forced any changes in the conclusions?

Look at the extent and quality of citations provided by the author. This applies particularly to articles in academic journals, where positions are usually supported by citations of others' work. These citations may indicate that a certain amount of research has been carried out beforehand, and that the ideas or results are based on genuine scholarship. If you doubt the quality of the work, these references might be worth looking at. How up-to-date are they? Do they cite independent work, or is the author exclusively quoting himself or the work of one particular researcher or research group?

Analyse the language used. Words and their use can be very revealing. Have subjective or objective sentence structures been employed? The former might indicate a personal opinion rather than an objective conclusion. Are there any tell-tale signs of propaganda? Bias might be indicated by absolute terms, such as 'everyone knows...'; 'I can guarantee that...' or, a seemingly unbalanced consideration of the evidence. How carefully has the author considered the topic? A less studious approach might be indicated by exaggeration, ambiguity, or the use of journalese and slang. Always remember, however, that content should be judged above presentation.

Look at who else has cited the author's work, and how. In many subjects, you can use the Web of Knowledge website (generally available via your university library or associated computer suites) to find out how often an article or author has been cited and by whom. You may then be able to consult these sources to see how others have viewed the original findings. Reviews of a subject area published after your source may also provide useful comments.

AND NOW ...

10.1 Use the checklist in Table 10.1 to assess a source about which you are uncertain. If you are unable to establish its reliability, you should research further around the topic.

10.2 Analyse the nature of your reading list. Each time you are provided with a reading list for a tutorial, assessment exercise, project or background reading, decide whether the sources on it should be considered as a primary or secondary, and why (see Table 10.1). If secondary, do they quote any of the primary sources? Try to get a copy of one of the primary sources, if available, and see if this reveals anything to you about the nature of knowledge, how it arises and how it is modified during translation.

10.3 Have a look at the primary literature in your subject area. This may be shelved in the library building or you may be expected to access it online (or both). Read one or two articles to gain a flavour of the format, style of writing, language and sources used. You will probably find the subject matter relatively impenetrable; although by the time you graduate you will probably have mastered much of the jargon used.

EFFECTIVE ACADEMIC READING

How to read efficiently and with understanding

The first stage in assimilating the ideas of other authors is reading. This chapter outlines the processes involved in reading and suggests methods that will help you deal more effectively with academic text.

KEY TOPICS

→ Surveying the overall organisation of a text
→ How to examine the structure of the writing itself
→ Speed-reading techniques
→ Reading online resources

KEY TERMS

Blurb   Finger tracing   Gist   Terminator paragraph   Topic paragraph
Topic sentence

Much of the material you will read as part of your studies will be books and chapters written following traditional academic style, and may appear, at first glance, to be heavy going. However, by taking advantage of the way printed academic resources are organised and understanding how text within them is structured, you should find it easier to read the pages of print in a way that will help you gain an understanding of the author's key points while saving you time.

Reading and note-taking

This chapter is concerned mainly with reading and comprehension as a prelude to note-taking (**Ch 12**). While it is possible to read and take notes at the same time, this is not always the most effective form of studying, as your notes may end up simply as a rewrite of the source text. Notes framed after you have scanned the prescribed section of text will be better if you have a clearer idea of their context and content.

SURVEYING THE OVERALL ORGANISATION OF A TEXT

A text may be suggested by tutors; alternatively, when expanding your lecture notes or revising, you may come across a resource in the library that looks as if it might be relevant. In either case, carry out a preliminary survey to familiarise yourself with what it contains. You can use elements of the structure to answer key questions about the content, as follows:

- **Title and author(s).** Does this text look as though it is going to be useful to your current task? Are the authors well-known authorities in the subject area?
- **Publisher's 'blurb'.** Does this indicate that the coverage suits your needs?
- **Publication details.** What is the date of publication? Will this book provide you with up-to-date coverage?
- **Contents listing.** Does this indicate that the book covers the key topic areas you need? Do the chapter titles suggest the coverage is detailed enough?
- **Index.** Is this comprehensive and will it help you find what you want, quickly? From a quick look, can you see references to material you want?
- **General impression.** Does the text look easy to read? Is the text easy to navigate via sub-headings? Is any visual material clear and explained well?

The answers to these questions will help you to decide whether to investigate further: whether you need to look at the whole book, or just selected parts; or whether the book is of limited value at the present time.

 What is your reading goal?

It is always a good idea to think about your purpose before you start reading any piece of text (see 'question stage' in Table 11.3).

- If you are looking for a specific point of information, this can often be done quickly, using the index or chapter titles as a guide.
- If you wish to expand your lecture notes using a textbook, you might read in a different way, which might result in note-taking (Ch 12).
- If your aim is to assimilate the author's embedded idea or ideas, then you may need to read more slowly and reread key parts.

Well-structured academic texts usually follow a standard pattern with an introduction, main body and conclusion in each element. Sometimes the introduction may comprise several paragraphs; sometimes it may be only one paragraph. Similarly, the conclusion may be several paragraphs or only one. Figure 11.1 illustrates a layout for a piece of text with five paragraphs, comprising an introduction and conclusion with three intervening paragraphs of varying length.

Within the structure of the text, each paragraph will be introduced by a topic sentence stating the content of the paragraph. Each paragraph performs a function.

Reader as author

Understanding the organisation of printed material and the structure of text are important for you as a reader or decoder of text, and they also come into play when you become an academic author and have to write down your own ideas clearly – they help your reader (often 'the marker') to decode your written text.

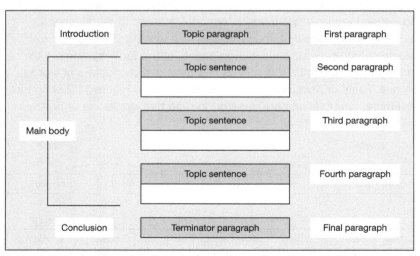

Figure 11.1 Sample textual layout. Most academic texts will be similarly organised, although, obviously, with more paragraphs.

For example, some paragraphs may describe, others may provide examples, while others may examine points in favour of a particular viewpoint and others points against that viewpoint.

The function of these paragraphs, and the sentences within them, is usually signalled by use of 'signpost words', which guide the reader through the logical structure of the text. For example, the word 'however' indicates that some contrast is about to be made with a point immediately before; 'thus' signals that a result or effect is about to be explained. A breakdown of text structure is given in Table 11.1.

Use this knowledge of text structure to establish general meaning.

● Read topic and terminator paragraphs, or even just their topic sentences, to gain a quick overview of the text.
● Scan through the text for key words related to your interest. This may indicate particular paragraphs worthy of detailed reading. Sometimes headings and sub-headings may be used, and these will facilitate a search of this kind.
● Look for signpost words to identify the underlying 'argument'.

SPEED-READING TECHNIQUES

Before describing techniques for improving reading speed, it is useful to understand how fast readers 'operate'. Instead of reading each word as a separate unit, these readers use what is called peripheral vision (what you see, while staring ahead, at the furthest extreme to the right and the left). This means that they absorb clusters of words in one 'flash' or 'fixation' on the text, as shown in Figure 11.2(a). In this example, four fixations are required to read that single line of text.

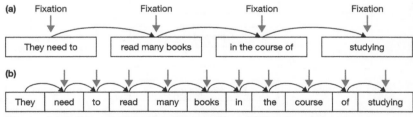

Figure 11.2 **Eye movements when reading. (a)** Reader who makes eye fixations on clusters of words. **(b)** Reader who reads every word one by one.

A reader who does this is reading more efficiently than the reader who reads word by word (Figure 11.2(b)). This reader makes 12 fixations along the line, which means that their reading efficiency is low. Research has also indicated that people who read slowly in this way are less likely to absorb information quickly enough for the brain to comprehend. Therefore, reading slowly can actually hinder comprehension rather than assist it.

As a practised reader, you will probably have developed these fast-reading skills to some degree. Other things you can do include 'finger tracing', where you run your finger below the line of text being read to follow your eyes' path across a page, starting and stopping a word or two from either side. This is said to increase your eye speed, keep your mind focused on the words being read and prevent you from skipping back to previous sentences or jumping forward to text that follows. Some people find it helpful to use a bookmark placed horizontally along the line they are reading, because it makes a useful guide that prevents the eye jumping ahead of the text they are reading.

Origin of speed-reading

The basic techniques were developed in the 1950s by Evelyn Wood, an American educator. She set up institutes to teach students to develop an ability to read hundreds of words per minute. Those who have studied her method include businessmen and politicians, who have to learn to read lengthy papers quickly but with understanding. US Presidents Jimmy Carter and John F. Kennedy were both regarded as famous speed-reading practitioners.

The average reading speed is said to be 265 words per minute (wpm). Reading speeds for university purposes may be slightly lower, as aspects like difficulty of the text, unfamiliarity with the terminology used and the complexity of the concepts being discussed in the text have the potential to slow down reading. However, as you become more familiar with the subject and the issues being covered in your course and, thus, with your supplementary reading, then your reading speed will increase.

Table 11.1 Sample reading text, showing reading 'signposts'. This text might represent the introduction to a textbook on modern communications in electrical engineering, journalism, marketing or psychology. The light shaded areas indicate the topic sentences; darker shading indicates the signpost words. You can also use this text of 744 words to assess your speed of reading (see Table 11.2).

Introduction Topic paragraph	Technological advances and skilful marketing have meant that the mobile phone has moved from being simply an accessory to a status as an essential piece of equipment. From teenagers to grandmothers, the nation has taken to the mobile phone as a constant link for business and social purposes. As a phenomenon, the ascendancy of the mobile phone, in a multitude of ways, has had a critical impact on the way people organise their lives.	Topic sentence
	Clearly, the convenience of the mobile is attractive. It is constantly available to receive or send calls. While these are not cheap, the less expensive text-message alternative provides a similar 'constant contact' facility. At a personal and social level, this brings peace of mind to parents as teenagers can locate and be located on the press of a button. However, in business terms, while it means that employees are constantly accessible and, with more sophisticated models, can access internet communications also, there is no escape from the workplace.	Topic sentence Signpost word Signpost word
	The emergence of abbreviated text-message language has wrought a change in everyday print. For example, pupils and students have been known to submit written work using text message symbols and language. Some have declared this to mark the demise of standard English. Furthermore, the accessibility of the mobile phone has become a problem in colleges and universities where it has been known for students in examinations to use the texting facility to obtain information required.	Topic sentence Signpost word Signpost word
	The ubiquity of the mobile phone has generated changes in the way that services are offered. For instance, this means that trains, buses, and restaurants have declared 'silent zones' where the mobile is not permitted, to give others a rest from the 'I'm on the train' style mobile phone conversation.	Topic sentence Signpost words
Transition paragraph	While the marked increase in mobile phone sales indicates that many in the population have embraced this technology, by contrast, 'mobile' culture has not been without its critics. Real concerns have been expressed about the potential dangers that can be encountered through mobile phone use.	Topic sentence Signpost words

	One such danger is that associated with driving while speaking on a mobile. A body of case law has been accumulated to support the introduction of new legislation outlawing the use of hand-held mobile phones by drivers while driving. The enforcement of this legislation is virtually impossible to police and, thus, much is down to the common sense and responsibility of drivers. Again, technology has risen to meet the contingency with the development of 'hands-free' phones that can be used while driving and without infringing the law.	Topic sentence
		Signpost word
	A further danger is an unseen one, namely the impact of the radiation from mobile phones on the human brain. Research is not well advanced in this area and data related to specific absorption rates (SARs) from the use of mobile phones and its effect on brain tissue is not yet available for evaluation. Nevertheless, although this lack of evidence is acknowledged by mobile phone companies, they advise that hands-free devices reduce the SARs levels by 98 per cent.	Topic sentence
		Signpost word
	Mobile phone controversy is not confined only to the potential dangers related to the unit alone; some people have serious concerns about the impact mobile phone masts have on the area surrounding them. The fear is that radiation from masts could induce serious illness among those living near such masts. While evidence refuting or supporting this view remains inconclusive, there appears to be much more justification for concern about emissions from television transmitters and national grid pylons, which emit far higher levels of electromagnetic radiation. Yet, little correlation appears to have been made between this fundamental of electrical engineering and the technology of telecommunications.	Topic sentence
		Signpost word
		Signpost word
Conclusion **Terminator paragraph**	In summary, although it appears that there are enormous benefits to mobile phone users, it is clear that there are many unanswered questions about the impact of their use on individuals. At one level, these represent an intrusion on personal privacy, whether as a user or as a bystander obliged to listen to multiple one-sided conversations in public places. More significantly, there is the potential for unseen damage to the health of individual users as they clamp their mobiles to their ears. Whereas the individual has a choice to use or not to use a mobile phone, people have fewer choices in relation to exposure to dangerous emissions from masts. While the output from phone masts is worthy of further investigation, it is in the more general context of emissions from electromagnetic masts of all types that serious research needs to be developed.	Topic sentence
		Signpost words
		Signpost words
		Signpost word
		Signpost word

Increasing your reading speed using finger tracing

■ Select a reading passage of about two pages in length (you could use the sample text in Table 11.1). Note your starting and finishing time and calculate your reading speed using Method B in Table 11.2.

■ Take a break of 40–60 minutes. Return to the text and run a finger along the line of text much faster than you could possibly read it.

■ Repeat, but more slowly, so that you can just read it ('finger tracing'). Again, note your starting and finishing times, and work out your reading speed. You should find that your reading speed has increased from the first reading.

■ Carry out this exercise at the same time of day over a week, using texts of similar length and complexity.

You can assess your normal reading speed using either method described in Table 11.2. The text of Table 11.1 is a suitable piece of writing whose word length is already known, should you wish to try method B. If your reading speed seems slow, you can work on improving it by using a similar level and length of text at the same time each day. Go through the reading speed process and, gradually, you should see your average creeping up.

Things that can reduce your reading speed

As well as trying methods to read faster, you should be aware of circumstances that might slow you down. These include:

■ distractions such as background noise of television, music or chatter

■ sub-vocalisation (sounding out each word as it is read aloud)

■ reading word by word

■ over-tiredness

■ poor eyesight – if you think your eyes are not 20:20, it might be worth going for an eye test; your eyes are too important to neglect and a pair of reading glasses may make a huge difference to your studying comfort

■ poor lighting – if you can, read using a lamp that can shine directly on to the text; reading in poor light causes eye strain and this, in turn, limits concentration and the length of reading episodes

Table 11.2 **How to calculate your reading speed.** Two examples.

Method A (specified reading time)	
(a) Select a chapter from a textbook (this is better than a newspaper or journal because these are often printed in columns)	
(b) Calculate the average number of words per line, e.g. 50 words counted over 5 lines	= 10 words per line
(c) Count the number of lines per page	= 41 total lines
(d) Multiply (b × c) = 10 × 41	= 410 words per page
(e) Read for a specific time (to the nearest minute or half-minute) without stopping	= 4 minutes' reading
(f) Number of pages read in 4 minutes	= 2.5 pages read
(g) Multiply (d × f) = 410 × 2.5	= 1025 total words read
(h) Divide (g ÷ e) = 1025 ÷ 4	**= 256 words per minute**
Method B (specified text length)	
(a) Find a piece of text of known word length (see method A)	= 744 words
(b) Note the time taken to read this in seconds	= 170 seconds
(c) Convert the seconds to a decimal fraction of minutes = 170 ÷ 60	= 2.8 minutes
(d) Divide (a ÷ c) = 744 ÷ 2.8	**= 266 words per minute**

Other strategies for reading and absorbing content quickly include:

- **Skimming.** Pick out a specific piece of information by quickly running your eye down a list or over a page looking for a key word or phrase, as when seeking a particular name or address in a phone book.

- **Scanning.** Let your eye run quickly over a chapter, for example before you commit yourself to study-read the whole text. This will help you to gain an overview of the chapter before you start.

- **Picking out the topic sentences.** As seen above and in Figure 11.1 and Table 11.1, by reading the topic sentences you will be able to flesh out your overview of the text content. This will aid your understanding before you study-read the whole text.

- **Identifying the signpost words.** As noted above, these help guide you as the reader through the logical process that the author has mapped out for you.

- **Recognising clusters of grammatically allied words.** Subliminally, you will group words in clusters according to their natural sense. This will help you to read by making fewer fixations and will improve your reading speed.

- **Taking cues from punctuation.** As you read, you will gain some understanding by interpreting the text's structure using the cues of full stops and commas, for example.

To be effective, reading quickly must be matched by a good level of comprehension; conversely, reading too slowly can hamper comprehension. You need to incorporate tests of your understanding to check that you have understood the main points of the text. One approach to reading that incorporates this is called the SQ3R method – survey, question, read, recall and review (Table 11.3). This incorporates memory and learning skills simultaneously.

Table 11.3 Reading for remembering: the SQ3R method. The reader has to engage in processing the material in the text and is not simply reading on 'autopilot', with very little being retained. Note-making is covered further in Chapter 12.

Survey stage
• Read the first paragraph (topic paragraph) and last paragraph (terminator paragraph) of a chapter or page of notes • Read the intervening paragraph topic sentences • Focus on the headings and sub-headings, if present • Study the graphs and diagrams for key features
Question stage
• What do you know already about this topic? • What is the author likely to tell you? • What specifically do you need to find out?
Read stage
• Read the entire section *quickly* to get the gist of the piece of writing; finger-tracing techniques may be helpful at this point • Go back to the question stage and revisit your initial answers • Look especially for keywords, key statements, signpost words • Do not stop to look up unknown words – go for completion
Recall stage
• Turn the book or your notes over and try to recall as much as possible • Make key pattern headings/notes/diagrams/flow charts (Ch 12) • Turn over the book again and check over for accuracy of recall; suggested recall periods – every 20 minutes
Review stage
• After a break, try to recall the main points

READING ONLINE RESOURCES

Of course, you can always print out material sourced from the Web, in which case, similar principles apply to those described elsewhere in this chapter. However, due to cost or environmental considerations, or simply the fact that that you need to assess the material before committing yourself to a printout, you may prefer to read directly from the screen. The following points are worth considering when doing this:

- Web page designers often divide text into screen-sized chunks, with links between 'pages'. This can make it difficult to gain an overall picture of the topic being covered. Make sure you read through the whole of the material before forming a judgement about it.

- One benefit of web-based material is that it is often written in a 'punchy' style, with bulleted lists and easily assimilated take-home messages, often highlighted with graphics. Bear in mind, however, that content may lack the detail required for academic work, for example in the number and depth of any examples given.

- The ease of access of web-based materials might cause a bias in your reading – perhaps towards more modern sources, but also, potentially, away from the overtly academic – always check to see whether 'standard' printed texts are advised on reading lists or are available in your library.

- The skimming method described on page 137 can be accelerated if you use the 'find' function (control + F in MS Word and Internet Explorer) to skip to key words.

- If you are likely to spend lengthy spells at a screen, make sure you are positioned well, with your eyes roughly level with the mid point of the screen.

- Take frequent breaks – stand up, walk around for a while and then return to the task.

- If you wear spectacles, you may find that an additional prescription for use when reading on-screen material is helpful. You can find out more about this from your institution's health and safety website or from an optician.

If you do decide to print out a resource, check on the screen for an icon that might give you a 'print-friendly' version.

PRACTICAL TIPS FOR READING EFFECTIVELY AND WITH UNDERSTANDING

Be selective and understand your purpose. Think about why you are reading. Look at the material you have already collected relating to the subject or topic you aim to study. For example, this should include lecture notes, which ought to remind you of the way a topic was presented, the thrust of an argument or a procedure. Are you reading to obtain a general overview or is it to identify additional specific information? Use a technique and material that suits your needs.

Adjust your reading speed according to the type of text you have to read. A marginally interesting article in a newspaper will probably require less intensive reading than a key chapter in an academic book.

Grasp the general message before dealing with difficult parts. Not all texts are 'reader friendly'. If you find a section of text difficult to understand, skip over that bit; toiling over it will not increase your understanding. Continue with your reading and when you come to a natural break in the text, for example the end of a chapter or section, then go back to the 'sticky' bit and reread it. Usually, second time round, it will make more sense because you have an overview of the context. Similarly, don't stop every time you come across a new word. Read on and try to get the gist of the meaning from the rest of the text. When you have finished, look the word up in a dictionary. You may wish to keep a list of these words and their definitions to help expand your vocabulary.

Take regular breaks. Reading continuously over a long period of time is counterproductive. Concentration is at a peak after 20 minutes, but wanes after 40 minutes. Rest frequently, but make sure that your breaks do not become longer than your study stints.

Follow up references within your text. When you are reading, you need to be conscious of the citations to other authors that might be given in the text; not all will be relevant to your reading purpose, but it is worth quickly noting the ones that look most interesting as you come across them. You'll usually find the full publication details in the references at the end of the chapter/article or at the end of the book. This will give you sufficient information to supplement your reading once you have finished reading the 'parent' text.

11.1 Monitor your reading speed. Choose a suitable text and calculate your speed using either method A or B in Table 11.2. If you feel your speed is relatively slow, try out some of the methods suggested in the speed-reading section of this chapter. After a period of using these methods, and deciding which suit you, check your speed to see if you have improved.

11.2 Practise surveying a text using a book from your reading list. Rather than simply opening your reading resource at the prescribed pages, spend five or ten minutes surveying the whole book. Think about how the author has organised the content and why. Keep this in mind when reading the text, and reflect on whether this has improved your comprehension and assimilation of the content.

11.3 Look for the clues in paragraph topic sentences. Next time you examine a piece of text, read the paragraph topic sentences first to see if you can gain an initial picture of the author's key ideas via this shortcut. This will also help you to pinpoint the key paragraphs to read in detail so you can assimilate the points in greater depth.

NOTE-MAKING FROM TEXTS

How to create effective notes for later reference

Keeping a record of the content of your reading is essential – there is simply too much information to remember and retain. This chapter outlines practical ways in which you can keep a record of what you read and think in appropriate note form so that it is meaningful to you at a later date. You should also note connections, critical thoughts and ideas that arise while you read.

KEY TOPICS

→ Why are you taking notes?

→ What do you need to record?

→ How are you going to lay out your notes?

KEY TERMS

Annotate   Citation   Citing   Landscape orientation   Mnemonic
Portrait orientation

Most courses provide a reading list of recommended resources. Depending on your subject, these include textbooks, journal articles and web-based materials. Sometimes you will be given specific references; at other times you will have to find the relevant material in the text for yourself. The techniques described in Chapter 11 will help you identify the most relevant parts of the text quickly and provide basic information for your note-making.

You will develop note-making skills as you progress in your studies. It takes time and experimentation to achieve a method that suits you. This will need to fit with your learning style (p. 46), the time that you can allocate to the task and be appropriate for the material and the subject area you are tackling. This chapter suggests a range of methods you can choose from in order to abstract and write down the key points from your sources.

WHY ARE YOU TAKING NOTES?

Students usually make notes for assignment writing and/or revision. Therefore, some texts will simply be 'dip in and out', while some will require intensive reading. You need to decide what your purpose is in making the notes. For example, it may be to:

- frame an overview of the subject;
- record a sequence or process;
- record what is novel in a piece of work (Ch 2);
- compare different viewpoints and/or arrive at your own (Ch 5);
- extract the logic of an argument or position (Ch 6);
- understand the meaning of data (Ch 7);
- borrow quotes (with suitable citation – see Ch 14);
- add your own commentary on the text.

This will influence the style, detail and depth of your notes. Whatever your purpose, a key aspect of note-making is that it makes you think about what you are reading. The act of translating and reducing text into your own words forces you to consider the content more deeply than when reading superficially.

WHAT DO YOU NEED TO RECORD?

One of the pitfalls of making notes is that people often start off with a blank sheet, pen in hand, and then begin to note 'important' points as they read. Within a short time, they are rewriting the book. To avoid this, the trick is to:

- identify your purpose;
- decide on the most appropriate note-making style and layout for the task;
- scan the section to be read;
- establish the writer's purpose, for example:
  - a narrative of events or process
  - a statement of facts
  - an explanation of reasoning or presentation of a logical argument
  - an analysis of an issue, problem or situation
  - a critique of an argument;

- work out their 'take' on the subject, and how this relates to your purpose;
- jot down ideas that arise during your reading;
- make links between this text and others, if any;
- ensure you paraphrase in your own words rather than transcribe, and if you do transcribe, use quote marks and note reference details (Chs 13 and 14).

HOW ARE YOU GOING TO LAY OUT YOUR NOTES?

There are several strategies that you might consider using. Figures 12.1–12.7 illustrate some examples. Not all will be relevant to your subject, but some will. Some may not seem directly suitable, but, with a little adaptation, they may work for you. Table 12.1 compares the advantages and disadvantages of each method.

Essentials of note-making

If you develop good practice in making your notes, it will save time.
- On all notes record the full details of source, namely:
  - author surname and initials
  - title in full with chapter and pages
  - date of publication
  - publisher and place of publication.

You will need this information to enable you to cite the source of information if you decide to use any of this information in your own writing (Ch 14).

- Add the date(s) you made the notes to record their sequence.
- Your notes have to be as meaningful in six days, weeks or months. Personalise them by using:
  - underlining
  - highlighting
  - colour coding
  - numbered lists
  - bullet points
  - mnemonics
  - distinctive layout
  - boxes for important points.

Note-making formats

Sometimes notes may be better suited to being laid out on paper in the landscape rather than the portrait position. This clearly suits methods such as mind maps (Figure 12.5). Similarly, you can take advantage of the landscape format when making matrix (grid) notes (Figure 12.6) by creating columns across the page.

It may be that a specific note-making strategy has attractions for you because it seems to fit with your learning preference. For example, someone with 'read–write preference' in the VARK system (p. 46) might prefer to use keyword or linear notes (Figures 12.1 or 12.2), while a 'visual learner' might prefer the concept map shown in Figure 12.5.

Other methods might suit a specific task: an assignment that requires you to analyse a complex set of viewpoints or positions might best be approached using the matrix approach shown in Figure 12.6, while one that asked you to review two sides of an argument could be tackled using the herring-bone map shown in Figure 12.7, or a variant of it.

Topic: DEPOPULATION OF THE COUNTRYSIDE   Source: Ormiston, J., 2002. Rural Idylls. Glasgow: Country Press.

Problem:
　　　　Population falling in rural areas
　　　　Traditional communities disintegrate
　　　　Incomer settlement – dormitory villages

Reasons:
　　　　Mechanisation of farming
　　　　Creation of farming combines
　　　　Bigger farms, fewer employed
　　　　Decline of traditional farming & related activities

Effects:
　　　　Families dispersed – fewer children
　　　　Closure of shops, post offices, schools, surgeries
　　　　Transport links less viable

Solutions:
　　　　Housing subsidies to encourage families to remain
　　　　Diversify economic activity, e.g. tourism/action holidays
　　　　Stimulate rural economy – farm shops, farmers' markets
　　　　Diversify from traditional crops – seek new markets

Figure 12.1 Example of keyword notes

Table 12.1 A comparison of the different methods of note-making from texts (illustrated in Figures 12.1–12.7)

Note type	Figure	Advantage	Disadvantage
Keyword notes	12.1	Good as a layout for easy access to information	Dependent on systematic structure in text
Linear notes	12.2	Numbered sequence – good for classifying ideas	Restrictive format, difficult to backtrack to insert new information
Time lines	12.3	Act as memory aid for a sequence of events; stages in a process	Limited information possible
Flow-chart notes	12.4	Allow clear path through complex options	Take up space; may be unwieldy
Concept maps/ mind maps	12.5	Good for recording information on a single page	Can become messy; can be difficult to follow; not suited to all learning styles
Matrix notes/ grid notes	12.6	Good layout for recording different viewpoints, approaches, applications	Space limitations on content or amount of information
Herringbone maps	12.7	Good for laying out opposing sides of an argument	Space limitations on content or amount of information

(a)

Topic: OBESITY IN CHILDREN

Source: Skinner, J., 2001. Diet and Obesity. Edinburgh: Castle Publishing.

1. Lifestyle
   1.1 Television, computer-games generation
   1.2 Unsupervised leisure time – sedentary
2. Diet
   2.1 Constant 'grazing' – junk food
   2.2 Additives/processed foods
   2.3 Lack of adequate fresh food, including fruit & vegetables
3. Exercise
   3.1 Sport by spectating rather than participating
   3.2 Decline in team sports in schools
   3.3 Children over-protected from 'free play' outdoors
4. Family
   4.1 Parents overeat; children likewise
   4.2 Instant food
   4.3 Food as an incentive & reward
5. Schools
   5.1 School meals spurned in favour of snack bar/chip shop
   5.2 Health-eating programmes as part of curriculum
6. Health service
   6.1 Less emphasis on prevention
   6.2 Limited health education of parents and children

(b)

Topic: GENERAL FEATURES OF ORGANIC MATERIALS

Source: Barker, J., 2001. Chemistry for University. Manchester: Midland Publishing.

1. Solid state – molec. crystal – powder, poly. Thin films
2. Unique physical properties – exploit for high-tech applications
3. Advantages
   3.1 Versatile properties – reg. by organic chemistry
   3.2 Readily accessible – via organic synthesis
   3.3 Low cost – cheap raw materials
   3.4 Tractable – fusable, soluble: easy to fab.
4. Disadvantage
   4.1 Relatively fragile
5. Important types
   5.1 Conducting CT salts
   5.2 Conducting poly

(c)

Topic: OPERATIONAL AMPLIFIERS

Source: Scott, D.I., 1977. Operational Amplifiers. Coventry: Circuit Publishers.

1. Usually an integrated circuit; can be discrete
2. Uses all technologies: bipolar; FET; MOS; BI-FET
3. Effectively a highly stable differential amplifier
4. Advantages
   4.1 High voltage gain – typ. 100,000
   4.2 High input impedance – typ. 1 MΩ – can be much higher, FET, MOS
   4.3 Low output impedance – typ. 600 Ω
   4.4 Low drift, BI-FET best
   4.5 Wide voltage supply range
5. Disadvantages
   5.1 Relatively narrow bandwidth – GBP typ. 1 MHz (but operates to DC)
   5.2 Very unstable in discrete versions – requires matched transistors
6. Common types
   6.1 741 – most common
   6.2 LM 380 – common AF AMP
   6.3 TDA 2030 – common power amp. – 20 W into 4 Ω

Figure 12.2 Examples of linear notes. These are drawn from three diverse disciplines where topics lend themselves to hierarchical approaches.

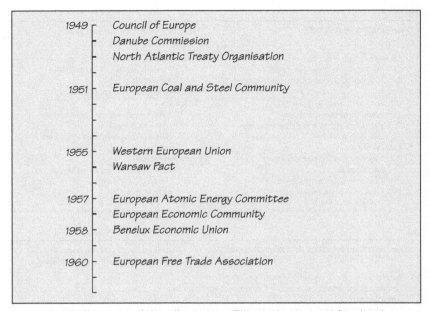

Figure 12.3 Example of time line notes. This design is good for showing a sequence of events, in this case the development of European organisations.

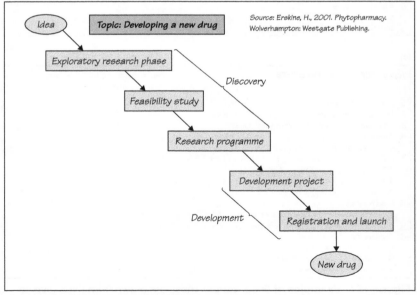

Figure 12.4 Example of flow chart notes. These are particularly useful for describing complex processes in visual form.

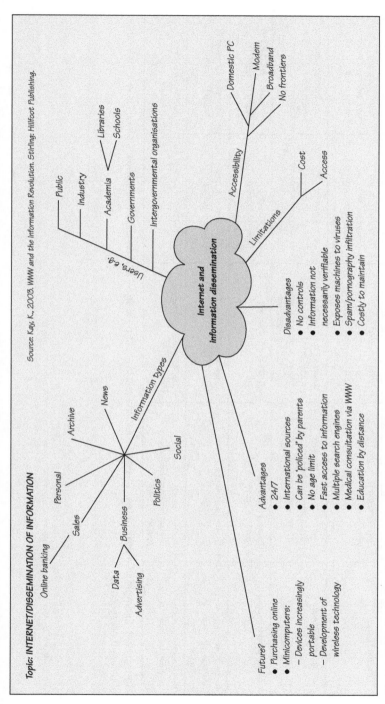

Topic: INTERNET/DISSEMINATION OF INFORMATION

Source: Kay, K., 2003. WWW and the Information Revolution. Stirling: Hillfoot Publishing.

Internet and information dissemination

Users, e.g.:
- Public
- Industry
- Academia
  - Libraries
  - Schools
- Governments
- Intergovernmental organisations

Accessibility
- Domestic PC
- Modem
- Broadband
- No frontiers

Limitations
- Cost
- Access

Disadvantages
- No controls
- Information not necessarily verifiable
- Exposes machines to viruses
- Spam/pornography infiltration
- Costly to maintain

Information types
- Archive
- News
- Personal
- Sales
- Online banking
- Data
- Advertising
- Business
- Politics
- Social

Advantages
- 24/7
- International sources
- Can be 'policed' by parents
- No age limit
- Fast access to information
- Multiple search engines
- Medical consultation via WWW
- Education by distance

Future?
- Purchasing online
- Minicomputers:
  - Devices increasingly portable
  - Development of wireless technology

Figure 12.5 Example of a concept map. This may also be called a mind map.

Source: Walker, I.M.A., 2005, Urban Myths and Motorists. London: Green Press.

Topic: TRAFFIC CONGESTION

Solutions	Council view	Police view	Local business view	Local community view
Pedestrianisation	+ Low Maintenance − Initial outlay	+ Easier to police + Less car crime + CCTV surveillance easier	+ Safer shopping and business activity − Discourages motorist customers	+ Safer shopping + Less polluted town/city environment
Park and ride schemes	+ Implements transport policy − Capital investment to initiate − Car park maintenance	+ Reduce inner-city/town traffic jams + Reduce motor accidents − Potential car park crime	− Loss of custom − Lack of convenience − Sends customers elsewhere	+ Less polluted town/city environment − Costly
Increase parking charges	+ Revenue from fines − Costly to set up	− Hostility to enforcers	− Loss of custom − Delivery unloading problematic	− Residents penalised by paying for on-street parking
Restrict car journeys, e.g. odd/even registrations on alternate days	+ Easy to administer	+ Easy to police	− Seek exemption for business vehicles	+ Encourage car-sharing for daily journeys − Inconvenience
Levy congestion charge for urban journeys	+ Revenue raised − Cost of implementing tracking system	− Traffic jams on alternative routes	− Cost of loss of custom	− Inhibit work/leisure activities − Cost

Figure 12.6 Example of matrix notes. This particular analysis lays out positive (+) and negative (−) viewpoints on an issue from a range of different perspectives.

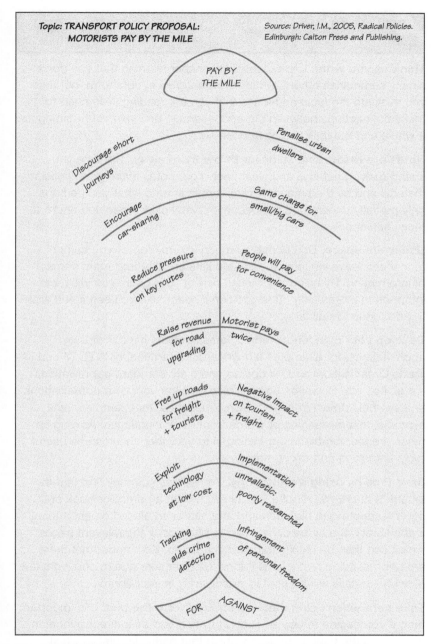

Topic: TRANSPORT POLICY PROPOSAL:
MOTORISTS PAY BY THE MILE

Source: Driver, I.M., 2005, Radical Policies.
Edinburgh: Calton Press and Publishing.

PAY BY THE MILE

Discourage short journeys

Penalise urban dwellers

Encourage car-sharing

Same charge for small/big cars

Reduce pressure on key routes

People will pay for convenience

Raise revenue for road upgrading

Motorist pays twice

Free up roads for freight + tourists

Negative impact on tourism + freight

Exploit technology at low cost

Implementation unrealistic: poorly researched

Tracking aids crime detection

Infringement of personal freedom

FOR   AGAINST

Figure 12.7 Example of a herringbone map. This design is good for showing, as in this case, two sides to an argument.

PRACTICAL TIPS FOR MAKING PERSONALISED NOTES

Think as you write. It is essential for deeper learning that you don't simply summarise others' writing and thoughts in note form, but that you evaluate the facts and ideas that you are reading. You need to make connections between different sources, between your reading as a whole and the task you have been set.

Notes are resources, so never throw them away. The time you spend making notes is an investment. Your notes make good revision material and by the time the exam comes around what you perhaps only partially understood will become crystal clear when you return to these earlier notes.

Use white space. Don't cram as much information as you can on to a sheet; leave white space around lists or other important items of information. By using the 'visual' part of your brain, you will recall information more easily. This additional space can be used if you wish to add further detail later.

Develop your own 'shorthand'. Some subjects have their own abbreviations, for example MI (myocardial infarction) or WTO (World Trade Organisation) and, of course, there are standard abbreviations – e.g., i.e., etc. However, you will also develop your own abbreviations and symbols drawn from your own experience, for example maths symbols, text messaging or words from other languages. As long as these are memorable and meaningful to you, then they can be useful tools in making and taking notes.

Save time by using a photocopy. Sometimes you may find that the extent of notes you require is minimal, or that a particular book or other resource is in high demand and has been placed on short loan in the library. It may be convenient to photocopy the relevant pages, which can then be highlighted and annotated. Remember that there are photocopying restrictions imposed on readers due to copyright law (Ch 14) – details will be posted prominently in your library.

Take care when using material straight from the text. It is important that, if you decide to use an excerpt from a text as a direct quotation, you record the page number on which that particular piece of text appeared in the book or article you are citing. You should include the author, date of publication and page number alongside. More information on citing sources is given in Chapters 13 and 14.

12.1 Find out about abbreviations. Find a general dictionary that gives a comprehensive list of abbreviations and identify ones that you might use; find a subject-specific dictionary and identify whether it provides lists of specialist abbreviations. This will mean that you'll know where to look if you come across an abbreviation that is unfamiliar to you.

12.2 Compare notes with a friend. Everyone has a different method of note-making that they have personalised to suit their own style. Compare your note-making style with that of a classmate – preferably on the same piece of text. Discuss what you have recorded and why – this may bring out some differences in reasoning, understanding and logic.

12.3 Try something new. You may feel that you already have a fairly reasonable note-making strategy in place, but as time goes on you may find that it is not quite as suitable for the type of reading you are now required to do. If this turns out to be the case, try out some of the alternative styles demonstrated in this chapter to see if these are better suited to your study tasks.

13

PLAGIARISM AND COPYRIGHT INFRINGEMENT

How to avoid being accused of 'stealing' the ideas and work of others

An understanding of plagiarism and copyright issues is vital when expressing your own ideas. Due reference must be made to the work of others and there are limits to the extent you may copy material. Failure to take account of academic conventions and the legal rights of others can result in severe penalties.

KEY TOPICS

→ What is plagiarism?

→ Strategies to ensure that you avoid plagiarism

→ How to paraphrase

→ Examples of summarising and paraphrasing

→ What is copyright infringement?

KEY TERMS

Copyright   Paraphrase   Paraphrasing   Plagiarism   Quoting   Summarising   Synonym   Verbatim

Plagiarism and copyright are two related topics that are extremely important academically and legally, but which are often misunderstood by students. They have become more significant in recent years due to technological advances such as digital scanners, photocopiers and electronic file exchange, which make it simple to 'cut and paste' and copy materials. This means it is easier to commit the offence of plagiarism unknowingly. You need to be fully aware of the issues involved so you can acknowledge intellectual property appropriately and avoid losing marks or being involved in further disciplinary action.

WHAT IS PLAGIARISM?

Plagiarism can be defined as: 'the unacknowledged use of another's work as if it were one's own' (University of Dundee, 2005). Alongside other forms of academic dishonesty, universities regard intentional plagiarism as a very serious offence. The regulations normally prescribe a range of penalties depending on the severity of the case, from a simple reduction in marks, to the ultimate sanctions of exclusion from the university or refusal to award a degree. You will find the exact penalties specified in departmental or school handbooks.

Plagiarism is thus something to be avoided, and it is assumed that no one would deliberately set out to cheat in this way. The problem is that it is easy to plagiarise unwittingly. Regarding such 'unintentional plagiarism', you should note the following:

● The concept of 'work' in the definition of plagiarism given above includes ideas, writing or inventions, and not simply words.

● The notion of 'use' in the definition does not only mean 'word for word' (an exact copy) but also 'in substance' (a paraphrase of the notions involved).

● Use of another's work *is* acceptable, *if* you acknowledge the source.

The first two of these aspects give an indication of the potential dangers for students, but the third provides a remedy. To avoid the risk of unintentional plagiarism, adopt the following advice: if you think a particular author has said something particularly well, quote them directly *and* provide a reference to the relevant article or book beside the quote (Ch 14).

Note that the convention in academic writing is to use inverted commas (and sometimes italics) to signify clearly that a quotation is being made. The reference or citation is generally given in one of several standard forms described in Chapter 14.

Cutting and pasting

The practice of cutting (copying) and pasting electronically (for example, taking material from websites) and using this in an essay without citing it is regarded as plagiarism and will be punished if detected. Universities now have sophisticated electronic means of identifying where this has occurred.

Punishments for copying

Copying an essay or other piece of work by a fellow student (past or present) is cheating. The punishment is often an assessment mark of zero *for both parties*, and further disciplinary measures may be taken. If you let someone copy your work, you are regarded as just as culpable as the 'real' cheat – so consider the risk to your academic future if you misguidedly allow someone to copy your work.

STRATEGIES TO ENSURE THAT YOU AVOID PLAGIARISM

Once you have identified the source material that you wish to use in your assignment, you will need to identify the function that the citations related to this material will perform in your work. For example, you will need to ask yourself whether the text you wish to cite endorses an idea, contradicts it or is neutral. In some cases you will need to make a decision about how you will incorporate the ideas from your source material within your own text. There are essentially three options:

- Quoting
- Summarising
- Paraphrasing

Characteristics of these methods of using sources are shown in Table 13.1.

Regardless of which of these approaches you choose to adopt, within the layout conventions of the citation and referencing style you are expected to adopt, you will require the following information:

- Author
- Date
- Title
- Place of publication
- Publisher
- Page number(s).

It is a good idea to note these details when you first consult the source, or you may waste time seeking them out later.

Table 13.1 Characteristics that typify quoting, summarising and paraphrasing

Method	Characteristics

Quotation (see Ch 14)	• 'short' quotes – include in the text
	• 'long quotes' (usually 30+ or 40+ words) in some style guides require to be indented; in others they may be italicised and indented.
	• Punctuation conventions
	   – Single quotation marks (British English)
	   – Double quotation marks (American English)

Summarising	• Broad overview, briefly stating the main points from the original • Less detailed than a paraphrase • Ideas expressed using your own words • Technical terms can be retained, but otherwise ideas are expressed using different sentence structure and vocabulary
Paraphrasing	• Broad theme condensed from the original • More detailed than a summary • Ideas expressed using your own words • Technical terms can be retained but otherwise ideas are expressed using different sentence structure and vocabulary

HOW TO PARAPHRASE

1 Read the text to establish overall meaning; it may help to use the speed-reading strategy of reading *topic sentences* first of all to gain this overview (see Ch 11).

2 Turn over the text and note down key ideas.

3 Re-read the text intensively for greater detail.

4 Turn over the text and, from memory, note points that support the key ideas. This encourages you to use your own words and makes you less dependent on words from the text.

5 Note how you intend to use these ideas in your work.

6 Record bibliographical details for your reference list (see Ch 14).

Sometimes it is helpful when constructing paraphrased text to begin with the concluding idea of the text and work through the key ideas from that perspective, rather than in the logical sequence of the original. In this way you are less likely to lapse into the pitfalls of word substitution or over-quotation.

How much quotation is acceptable?

Too much quotation is regarded as plagiarism, even if all the source information is provided. Aim to limit use of quotation to 10 per cent of the total work as an absolute maximum. In many cases the proportion will be well below the threshold.

EXAMPLES OF SUMMARISING AND PARAPHRASING

The excerpt of original text in Table 13.2 represents material that a student might wish to use in relation to an assignment on the relative merits of e-books and traditional bound volumes, demonstrating poor and good examples of summarising and paraphrasing technique.

Avoid a word substitution exercise when citing the work of others either in summarising or in paraphrasing; this is plagiarism. You need to show that you have engaged in a critical analysis of the material and demonstrate this by using the citation material to good effect in structuring your discussion. In the good models shown in Table 13.2, the writer has processed the ideas from the original text and presented them in a fresh manner, demonstrating engagement with the meaning of the original text and hence independent thinking.

WHAT IS COPYRIGHT INFRINGEMENT?

Copyright law 'allows you to protect your original material and stop others from using your work without your permission' (Intellectual Property Office, 2009). Copyright infringement is regarded as equivalent to stealing, and legal rights are sometimes jealously guarded by companies with the resources to prosecute.

In the UK, authors have literary copyright over their material for their life, and their estate has copyright for a further 70 years. Publishers have typographical copyright for 25 years. This is why the copyright symbol © is usually accompanied by a date and the owner's name. You'll find this information on the publication details page at the start of a book.

Table 13.2 Examples of summarising and paraphrasing. Further guidance on appropriate methods for paraphrasing text is provided in the companion book *How to cite, reference and avoid plagiarism at university* (McMillan and Weyers, 2013).

Original text
E-books are a function of the internet era and make access to otherwise unattainable material possible to wide audiences. The globalisation of literature means that individual authors can present their work to a wider audience without incurring abortive publication costs. This facility constitutes a considerable threat to publishers of traditional books.
Source: Watt, W. (2006) *The demise of the book*. Dundee: Riverside Press (p. 13)

Summarising		
Poor model of summarising	**Explanation**	**Good model of summarising**
It has been suggested that **e-books are a function of the internet era** and that **globalisation of literature** allows authors to **present their work to a wider audience** without having to incur **abortive publication costs**.	In this example, direct quotation (shown in bold) comprises 60 per cent of the total word count – this is excessive and could be regarded as a form of plagiarism. This fault is compounded because the writer has failed to give the source of the quotations.	With the advent of e-books, individual authors are faced with new approaches to publication of their work (Watt, 2006).

Paraphrasing		
Poor model	**Explanation**	**Good model**
E-books are part of the internet age and allow people from all over the globe to use them. This means that writers show their writing on the internet and so they do not have such high publishing costs. This feature means that publishers of old-fashioned books are under threat (Watt, 2006).	In this example, use of synonyms (underlined) in a superficial manner constitutes another form of plagiarism. Despite correctly citing the source, the writer has simply 'stolen' the essential meaning without engaging in any analysis or original thinking.	Watt (2006) notes that there is concern amongst publishers of hard-copy printed books that the advent of e-books marks the end of their monopoly of the literature market, since authors can publish directly on the internet, thus avoiding publishing costs.

Use of the copyright symbol

The © symbol indicates that someone is drawing your attention to the fact that something is copyright. However, even if © does not appear, the material may still be copyright.

You will be at risk of breaking the law if you copy (for example, photocopy, digitally scan or print out) material to which someone else owns the copyright, unless you have their express permission, or unless the amount you copy falls within the limits accepted for 'fair dealing'.

'Educational copying', *for non-commercial private study or research*, is sometimes allowed by publishers (they will state this on the material, and may allow multiple copies to be made). Otherwise, for single copies *for private study or research*, you should only copy what would fall under the 'fair dealing' provision, for which there is no precise definition in law.

Private study or research

This means what it says: the limits discussed here apply to that use and not to commercial or other uses, such as photocopying an amusing article for your friends. Copying of software and music CDs (including 'sharing' of MP3 files) is most often illegal, although you are usually permitted to make a *personal* back-up copy of a track or CD you already own.

Approved copyright exceptions

Certain copying for academic purposes may be licensed by the Copyright Licensing Agency (CLA) on behalf of authors. Other electronically distributed material may be licensed through the HERON (Higher Education Resources On-Demand) scheme. In these cases you may be able to copy or print out more than the amounts listed opposite, including multiple copies. Your university may also 'buy in' to licensing schemes, such as those offered by the NLA (Newspaper Licensing Agency) and the Performing Rights Society. As these can refer to very specific sources, consult your library's staff if in doubt.

Established practice suggests that you should copy no more than 5% of the work involved, or:

- one chapter of a book;
- one article per volume of an academic journal;
- 20% (to a maximum of 20 pages) of a short book;
- one poem or short story (maximum of 10 pages) from an anthology;
- one separate illustration or map up to A4 size (note: illustrations that are parts of articles and chapters may be included in the allowances noted above);
- short excerpts of musical works – not whole works or movements (note: copying of any kind of public performance is not allowed without permission).

These limits apply to single copies – you can't take multiple copies of any of the above items, nor pass on a single copy for multiple copying to someone else, who may be in ignorance of the source or of specific or general copyright issues.

In legal terms, it doesn't matter whether you paid for the source or not: copyright is infringed when the whole or a substantial part is copied without permission – and 'substantial' here can mean a qualitatively significant section even if this is a small part of the whole.

The same rules apply to printing or copying material on the Web unless the author gives explicit (that is, written) clearance. This applies to copying images as well as text from the internet, although a number of sites do offer copyright-free images. A statement on the author's position on copying may appear on the home page or a page linked directly from it.

Complexity of copyright law

Note that the material in this chapter is a summary of some basic aspects of a complex body of law, and much may depend on individual circumstances.

Avoid copying material by electronic means. You may only do this if you are prepared to quote the source. If you use the material in your work, and fail to add an appropriate citation, this would be regarded as plagiarism and hence cheating.

When making notes, always write down your sources. You may risk plagiarising if you cannot recall or find the source of a piece of text. Avoid this by getting into the habit of making a careful note of the source on the same piece of paper that you used to summarise or copy it out. Always use quote marks ('...') when taking such notes verbatim from texts and other materials, to indicate that what you have written down is a *direct copy* of the words used, as you may forget this at a later time. You do not need to quote directly in the final version of your work, but if you paraphrase you should still cite the source.

Try not to paraphrase another person's work too closely. Taking key phrases and rearranging them, or merely substituting some words with synonyms is still regarded as plagiarism.

Follow the academic custom of citing your sources. You should do this even if you prefer to use your own wording rather than a direct copy of the original. The reference to the source signifies that you are making that statement on the basis of the ideas reported there. If you are unclear about the different methods of mentioning sources and constructing a reference list, consult Chapter 14.

Avoid overuse of quotations. Plagiarism still occurs if a considerable percentage of your assignment is comprised of quotations. In general, quotations should be used sparingly.

Double-check on your 'original' ideas. If you have what you think is a novel idea, do not simply accept that your brainwave is unique. It's common for people to forget the original source of an idea, which may resurface in their mind after many years and perhaps in a different context – this may have happened to you. Think carefully about possible sources that you may have forgotten about; ask others (such as your tutor or supervisor) whether they have come across the idea before; and consult relevant texts, encyclopaedias or the internet.

13.1 Double-check your department's (or university's) plagiarism policy. This should spell out the precise situations in which you might break rules. It may also give useful information on the preferred methods for citing sources.

13.2 Next time you are in the library, read the documentation about photocopying often displayed beside the photocopiers. This will provide detailed information about current legislation and any local exceptions.

13.3 Modify your note-making technique. Highlight and put any direct transcriptions in quotes. Add full details of the source whenever you make notes from a textbook or paper source.

CITING AND LISTING REFERENCES

How to refer appropriately to the work of others

In academic writing you must support your discussion of others' ideas and findings by referring to the relevant literature. Several styles are in use and which one you will be required to adopt will depend on the conventions within your discipline. This chapter outlines four of the more common styles, showing you how to cite your source in the text and list these in your reference list or bibliography.

KEY TOPICS

→ Why you need to cite your sources

→ Using information within your text

→ How to cite the work in the text

→ Different reference styles

KEY TERMS

Bibliography Citation Ellipsis *ibid.* Indentation *op. cit.*
Reference list Secondary reference Superscript

When you write any kind of academic paper you must expect to give the sources of information and ideas you have drawn from your in-depth reading on the subject. You have to give your reader sufficient information to be able to locate your source. This is done in the body of the text at the point where you refer to (cite) the source, and then give full details of it either in a footnote, endnote or separate reference list at the end of the paper. Styles vary (see Table 14.1), but the preferred style for your discipline will be stipulated in your course handbook, or may be recommended by your lecturer or supervisor. However, you must be able to recognise the alternative styles in order to interpret similar information given in sources that you read.

Definitions

Citation – the use of the idea presented by an author and expressed *in your own words* to support a point in your own work. Rules about how to incorporate citations in your text are given in this chapter.

Quotation – the use of words drawn from the source you need. The words should remain faithful to the original. For layout of quotes see p. 168.

Bibliography – a listing at the end of your work of all source materials that you have consulted as preparation for your paper. You do not need to have referred to all these sources directly in your text. In some styles the terms 'bibliography' or 'works cited' are used instead of the term 'reference list'.

Reference list – all the books, journals, web and online materials you have referred to in your paper. This list is usually at the end of the work.

Secondary reference – where the original text is not available and the reference you give relates to a citation of this in material which you *have* read.

WHY YOU NEED TO CITE YOUR SOURCES

Academic convention requires you to give this information in order to:

● acknowledge the use of other people's work – you must demonstrate clearly where you have borrowed text or ideas from others; even if you cite an author's work in order to disagree with it, you have made use of their intellectual property and you must show that you recognise this (there is more discussion on intellectual property and plagiarism in **Ch 13**);

● help your readers understand how your argument/discussion was assembled and what influenced your thinking – this will help them form opinions about your work;

● help your reader/marker evaluate the extent of your reading. This may help them to assess your work and to advise you on further or more relevant reading;

● provide your readers with sufficient information to enable them to consult the source materials for themselves, if they wish.

In many cases, if you do not provide a reference list you will lose marks. This must be in your department's preferred style (Table 14.1).

Table 14.1 **Choosing a referencing style.** Departments normally specify the referencing style. Where no guidance is given, the choice is up to you. This table shows the most significant features, advantages and disadvantages of four common styles used in all forms of academic writing, including undergraduate and postgraduate assignments. It applies to all forms of writing – from essays to theses.

Method	Features	Advantages	Disadvantages
Harvard (Table 14.2)	• **Name/date** system used in the text (page number included only if making a reference to a specific quote or data) • Name of author can be included as part of the sentence (date in round brackets immediately after the name) or • Name and date both placed in round brackets at the end of the sentence	• Minimal typing: once-only entry in alphabetical order by author name in the reference list • Easy to identify contributors in a field from the citations shown in the text • Easy to make adjustments in the text and the reference list	• Name/date references can be intrusive in text • Not well-suited to citing archive material, e.g. historical documents, which may not have full details sufficient to comply with the system
Modern Languages Association (MLA) (Table 14.3)	• **Name/page** system in text; date at end of reference • Name of author can be included as part of the sentence (page number comes in brackets at the end of the sentence or clause) or • Name and page number(s) (no punctuation) both placed in brackets at the end of the sentence	• Minimal typing as details are printed only once in alphabetical order by author name in the reference list, which makes it easy to locate the source information • Easy to identify contributors in a field from the citations shown in the text	• Date of publication of source not in the text and not immediately evident in the reference list because of the position at the end of the reference • Indentation in 'follow-on' lines in the reference list can give a 'ragged' appearance to the layout of the reference list

Vancouver (Table 14.4)	• **Numerical** system with full-size numerals in brackets after the reported point • If another reference is made to a source in the text, the second and subsequent references use the number given to the reference when it was used for the first time	• Numbers are less intrusive in the text • Numbers are listed in numerical order at the end of the text, thus it is easy to locate the reference	• No bibliographical information in the text, thus difficult to gauge significance of the sources • Cumbersome to apply • Use of one number each time the source is used • Involves a considerable amount of checking and slows down the writing process
Chicago (Table 14.5)	• **Superscript** numbers used in the text • Relates superscript numbers to footnotes on the same page • Provides reference information in footnotes and reference list (note that the format differs between footnotes and reference list)	• Numbering system is unobtrusive and does not interrupt the flow of the text • Use of *op. cit.* and *ibid.* in the referencing saves retyping of bibliographical information	• First mention of a source gives full details, subsequent references give only name/page • More difficult to track the main contributors • Layout of footnote references differs from the bibliographical reference (if used) • Intensive checking to ensure that all superscript references are consistent after any changes

Essentially there are two means by which you can introduce the work of others into your text – by *quoting* exact words from a source, or by *citation*, which involves summarising or paraphrasing (Ch 13) the idea in your own words. In both instances you need to indicate the source material by means of the chosen style of citation (Table 14.1).

> The cultural values identifiable in one minority group create what has been called the 'invisible clamour' (Henze, 1990) as they conflict with those of the dominant culture.

Figure 14.1 How to present a short quotation in text form.

Quotation in the text

There are two possibilities. If the quotation is a short quotation, the exact words are placed within single inverted commas within the sentence (e.g. xxxx 'zzzz zz zzzz zz zzzz' xxx (see Figure 14.1). If you are using a longer quotation, usually 30 words or more, then no inverted commas are used. The status of the text as a quotation is indicated by the use of indentation where several lines

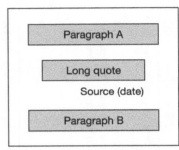

Figure 14.2 How to present a long quotation, shown in outline form.

quoted from another source are indented within your own text and in single-line spacing (see Figure 14.2). If you deliberately miss out some words from the original, the 'gap' is represented by three dots. This is called an ellipsis. For example:

xxxxxxxx xxxxx xxxxx xxxx xxx xx xxxxxxxxx xxxx xx xxxxx xx xx xxxx xxxxxx:

... zzzz z zzzzzz zzzzzzz zzz zzzzzzz zzzz zz z zz zzzz z zzzz zz z zzzzzz.
(source)

xxxxxxxx xxxxx xxxxx xxxx xxx xx xxxxxxxxx xxxx xx xxxxx xx xx xxxx xxxxxx.

 Quoting within a quote

The convention of British English is to use single inverted commas to cover the whole quotation and double inverted commas (quotation marks) for the quotation within the quotation. For example, 'xxxxxx "zzzz" xxx'. The convention in American English is the opposite.

Definition

Ellipsis – the three dots used to substitute for words that have been omitted from a quotation are called an 'ellipsis' and are often used at the beginning of a quote, as in the example opposite, or where some information that is irrelevant to your point has been omitted for brevity. Obviously, you should not omit words that change the sense of the quotation. For example, omitting the word 'not' in the following quotation would entirely change its sense: 'The adoption of the Euro as the common currency of the EU is *not* universally acceptable'.

Footnotes and endnotes

In some disciplines, footnotes and endnotes, generally using superscript numbers, lead readers to the source information. However, in other disciplines, footnotes and endnotes are used simply to provide additional information, commentary or point of discussion about the content of the text. Footnotes generally appear at the bottom of the page where the link appears; endnotes are recorded in number order at the end of the body of the work.

HOW TO CITE THE WORK IN THE TEXT

There are essentially two ways in which to do this: the information-prominent and author-prominent methods. These depend on the style of referencing you have elected to follow. Four commonly used styles are laid out in Tables 14.2–14.5. The broad principles, following the Harvard method, are outlined below.

- **Information-prominent method.** Here the statement is regarded as being generally accepted within the field of study. For example:

  Children express an interest in books and pictures from an early age (Murphy, 1995).

- **Author-prominent method.** Here the author and date of publication form part of the construction of the sentence. This formulation can be used with appropriate reporting words (see tip box) to reflect a viewpoint. For example:

  Murphy (1995) claimed that children as young as six months are able to follow a simple story sequence.

Reporting words

There is a considerable range of verbs that can be used to report the views of others. Here are some examples:

allege	consider	demonstrate	judge	show	surmise
assert	contend	explain	propose	state	warn
claim	declare	find	report	suggest	

Note that some of these words are 'stronger' than others and you need to consider carefully which you use so that they reflect your view of the reported work.

Sometimes you will not be able to access the original source of a piece of information, quote or viewpoint, but will have read another source which provides it. This could be because the original is out of print or unavailable to you for other reasons. In this case, the item that is cited is the text that you read personally. Historically, such secondary referencing, sometimes called secondary citation, was actively discouraged or disallowed. However, views are becoming more relaxed as the need for secondary quotation is becoming more common due to the ease of access to online literature, and reduction in hard-copy library collections.

Examples of secondary referencing formats

These examples use the form of words 'cited in' but it would be equally acceptable to use the form 'quoted in' where material had been quoted. Note that, as shown below, secondary referencing can be used for paraphrased citations as well as for direct quotations.

Illustration of an **information-prominent** secondary citation:

One of the most powerful criticisms is that reading on-screen is, for many people, a painful activity (Owen, 2007 cited in Peel, 2009).

Illustration of an **author-prominent** secondary citation:

Owen (2007 cited in Peel, 2009) considered that 'one of the most powerful criticisms of reading on-screen is that, for many people, this is a painful activity'.

DIFFERENT REFERENCE STYLES

Styles of citing and listing references have evolved as technology and preferences have altered. Thus, some have followed different conventions such as using name/date, name/page, numerical notation to cite sources within text. These different approaches are reflected in different conventions in the layout of the corresponding reference or bibliography lists.

Styles have been dictated by disciplines and their associated journals and this has led to modifications that create many variants of the original formats. Other styles, such as the American Psychological Association (APA) and the Modern Humanities Research Association (MRHA) used for literature and language, are extremely prescriptive. Their respective style guides specify a wide variety of features including such aspects as font, page layout, spelling, the use of active in preference to passive voice and much more.

The tables on the following pages illustrate four of the more commonly used styles:

● Harvard (Table 14.2, pp. 172–3)
● Modern Languages Association (Table 14.3, pp. 174–5)
● Vancouver (Table 14.4, pp. 176–7)
● Chicago (Table 14.5, pp. 178–81).

The specifications associated with these referencing systems continue to change, often to keep up with new forms of electronic information (such as blogs and tweets in recent years). For example, in relation to the citation of websites, there has been a shift towards the use of Data Objective Indicators (DOIs) rather than URLs. These are alphanumeric and unique to a document, allowing it to be accessible even if a website or database 'dies'.

In addition to the styles and layouts shown in this chapter, further detailed discussion and examples can be found in McMillan and Weyers (2013b).

Software referencing packages

These can be used to fit your reference list to any of several conventions. However, it is worth reflecting on whether it is good use of your time to learn how to use a relatively complex package and key in the data to 'feed' the package, when you could achieve a similar end result with common-sense use of a list typed straight into a word-processed table, which can then be sorted alphabetically (usually sufficient for most needs).

Table 14.2(a) Outline of the Harvard style for citing references. This referencing system has the advantage of being simpler, quicker and possibly more readily adjustable than other systems. It is used internationally in a wide range of fields and provides author and date information in the text. Note that there are various interpretations of the style. This one generally follows BS5605:1990.

How to cite the reference in the text	How to lay out references
The cause of European integration has been further hampered by the conflict between competing interests in a range of economic activities (Roche, 2009). However, Hobart and Lyon (2012) have argued that this is a symptom of a wider disharmony which has its roots in socio-economic divisions arising from differing cultural attitudes towards the concept of the market economy. Morrison *et al.* (2011) have identified 'black market' economic activity in post-reunification Germany as one which exemplified this most markedly. Scott (2012) suggests that the black economy which existed prior to reunification operated on strong market economy principles. However, Main (2008 cited in Kay, 2010) has supported the view that black market economies are not culture dependent. Statistics presented by Johannes (2010) suggest that, in the UK, as many as 23 per cent of the population are engaged at any one time in the black economy. European-wide statistics indicate that figures for participation in the black economy may be as high as 30 per cent (Brandt, 2011).	Brandt, K-H., 2011. *Working the system* [online book]. Cardiff: Thornhill Press. Available at: http://www.hvn.ac.uk/econ/trickco.htm [Accessed 1 April 2011]. *Ferry Times*, 2012. Where the money moves. *Ferry Times*, 12 April, p. 24. Hobart, K. and Lyon, A., 2012. *Socio-economic divisions: the cultural impact.* London: Thames Press. Johannes, B., 2010. Functional economics. In M. Edouard ed., *The naked economy*. Cologne: Rhein Verlag, pp. 120–30. Kay, W., 2010. *The power of Europe*. Dover: Kentish Press. Morrison, F., Drake, C., Brunswick, M. and Mackenzie, V., 2011. *Europe of the nations*. Edinburgh: Lothian Press. Roche, P., 2009. *European economic integration*. London: Amazon Press. Saunders, C., ed., 2006. *The economics of reality*. Dublin: Shamrock Press. Scott, R., 2012. Informal integration: the case of the non-monitored economy. *Journal of European Integration Studies*, 3 (2), pp. 81–9.
Quotations in the text	
The movement of money within the black economy is regarded by Finance Ministers in Europe as 'a success story they could emulate' (*Ferry Times*, 12.4.11). According to Saunders (2006, p. 82), 'black economies build businesses'.	

Notes:
- In this version of the Harvard style only the first word of a book title is capitalised. With the exception of proper nouns, other words are in lower case. Titles of books and journals are italicised. Each entry is separated by a double line space.
- If you need to cite two (or more) pieces of work published within the same year by the same author, then the convention is to refer to these texts as 2012a, 2012b and so on.
- In some interpretations of this style the first line of every entry is indented five character spaces from the left margin.
- The first date in the internet citation is the date of publication, *if available*. Thus, the 'Accessed' date as shown in the second internet reference example will always be the same or later than the published date, never earlier.

Table 14.2(b) How to list different types of source following the Harvard style

Hard copy resources	Basic format: author surname | author initial | date | title | place of publication | publisher |
Book by one author	Roche, P., 2009. *European economic integration*. London: Amazon Press.
Book by two authors	Hobart, K. and Lyon, A., 2012. *Socio-economic divisions: the cultural impact*. London: Thames Press.
Book with more than three authors	Morrison, F., Drake, C., Brunswick, M. and Mackenzie, V., 2011. *Europe of the nations*. Edinburgh: Lothian Press.
Book under editorship	Saunders, C., ed., 2006. *The economics of reality*. Dublin: Shamrock Press.
Chapter in a book	Johannes, B., 2010. *Functional economics*. In M. Edouard, ed., *The naked economy*. Cologne: Rhein Verlag, 120–30.
Secondary reference	Kay, W., 2010. *The power of Europe*. Dover: Kentish Press.
Journal article	Scott, R., 2012. Informal integration: the case of the non-monitored economy. *Journal of European Integration Studies*, 3 (2), 81–9.
Newspaper article	*Ferry Times*, 2012. Where the money moves. *Ferry Times*, 12 April, p. 24.
Online and electronic resources	
Internet references including e-books	Brandt, K-H. 2011. *Working the system* [online book]. Cardiff: Thornhill Press. Available at: http://www.hvn.ac.uk/econ/trickco.htm [Accessed 1 April 2011].
Internet references: e-journals online only	Ross, F., 2009. Coping with European fallout. *Journal of European Amity* [online], 5 (14). Available at: http://jea,org/archive00000555/ [Accessed 11 Jan. 2010].
Journal article in print and online	Hunter, M., 2008. Europe: a group of friends or rivals?, *Journal of European Collaboration*, 3 (35). Available at: http://www.jec.org/3/35/hunter [Accessed 11 April 2011].
Film, video or radio programme	Euro Yeti, 2010. Television programme. Kanal Alpha, Munich, 1 May.
Website	Transnational Co-operatives. 2010. Available at: www.tca.org [Accessed 1 April 2012].

Table 14.3(a) Outline of the Modern Languages Association (MLA) style for citing references. This style provides author and page information in the text, but no date is included, only the page number(s). List alphabetically by the author's surname in the 'Works cited' (MLA term for 'Reference list').

How to cite the reference in the text	How to lay out the works cited
The cause of European integration has been further hampered by the conflict between competing interests in a range of economic activities (Roche 180). However, Hobart and Lyon have argued that this is a symptom of a wider disharmony which has its roots in socio-economic divisions arising from differing cultural attitudes towards the concept of the market economy (101). Morrison *et al.* have identified 'black market' economic activity in post-reunification Germany as one which exemplified this most markedly (99–101). Scott suggests that the black economy which existed prior to reunification operated on strong market economy principles (83). However, Main has supported the view that black market economies are not culture dependent (qtd. in Kay 74). Statistics presented by Johannes suggest that, in the UK, as many as 23 per cent of the population are engaged at any one time as part of the black economy (121). European-wide statistics indicate that figures for participation in the black economy may be as high as 30 per cent (Brandt 12).	Brandt, K-H. 'Working the System.' Haven University 31 December 2010. Web. 1 April 2012. Hobart, K. and A. Lyon, *Socio-economic Divisions: the cultural impact*. London: Thames Press, 2012. Print. Johannes, B. 'Functional Economics.' *The Naked Economy*. Ed. M. Edouard. Cologne: Rhein Verlag, 2010: 120–30. Print. Kay, W. *The Power of Europe*. Dover: Kentish Press, 2010. Print. Morrison, F., *et al. Europe of the Nations*. Edinburgh: Lothian Press, 2011. Print. Roche, P. *European Economic Integration*. London: Amazon Press, 2009. Print. Saunders, C. ed. *The Economics of Reality*. Dublin: Shamrock Press, 2006. Print. Scott, R. 'Informal Integration: the case of the non-monitored economy.' *Journal of European Integration Studies* 2 (2012): 81–9. Print. 'Where the money moves.' *Ferry Times* 12 April 2011: 24.

Quotations in the text
The movement of money within the black economy is regarded by Finance Ministers in Europe as "a success story they could emulate" (*Ferry Times* 24).
Some commentators appear to give approval to non-conventional economic activity: "black economies build businesses" (Saunders 82).
Long quotatations (normally more than four typed lines) should be presented as indented text without quotation marks, that is, 2.5 cm from left margin and printed using double line spacing.

Notes:
- Successive lines for the same entry are indented by five character spaces.
- If two (or more) pieces of work published within the same year by the same author are cited, refer to these texts as 2012a, 2012b and so on.
- Titles are *italicised* (not underlined).
- MLA Style has discontinued use of URLs in citations for electronic resources.

Table 14.3(b) How to list different types of source following the Modern Languages Association (MLA) style

Hard copy resources	Basic format: author surname | author initial | title | place of publication | publisher | date | mode of publication |
Book by one author	Roche, P. *European Economic Integration*. London: Amazon Press, 2009. Print.
Book by two authors	Hobart, K. and A. Lyon. *Socio-economic Divisions*. London: Thames Press, 2012. Print.
Book with more than four authors	Morrison, F. *et al*. *Europe of the Nations*. Edinburgh: Edinburgh City Press, 2011. Print.
Book under editorship	Saunders, C. ed. *The Economics of Reality*. Dublin: Shamrock Press, 2006. Print.
Chapter in a book	Johannes, B. "Functional Economics." *The Naked Economy*. Ed. Maurice Edouard, Cologne: Rhein Verlag, 2010. 120–130.
Anthology or collection	Henderson, J., ed. *The Euromarketplace*. Bochum: Wurtzig GMbH. 2010. Print.
Essay in a collection	Spark, L. "Talking shop." *Accessing Europe*. Ed. A. Dye. Perth: Glen Press, 2009. 55–65. Print.
Secondary reference	Kay, W. *The Power of Europe*. Dover: Kentish Press, 2010. Print.
Journal article	Scott, R. "Informal Integration: the case of the non-monitored economy." *Journal of European Integration Studies* 2 (2012): 81–89. Print.
Newspaper article	"Where the money moves." *Ferry Times* 12 April 2011: 24. Print.
Online and electronic resources	
Internet reference including ebooks	Brandt, K-H. *Working the System*. Haven University 31 December 2010. Web. 1 April 2011.
Internet references: e-journals online only [n.p. = no publisher]	Ross, F. "Coping with European Fallout." *Journal of European Amity* [online only journal] 5.14 (2009) n.p. Web. 11 Jan 2010.
Journal article in print and online	Hunter, M. "Europe: a group of friends or rivals?" *Journal of European Collaboration*, 35.3 (2008): 120–129. Web. 11 April 2011.
Film	*Euro Yeti*, Dir. David Royale, Perf. Ian Brown and Donna White. Kanal Alpha, 2010. DVD.
Television/radio programme	"Europe and the Stars." *Euroknowledge Series*. Munich. 1 May 2011. Television.
Website	Co-operation Across Frontiers Online Transnational Co-operatives, 2010. Web. 1 April 2012.

Table 14.4(a) Outline of the Vancouver style (numeric) for citing references.
This system is widely used in Medicine and the Life Sciences, for example. In the text, numbers are positioned in brackets, that is, like this (1). These numbers relate to corresponding numbered references in the reference list. This style has the advantage of not interrupting the text with citation information. However, this means that the reader cannot readily identify the source without referring to the reference list. The Vancouver style resembles in some ways the style adopted by the Institute of Electrical and Electronic Engineers (IEEE).

How to cite the reference in the text	How to lay out references
The cause of European integration has been further hampered by the conflict between competing interests in a range of economic activities (1). However, Hobart and Lyon (2) have argued that this is a symptom of a wider disharmony which has its roots in socioeconomic divisions arising from differing cultural attitudes towards the concept of the market economy. Morrison *et al.* (3) have identified 'black market' economic activity in post-reunification Germany as one which exemplified this most markedly. Scott (4) suggests that the black economy which existed prior to reunification operated on strong market economy principles. However, Kay (5) has supported the view of Main that black market economies are not culture dependent. Statistics presented by Johannes (6) suggest that, in the UK, as many as 23 per cent of the population are engaged at any one time as part of the black economy. European-wide statistics indicate that figures for participation in the black economy may be as high as 30 per cent (7).	1 Roche P. European economic integration. London: Amazon Press; 2009. 2 Hobart K. and Lyon A. Socio-economic divisions: the cultural impact. London: Thames Press; 2012. 3 Morrison F., Drake C., Brunswick M. and Mackenzie V. Europe of the nations. Edinburgh: Lothian Press; 2011. 4 Scott R. Informal integration: the case of the non-monitored economy. Journal of European Integration Studies. 2012; 2, 81–9. 5 Kay W. The power of Europe. Dover: Kentish Press; 2010. 6 Johannes B. Functional economics. In Edouard M. The naked economy. Cologne: Rhein Verlag; 2010 p. 120–30. 7 Brandt K-H. Working the system. 2010 [cited 1 April 2011]. Available from: http://www.hvn.ac.uk/econ/trickco.htm. 8 Where the money moves. Ferry Times. 2011 April 12; 24. 9 Saunders C, editor. The economics of reality. Dublin, Shamrock Press; 2006.
Quotations in the text	
The movement of money within the black economy is regarded by Finance Ministers in Europe as 'a success story they could emulate' (8). According to Saunders, 'black economies build businesses' (9).	

Notes:
- If two (or more) pieces of work published within the same year by the same author are cited, refer to these texts as 2012a, 2012b and so on.
- In some interpretations of this style, superscript numbers [8] are used instead of the full-size number in brackets (8) shown in the example in Table 14.4(a).
- In this system, titles are *not* italicised and only initial letter of first word is capitalised, unless a proper noun is used in the title.
- If a source is repeated, the number reference is reused for each occurrence of the repetition, regardless of its previous position in the text.

Table 14.4(b) How to list different types of source following the Vancouver style

Hard copy resources [# to demonstrate number of citation in the text]	The reference list or bibliography following the Vancouver style
	Basic Format: Author surname | author initial | title | place of publication | publisher | date |
Book by one author	# Roche P. European economic integration. London: Amazon Press, 2009.
Book by two authors	# Hobart K. Lyon A. Socio-economic divisions: the cultural impact. London, Thames Press, 2012.
Book with more than three authors	# Morrison F, Drake C, Brunswick M, and Mackenzie V. Europe of the nations. Edinburgh, Edinburgh City Press, 2011.
Book under editorship	# Saunders C, editor. The economics of reality. Dublin, Shamrock Press, 2006.
Chapter in a book	# Johannes B. Functional economics. In: Edouard, M. The naked economy. Cologne: Rhein Verlag; 2010. p. 120–30.
Secondary reference	# Kay W. The power of Europe. Dover: Kentish Press; 2010.
Journal article	# Scott R. Informal integration: the case of the non-monitored economy. Journal of European Integration Studies. 2012; 2: 81–89.
Newspaper article	# Where the money moves. Ferry Times. 2011 April 12; 24.
Online and electronic resources	
Internet reference: e-books	# Dohmen W. Working for Europe. [book on the internet]. Brighton: Rock Press; 2011 [cited 2012 Apr 1]. Available from: http://www.brpress.org/dohmen/12/2011/
Internet reference: e-journal online only	# Hunter MM. Europe: a group of friends or rivals? J Ethical Enquiries 2010 [cited 2012 Oct 22]; 252 [about 10 screens]. Available from: http://www.ethicalenquiries.org/content/hunter/192784/
Journal article online in print and online	# Jenson TA. Europeans on the move. Migrant Working Association [Internet] 2010 August; [cited 2012 February 14]; 3(2): 199–208. Available from http://www.mwa.ac/vol3/issue2/199/
Video recording	# Europeans going it alone. [DVD] Bern: Alpine Productions; 2010.
Website	# Duncan SJ. Designing Europe. [Internet]. [Place unknown]: Transnational Co-operatives; 2009 [updated 2011 Dec. 14; cited January 2012]. Available from: www.tca.org

Table 14.5(a) Outline of the Chicago style (scientific) for citing references. This footnote style of referencing enables the reader to see the full bibliographical information on the first page the reference is made, but subsequent references to the same source do not give the same detail. If the full bibliographical information is not given in the footnote for some reason, a full bibliography is given at the end of the work. The *Chicago Manual of Style* (2010) stipulates double-space throughout – texts, notes and bibliography. To save space here, this example has been laid out in single-line spacing.

How to cite the reference in the text using footnotes	Quotations in the text
The cause of European integration has been further hampered by the conflict between competing interests in a range of economic activities. [1] However, Hobart and Lyon[2] have argued that this is a symptom of a wider disharmony which has its roots in socio-economic divisions arising from differing cultural attitudes towards the concept of the market economy. Morrison *et al*.[3] have identified 'black market' economic activity in post-reunification Germany as one which exemplified this most markedly. Scott[4] suggests, however, that the black economy which existed prior to reunification operated on strong market economy principles, while Main[5] has supported the view that black market economies are not culture dependent. Statistics presented by Johannes[6] suggest that as many as 23 per cent of the population are engaged at any one time as part of the black economy. This does not support the findings of Hobart and Lyon,[7] but it has been suggested by Scott[8] that this is probably an exaggerated statistic which it is impossible to verify. Scott[9] estimates a more modest 10 per cent of people of working age are actively involved in the black economy. Brandt[10] has conducted research into the phenomenon of the black economies of Europe but has been unable to confirm such estimates.	The movement of money within the black economy is regarded by Finance Ministers in Europe as "a success story they could emulate".[11]
	According to Saunders, "black economies build businesses".[12]
	[11] "Where the money moves." *Ferry Times*, (Edinburgh) 12 April 2011, 24.
	[12] C. Saunders, ed. *The Economics of Reality* (Dublin: Shamrock Press, 2006), 82.
	How to lay out the reference list or bibliography (note that layout differs for the footnotes)
	Brandt, K-H. "Working the System." Last modified September 30, 2010 http://www.hvn.ac.uk/econ/trickco.htm.
	Hobart, K. and Lyon, A. *Socio-economic Divisions: The Cultural Impact*. London: Thames Press, 2012.
	Johannes, B. "Functional Economics" in *The Naked Economy*, edited by M. Edouard. Cologne: Rhein Verlag, 2010.
	Main, K. *"Power, Politics and People"*. Plymouth: Maritime Press Co., 2008, quoted in W. Kay, *The Power of Europe*. Dover: Kentish Press, 2010, 218.
[1] P. Roche, *European Economic Integration* (London: Amazon Press, 2009), 180.	
[2] K. Hobart, and A. Lyon, *Socio-economic Divisions: The Cultural Impact* (London: Thames Press, 2012), 101.	
[3] F. Morrison, *et al. Europe of the Nations* (Edinburgh: Lothian Press, 2011), 99.	

continued below

⁴ R. Scott, "Informal Integration: the case of the non-monitored economy," Journal of European Integration Studies, 2 (2012): 81.

⁵ K. Main, *Power, Politics and People* (Plymouth: Maritime Press Co., 2008), 74, quoted in W. Kay, *The Power of Europe* (Dover: Kentish Press, 2010) 218.

⁶ B. Johannes, "Functional Economics" in *The Naked Economy*, ed. M. Edouard, 121 (Cologne: Rhein Verlag, 2010).

⁷ Hobart and Lyon *op. cit.*, 102.

⁸ Scott, *op. cit.*, 83.

⁹ *Ibid.*

¹⁰ K-H. Brandt, "Working the System." last modified Sep 30, 2010, http://www.hvn.ac.uk/econ/trickco.htm.

Morrison, F., *et al. Europe of the Nations.* Edinburgh: Lothian Press, 2011.

Roche, P. *European Economic Integration.* London: Amazon Press, 2009.

Saunders, C., ed. *The Economics of Reality.* Dublin: Shamrock Press, 2006.

Scott, R. 'Informal Integration: the case of the non-monitored economy.' *Journal of European Integration Studies* 2, No. 1 (2012), 81–9.

'Where the money moves,' *Ferry Times*, (Edinburgh) 12 April 2011, 24.

Table 14.5(b) How to list different types of source following the Chicago style (16th edition)

Hard copy resources [# symbol denotes number of footnote]	The Chicago style uses footnote style referencing. Below are the references as these would appear in the *footnotes*. Note that the layout differs for the presentation of the information in a *bibliography* using the Chicago style.	
	Basic footnote format: # author initial | author surname | title | (place of publication | publisher | date of publication) | page number | *Listed in numerical order as marked in text.*	Basic reference list format: author surname | author initial | date | title | place of publication | publisher | *Listed in alphabetical order by author surname.*
Book by one author	# P. Roche, *European Economic Integration* (London: Amazon Press, 2009), 180.	Roche, P. *European Economic Integration.* London: Amazon Press, 2009.
Book by two authors	# K. Hobart, and A. Lyon, *Socio-economic Divisions: the cultural impact* (London: Thames Press, 2012), 101.	Hobart, K. and A. Lyon. *Socio-economic Divisions: the cultural impact.* London: Thames Press, 2012.
Book with four or more authors	# F. Morrison et al., *Europe of the Nations* (Edinburgh: Lothian Press, 2011), 99.	Morrison, F.,* C. Drake, M. Brunswick, and V. Mackenzie. *Europe of the Nations.* Edinburgh: Lothian Press, 2011, 95–101. * alternatively: Morrison, F. et al.
Book under editorship	# C. Saunders, ed. *The Economics of Reality* (Dublin: Shamrock Press, 2006), 82.	Saunders, C, ed. *The Economics of Reality.* Dublin: Shamrock Press, 2006.
Chapter in a book	# B. Johannes, "Functional Economics," in *The Naked Economy*, ed. Maurice Edouard. (Cologne: Rhein Verlag, 2000), 121.	Johannes, B. "Functional Economics." In *The Naked Economy*, edited by Maurice Eduoard. Cologne: Rhein Verlag, 2010.
Secondary reference	# Main, K. "Power, Politics and People," (2008), quoted in W. Kay, *The Power of Europe* (Dover: Kentish Press, 2010), 218.	Main, K. "Power, Politics and People." (2008). Quoted in W. Kay *The Power of Europe.* Dover: Kentish Press, 2010, 218.
Journal article	# R. Scott, "Informal Integration: the case of the non-monitored economy," *Journal of European Integration Studies*, 2 No. 1 (2012): 81.	Scott, R. "Informal Integration: the case of the non-monitored economy." *Journal of European Integration Studies.* 2 No. 1 (2012): 81–96.
Newspaper article	# Craig L. Scott, "Where the money moves," *Ferry Times*, (Edinburgh) April 12, 2011, Financial section.	Scott, C.L. "Where the money moves." *Ferry Times*, (Edinburgh) April 12, 2011.

continued below

Online and electronic resources		
Internet reference: including e-books	# Willi Dohmen, *Working for Europe* (Brighton: Rock Press, 2011), doi: 10-006/500878-010-0120-6	Dohmen, Willi. *Working for Europe*. Brighton: Rock Press, 2011. doi: 10-006/500878-010-0120-6
Internet reference: e-journal online only	# Moyna Hunter, "Europe: a group of friends or rivals?" J Ethical Enquiries, 24 No. 5, 276, accessed Oct 22, 2012, www.ethicalenquiries.org/contents/hunter/192784.	Hunter M. "Europe: a group of friends or rivals?" *J Ethical Enquiries* 24 No. 5 (2010): 252–77 Accessed Oct 22 2012. http://www.ethicalenquiries.org/content/hunter/192784/
Journal article online in print and online	# Thomas A. Jenson, "Europeans on the move." Migrant Working Association 3 no. 2 (2010): 199, accessed February 14, 2012, http://www.mwa.ac/Vol3/issue2/199/.	Jenson, T.A. "Europeans on the move." Migrant Working Association 3 No. 2 (2010): 199–210. Accessed February 14, 2012. http://www.mwa.ac/uk/Vol3/issue2/199.
Film, video or radio programme	# *Europeans going it alone*, produced and directed by Berndt Brenner (2010; Bern: Alpine Productions, 2011), Film.	*Europeans going it alone*. Produced and directed by Berndt Brenner. 2010. Bern: Alpine Productions, 2011. Film.
Website	# "Designing Europe." Transnational Co-operatives. Last modified December 14, 2011, http://www.tca.org.	"Designing Europe." Transnational Co-operatives. Last modified December 14, 2011. http://tca.org.

Notes:

- Uses superscript numbers or full-size numbers within brackets in the text ordered consecutively. These relate to a footnote on the same page as the reference. Where references are repeated, then a new number is assigned each time it occurs in the text. Place the number **after a punctuation mark.**
- If you need to cite two (or more) pieces of work published within the same year by the same author, then refer to these texts as 2012a, 2012b and so on.
- Some abbreviations are used in this style. They are printed in italics, because these are Latin. The most commonly used are *op. cit.* (in the work already cited) and *ibid.* (in the same place – usually in the same place as the last fully cited reference.) Thus, in the example above [9] relates to [8] which, in turn, relates to [4].
- In the footnotes the author's first name or initial precedes the surname.
- Second or further lines in the reference list or bibliography should be indented five character spaces.
- For secondary referencing, when compiling the reference list cite both sources – the original source and the one that contained the reference (the source you read).

Record all bibliographical details as a matter of routine. However you copy your notes – electronically, by photocopy or by writing – ensure that you record all the necessary bibliographical information, or you will waste time later on backtracking to find it.

Compile your reference list as you go along. Keep a list of the works you have read. Simply create a table or list within your software package and type in the relevant details immediately you cite the source in the text. Doing this from time to time as you write saves you having to embark on a marathon of typing at the completion of the task (a table makes the formatting easier and allows easy insertion of additional records). You will need to make a decision about your choice of reference style (pp. 161–2) at an early stage.

Don't mix referencing systems. Whichever style you use, make sure you follow its conventions to the letter, including all punctuation details. When no guidance is given, consult Table 14.1 to evaluate the possibilities.

Source quotations. If you note down a quotation speculatively for later use, make sure that you write down full reference details alongside it. Never rely on your memory for remembering reference details. Check everything and write it all down.

Check the detail. Allow plenty of time for final checking, especially consistency of layout.

AND NOW ...

14.1 Identify the recommended referencing style for your subjects. These may differ from one discipline to another; one tutor to another. Go through your module handbooks and see what has been stated and how practices differ. Note that some subjects such as Law, History and English Literature often use specialised methods of citation and referencing. You will normally be given tuition in how to follow these practices. If no explicit information is given, analyse the way in which the list of books on your reading lists has been printed. If you compare this with the examples in Tables 14.2–14.5, you may be able to identify the style by name.

14.2 Look at textbooks or journal articles in your subject area to identify any deviations from the 'standard' referencing styles given in this chapter. You may find that in your field some modifications have been made to one of the styles outlined in this book. Discuss these modifications with a tutor in your department if you are unsure about which interpretation of a style you should follow.

14.3 Look at textbooks or journal articles in your subject area to identify which style is appropriate for quotations. Identify whether making direct quotations is common. In many academic areas, quotation from sources would be rare, and you need to be aware of this.

PUTTING YOUR THINKING INTO WORDS

15

TACKLING A WRITING ASSIGNMENT

How to respond to the specified task

Assignments at university challenge your ability to demonstrate critical thinking in your writing, in different written forms. This chapter looks at the fundamental stages in preparing to respond to any assignment.

KEY TOPICS

→ Realistic time planning

→ Deconstructing the assignment task

→ Exploring the topic

→ Finding the material and selecting what's relevant

→ Adopting an analytical approach

→ Taking word limits into account

KEY TERMS

Analyse Argue Describe Instruction word Restriction Topic

Written university assignments include essays, reports, project dossiers, short answer mini-essays, case studies, or dissertations (Ch 17). They give you an opportunity to demonstrate several critical thinking skills:

● your ability to research a specific aspect of the topic set in the assignment;

● your knowledge and understanding of a topic;

● your ability to synthesise original thoughts about the topic;

● your ability to organise supporting information and evidence in a structured piece of academic writing.

Especially for a longer piece of writing, or one which will count towards a module or degree mark, the additional skill of planning is required to ensure that you approach the task in a focused manner and submit your best possible work, on time.

Value of planning

Time spent deconstructing the task and planning your response will enable you to save time in the long-run and, as with most jobs, the quality of the preparation will be reflected in the quality of the end-product. It is well worth the time ensuring that you break down the question into its different elements.

REALISTIC TIME PLANNING

Consult the course handbook for the submission date. Work out how long you have between your starting point and the due date, and then work out how much of that time you can devote to completion of the work. Remember to take into account things you may need to do for other subjects, your need to attend lectures, tutorials, or practicals, and any part-time work commitments.

Next, divide the available time into periods and decide how much time you wish to allocate to each aspect of the task (Table 15.1). Map these time allowances onto the times you have available. This will ensure that you can realistically complete the work before the submission date, devote sufficient time to aspects such as editing and proof-reading (Ch 19) and avoid penalties that might be imposed because of late submission.

Table 15.1 Subdivisions of a large writing task

Aspect of task	Time required	When I plan to do this
Analysing the task		
Preliminary reading and note-making		
Planning the response to the task		
Doing supplementary reading		
Writing the first draft		
Reviewing the first draft		
Editing/proof-reading the final copy		
Printing/writing out the final copy		
Time margin for the unexpected		

DECONSTRUCTING THE ASSIGNMENT TASK

Once you have thought about the time you should allocate to the work, the next phase of analysing an assignment initiates a critical thinking approach to the task. Thus, analysis requires you to break down the specified task into its component parts. One way to do this is by asking yourself the following questions:

- **What's the *instruction*?** Many assignments are not in the form of questions but framed as instructions introduced by an instruction word. It is important to interpret these instruction words properly (see Table 15.2).
- **What's the *topic*?** This will clarify the context of the discussion you will need to construct.
- **What's the *aspect* of the topic?** This will help you define a more specific focus within the wider context.
- **What *restriction* is imposed on the topic?** This will limit the scope of your discussion.

The example in the tip box below shows you how this analysis might look for a sample question. You may already do this sort of thing subconsciously, but there is value in marking these elements out on paper. Firstly, it helps you to recognise the scope and limitations of the work you have been asked to complete. Secondly, it means that you can avoid producing a piece of work that waffles or strays from the point.

Once you have gone through this fairly quick process, you will be able to work on planning your writing and on adopting a suitable framework for your assignment (**Ch 17**).

Example

Assignment task: Assess the importance of post-operative care in the rehabilitation of orthopaedic patients.

Instruction: Assess

Topic: post-operative care

Aspect: importance

Restriction 1: rehabilitation

Restriction 2: orthopaedic patients

Table 15.2 Instruction words for assignments and exams. These words are the product of research into the frequency of use of the most common exam instruction words in university examinations. The definitions below are suggestions. You must take the whole question into account when answering. See also Table 2.1.

Instruction word	Definition – what you are expected to do
account [give an]	describe
brief account [give a]	describe in a concise way
account for	give reasons for
analyse	give an organised answer looking at all aspects
apply	put a theory into operation
assess	decide on value/importance
comment on	give your opinion
compare [with]	discuss similarities; draw conclusions on common areas
compile	make up [a list/plan/outline]
consider	describe/give your views on subject
contrast	discuss differences/draw own view
criticise	point out weak/strong points, i.e. balanced answer
define	give the meaning of a term, concisely
demonstrate	show by example/evidence
describe	narrative on process/appearance/operation/sequence...
devise	make up
discuss	give own thoughts and support your opinion or conclusion
evaluate	decide on merit of situation/argument
exemplify	show by giving examples
expand	give more information
explain	give reason for – say why
explain how	describe how something works
identify	pinpoint/list
illustrate	give examples
indicate	point out...but not in great detail
justify	support the argument for...
list	make an organised list e.g. events
outline	describe basic factors – limited information
plan	think how to organise something
report	make an account on process, event
review	write report – give facts and views on facts
show	demonstrate with supporting evidence
specify	give details of something
state	give a clear account of...
summarise	briefly give an account
trace	provide brief chronology of events/process
work out	find a solution, e.g. as in a maths problem

Generally, instruction words fall into four categories depending on what you are expected to achieve:

1 **do** – create something, draw up a plan, calculate;
2 **describe** – how something appears, happens or works;
3 **analyse** – look at all sides of an issue;
4 **argue** – look at all sides of an issue and provide supporting evidence for your position.

Table 15.2 shows a range of typical instruction words, with definitions for each one. You should make sure you know what is expected of you when any of these instructions are used, not only in terms of these definitions, but also in relation to the thinking processes expected (see **Ch 2** and especially Table 2.1). However, always remember to take the whole question into account when deciding this.

EXPLORING THE TOPIC

Having looked closely at the instruction, go back to the task and identify the topic, its aspect(s) and restriction(s). Thinking carefully here is important because students often misread the task and, although they may submit a good piece of work, their response may miss the focus of the assignment.

Next, create a brainstorm 'map' of the topic by writing down as many related aspects as you can in a free-flowing diagram (**Ch 4**, **Ch 12**). Revisit the instruction word and consider how this applies to your initial response to the task. This may seem to be a strange approach, but these immediate thoughts are principally your own 'take' on the topic, perhaps influenced by lectures, but before your ideas have been influenced by any reading material. The most important aspect is that you are beginning to exercise your critical thinking skills, by analysing for yourself what you think is important about this subject.

Brainstorming techniques

To create an effective brainstorm 'map', use a single sheet of A4 in the landscape orientation. This gives more space for lateral thinking and creativity. It also leaves more space for additions to be made at later stages. See Figure 12.2 for an example.

FINDING THE MATERIAL AND SELECTING WHAT'S RELEVANT

As a preliminary to tackling the prescribed reading list, you may find it useful to obtain some general background information about the topic. Typical sources for this might include handouts, PowerPoint slides, your lecture notes, subject textbooks and encyclopaedias.

Reading the detailed literature is the next activity. Where reading lists are provided, they are generally extensive to give some choice and to offer a range of approaches that might suit different groups of readers. Lists often include basic texts and then sources which go into greater depth. It is not usually expected that you read everything on these lists. In some subjects, you may only be expected to look at one or two recommended texts; in other subjects, book lists are lengthy and the volume of reading may seem daunting. However, this need not be the case if you approach the task systematically.

Unless specific chapters or pages are cited, students sometimes think that they need to read the whole book. This is usually not the case. Check whether your lecturer has specified sections or pages to consult (perhaps during a lecture). In not, use the contents page and the index in partnership to identify which sections are relevant to your topic. Some authors often put key pages in bold type in the index and this will help you to focus your reading rather than cover every reference.

Begin by doing the necessary reading (Chs 10 and 11) and associated note-making (Ch 12). This has to be focused and you need to be reading with discrimination. As you move from basic texts to more specialist books or journal articles that give more detailed analysis, your understanding of the topic will deepen. This may mean, for example, that you begin to build up a more informed picture of events, implications of a procedure or the possible solutions to a problem. What are you looking for? This could be, for instance, facts, examples, quotes, information to support a particular viewpoint, or counter-arguments to provide balance to your analysis of the topic.

 Direct quotation

It is important not to rely too heavily on quoting from the text. Firstly, if this is overdone, then it is plagiarism (Ch 13); secondly, it fails to give evidence that you understand the significance of the point being made.

As you become more familiar with the issues, the easier it will be to think analytically about what you are reading (Ch 2, Ch 10) and build your response to the task you have been set. Continue to add to your initial brainstorm.

ADOPTING AN ANALYTICAL APPROACH

Knowing what information to put aside and what to retain requires a more disciplined appraisal than the more wide-ranging approach you will have followed in your initial reading. Certain questions may help you to focus on what is important to the specified topic. For example:

- Who are the key actors in a sequence of events?
- What are the necessary criteria that explain particular situations?
- What explanations support a particular view?
- What patterns can be identified, for example, short-, medium- and long-term factors?

From your reading and note-making you will begin to find that different authors make similar or contradictory points. As you begin to identify the different schools of thought or approaches to an issue, you should begin to cross-reference your notes so that you can begin to group authors who subscribe to the same or similar viewpoints.

What are the Reporters' Questions?

Sometimes it is difficult to identify the important from the unimportant, the relevant from the irrelevant. A well-tried strategy, for many subjects, is to ask yourself the questions that trainee journalists are advised to use:

Who? Who is involved in relation to this topic, for example, people/organisations?

What? What are the problems/issues involved?

When? What is the time-frame to be considered?

Where? Where did it occur?

Why? What rationale/background is relevant to this issue/topic?

How? How has this situation been reached?

University work needs more than simple reproduction of facts. You need to be able to construct an argument and to support this with evidence (Ch 6). This means that you need to draw on the literature that you have read in order to support your position (Ch 14). In some instances, dependent on the topic and discipline, it may be appropriate to present differing viewpoints and evaluate arguments one over the others, and, if appropriate, address counter-arguments to these. What is important is to present a tight, well-argued case for the view you finally present as the one you favour (Chs 5 and 6).

TAKING WORD LIMITS INTO ACCOUNT

Word limits are imposed not to relieve lecturers of marking, but to train you to be concise in your writing and to analyse the topic carefully to decide what to keep in and what to leave out.

Falling short of the word limit is just as bad as over-running the maximum. Some students keep a running total of words they have used and as soon as they reach the minimum word limit, they stop abruptly. This is not a good approach because it is more likely to leave a ragged and poorly considered piece of text that comes to an unexpected halt rather than one which is well-planned, relevant and concisely written.

When planning and writing your first draft, keep only a casual eye on word count. When you come to editing that draft you can prune and re-shape your writing so that it becomes a tighter piece of prose that falls within the specified maximum–minimum word limits. If no word limit is specified, aim for a tight, well-argued submission that does not stray from the essence of the task.

Counting words

Most word processors include a word-count feature which updates as you write and edit. The latest version of Microsoft Word includes this at the bottom of the active page.

Select material form a wide range of sources. In the early years of university study many students follow the same practices as they used at school, often using a single core textbook, and putting too much reliance on handouts and notes, or even the direct copying of text. At university, you will be expected to read widely by identifying source material beyond titles given as a basic starting point and to quote and paraphrase material appropriately (Ch 13). It is worthwhile exploring your library on foot to browse in the areas related to your studies, where you may find a whole range of material that potentially expands your reading and understanding.

Keep records of what you read. It is exasperating to know that you have read something somewhere but cannot find it again. It is good to develop the habit of noting page number, chapter, title, author, publisher and place of publication on notes you make (Ch 12). This makes citation and referencing (Ch 14) much easier and less time-consuming.

Conserve notes of what you read. In the process of marshalling information for a writing task, you will probably obtain some material that proves to be irrelevant to the current writing task. Keep this in your filing system because this topic may come up again at a later date. For example, in exam revision, this personal cache of information could be useful in revitalising your knowledge and understanding of this topic.

Stick to your planned allocation of time for reading. This is a vital part of the writing process but recognise the dangers of prolonging the reading phase beyond your scheduled deadline. This is an avoidance strategy that is quite common. Students may delay getting down to planning the structure and moving on to the writing phase because they are uncomfortable with writing. Facing up to these next phases and getting on with them is usually much less formidable once you get started, so it is best to stick to your time plan and move on to the next phase in the planned sequence.

15.1 Practise categorising instruction words. Revisit Table 15.2 and mark out all those instruction words that would invite a response asking you to *do something practical*, those requiring you simply to *describe*, those that invite you to *analyse* and those that are directing you to *construct an argument*. This will help to give you a better picture of what is expected.

15.2 Examine some of the assignment titles that you will have to complete in a selected subject. Taking the whole question or instruction into account, identify what type of approach is needed – doing something practical, describing, analysing or arguing (see Ch 2). You may find that within the same question/task you will have to do some describing in order to analyse or argue. Try not to devote too much time on the descriptive element at the expense of analysis/argument. You could also do this activity with past exam papers as a useful revision strategy.

15.3 Try creating the wording for a task in a selected subject for yourself. Think about the clarity of your 'question' – is it ambiguous? Is it unclear? Identify your topic, aspect and restriction(s). Turning the student–examiner roles around can sometimes be a helpful way of developing understanding. This could be an excellent preparation for exams because it helps with anticipating possible questions and reflecting on how you would answer them.

16

ACADEMIC WRITING STYLE

How to adopt appropriate language conventions

Writing for academic purposes is a vital skill, yet the stylistic codes you need to follow are rarely comprehensively defined. This chapter will help you understand what it means to express your thoughts in an academic style and outlines some forms of language to avoid.

KEY TOPICS

→ What is academic style?

→ Objectivity and subjectivity in writing

→ Appropriate use of tense

→ Use of appropriate vocabulary

→ Transforming non-academic to academic language

→ Using language to express your thoughts clearly

KEY WORDS

Acronym   Colloquial   Idiom   Jargon   Noun   Phrasal verb
Pronoun   Register   Rhetorical question   Verb

Your thinking will be assessed in a number of ways, but this assessment will most commonly be based on a piece of written work. Those marking your work will be looking for evidence of critical and other forms of thinking, but will also expect you to adopt certain scholarly conventions in your writing. In short, they will expect you to follow academic writing style.

While it is possible to identify differences between 'scientific' and 'humanities' styles in the finer detail, this chapter covers the common features of all types of academic writing.

WHAT IS ACADEMIC STYLE?

Academic style involves the use of precise and objective language to express ideas. It must be grammatically correct, and is more formal than the style used in novels, newspapers, informal correspondence and everyday conversation. This should mean that the language is clear and simple. It does not imply that it is complex, pompous and dry. Above all, academic style is usually *objective*, using language techniques that maintain an impersonal tone and a vocabulary that is more succinct, rather than involving personal, colloquial, or idiomatic expressions. Table 16.1 provides a worked example.

The following sections discuss important aspects of academic writing. Consult Table 16.2 if any of the terms used are unfamiliar.

Table 16.1 Example of converting a piece of 'non-academic' writing into academic style. Note that the conversion results in a slightly longer piece of text (47 versus 37 words): this emphasises the point that while you should aim for concise writing, precise wording may be more important.

Original text (non-academic style)	'Corrected text (academic style)
In this country, we have changed the law so that the King or Queen is less powerful since the Great War. But he or she can still advise, encourage or warn the Prime Minister if they want.	In the United Kingdom, legislation has been a factor in the decline of the role of the monarchy in the period since the Great War. Nevertheless, the monarchy has survived and, thus, the monarch continues to exercise the right to advise, encourage and warn the Prime Minister.
Points needing correction	**Corrected points**
• Non-specific wording (*this country*) • Personal pronoun (*we*) • Weak grammar (*but* is a connecting word and should not be used to start a sentence) • Word with several meanings (*law*) • Duplication of nouns (*king or queen*) • Inconsistent and potentially misleading pronoun use (*he or she*, *they*) • Informal style (*can still*)	• Specific wording (country specified: *in the United Kingdom*) • Impersonal language (*legislation has*) • Appropriate signpost word (*nevertheless*) • Generic, yet well-defined term (*legislation*) • Singular abstract term (*monarchy*) • Repeated subject (*monarchy*) and reconstructed sentence • More formal style (*continues to exercise*)

British English (BE) versus American English (AE)

Academic writing in the UK nearly always adopts BE. The differences are most evident in spelling; for example, 'colour' (BE) and 'color' (AE). However, there are also differences in vocabulary, so that in AE people talk of 'professor' for 'lecturer'; and in language use, so that in AE someone might write 'we have gotten results', rather than 'we have obtained results'. In some disciplines, there is an attempt at standardisation, for example in chemistry the spelling of 'sulphur' (BE) has become 'sulfur' (AE) as this is now the international standard.

OBJECTIVITY AND SUBJECTIVITY IN WRITING

When writing academically, it is generally considered important that your personal involvement with your topic does not overshadow the importance of what you are commenting on or reporting. The main way of demonstrating this lack of bias is by using impersonal language. This means:

- Avoiding personal pronouns – try not to use the following words:
  - *I*/*me*/*one*
  - *you* (singular and plural)
  - *we*/*us*.
- Using the passive rather than active voice – try to write about the action and not about the actor (the person who performed the action – see overleaf).

Debate about use of active and passive in academic circles is lively. For the purposes of reflective writing, the dominant voice is more frequently used. However, this does not mean that the passive voice should never be used. For example, a student social worker might write 'I thought the court judgement was unfair on John. However, the sentencing was applied according to the law by the judge.' The first sentence is active; the second passive, and each has its place in the context. This is discussed further in Chapter 18.

Passive and active voice

This is best explained from examples:

The distress of the client was observed by me at this point. (passive)

The client was demonstrating her distress at this point. (active)

While some might argue that the first example is more formal, others might say that the active voice in the second example is clearer. In practice, both have their place and you might need to evaluate when one is more appropriate than the other. In some disciplines, for example, the tendency would be to use the active when talking about and with a client; then a formality shift takes place when discussing theory or say legal aspects, and the passive would be used.

You may find that the grammar checkers in some word-processing packages suggest that passive expressions should be changed to active. However, if you follow this guidance, you will find yourself having to use a personal pronoun, which may be inconsistent with impersonal academic style where this is expected in your work. If in doubt, consult with your tutors.

You can use other strategies to maintain an impersonal style in your writing. For general statements, you could use a structure such as *'it is ...'*, *'there is ...'* or *'there are ...'* to introduce sentences. However, beginning a paragraph with 'it' is not advised as, by definition, this word has to refer to a preceding word or idea; a new paragraph introduces a new point. To avoid the initial *'it'* position, change the sentence around so that *'It is important to note ...'* becomes *'The important point to note is ...'*.

For more specific points relating to statements you have already made, you could use the structures *'this is ...'* or *'these are ...'*, *'that is ...'* or *'those are ...'* with appropriate tense changes according to the context. Don't forget that when you use words like *'it'*, *'this'*, *'these'*, *'that'* or 'those', there should be no ambiguity over the word or phrase to which they refer.

Another way in which you can maintain objectivity by writing impersonally is to change the verb in the sentence to a noun and then reframe the sentence in a less personal way. You can see how this works in the following example.

The process carried out in a research study might be expressed as:

We collected data as the first step in the study. (Verb construction)

This could be converted to:

Data collection was the first step in the study. (Noun construction)

This kind of text-juggling will become second nature as you tackle more and more assignments.

APPROPRIATE USE OF TENSE

The tense of a verb conveys the timing of the event described (Table 17.2). The past tense is used in academic writing to describe or comment on things that have already happened. However, there are times when the present tense is appropriate. For example, in a report (Ch 17) you might write '*Figure 5 shows ...*', rather than '*Figure 5 showed ...*', when describing your results. A materials and methods section, on the other hand, will always be in the past tense, because it describes what you *did*. Within a report, where a reflective perspective is required, it may be appropriate to shift tense (Ch 17, Table 17.1).

In colloquial English, there is often a tendency to misuse tenses. This can creep into academic assignments, especially where the author is narrating a sequence of events. For example:

*Napoleon **orders** his troops to advance on Moscow. The severe winter **closes** in on them and they **come back** a ragbag of an army.* (Present tense in bold.)

Instead of:

*Napoleon **ordered** his troops to advance on Moscow. The severe winter **closed** in on them and they **came back** a ragbag of an army.* (Simple past tense in bold.)

While the first of these examples might work with the soundtrack of a documentary on Napoleon's Russian campaign, it is too colloquial for academic written formats.

USE OF APPROPRIATE VOCABULARY

Good academic writers think carefully about their choice of words. The 'plain English' movement recommends that words of Latin origin should be replaced by their Anglo-Saxon, or spoken, alternatives. However, this does not always contribute to the style and precision appropriate to academic authorship. For example, compare:

*If we **turn down** the volume, there will be no feedback.*

and

*If we **turn down** the offer from the World Bank, interest rates will rise.*

Both sentences make sense, but they use the two-word verb 'turn down' in different senses. These verbs are properly called phrasal verbs and they often have more than a single meaning. Furthermore, they are also used more in speech than in formal writing. Therefore, it would be better to write:

*If we **reduce** the volume, there will be no feedback.*

and

*If we **reject** the offer from the World Bank, interest rates will rise.*

By using 'reduce' and 'reject' the respective meanings are clear, concise and unambiguous. If you are restricted to a word limit on your work, using the one-word verb has additional obvious advantages.

Plain English

There has been a growing movement in recent times that promotes the use of 'plain English', and it has been very successful in persuading government departments and large commercial organisations to simplify written material for public reference. This has been achieved by introducing a less formal style of language that uses simpler, more active sentence structures, and a simpler range of vocabulary avoiding jargon. This is an admirable development. However, academic writing style needs to be precise, professional and unambiguous, and the strategies of 'plain English' campaigners may not be entirely appropriate to the style expected of you as an academic author. For the same reasons, some of the suggestions offered by software packages may be inappropriate to your subject and academic conventions.

The specialised vocabulary of your subject (its 'jargon') should be used with care. In particular, avoid confusing any use of a term in general conversational language with its specific meaning in your discipline (selected examples: 'accommodate'; 'cluster'; 'condition'; 'dispersion'; 'inclusion'; 'intervention'; 'portfolio'; 'procedure'; 'tracking'; 'variance'). Consider defining such words at the first point of use. When your audience includes non-specialists, try to avoid complicated jargon or provide a glossary.

Non-sexist language

The Council of Europe recommends that, where possible, gender-specific language is avoided. Thus: '*S/he will provide specimens for her/his exam*'. This is rather clumsy, but, by transforming the sentence into the plural, this is avoided, thus, '*They will provide specimens for their exams*'.

Alternatively, if appropriate, '*you/your*' could be used.

TRANSFORMING NON-ACADEMIC TO ACADEMIC LANGUAGE

Thinking about the style of your writing should be a feature of any review you make of drafts of your written work (Ch 19). Table 16.1 gives a specific example of text conversion from informal to formal style. Table 16.2 provides several pointers to help you achieve a more academic style.

One way of assimilating the accepted academic style for your discipline is to learn from the techniques adopted in the textbooks and journal articles that you read. For example:

- 'discussing' or 'concluding' text (whether signposted with a heading or not), will nearly always employ 'hedging' language (Table 16.2) to ensure that the author does not imply an absolute judgement on an issue;
- the Material and Methods section (common in scientific articles, Ch 17) will include highly detailed information expressed in a very concise manner;
- the text will be peppered with citations, using one of the common referencing styles (Ch 14).

Table 16.2 **Fundamentals of academic writing.** These elements of academic writing are laid out in alphabetical order.

Abbreviations and acronyms
It is acceptable to use abbreviations in academic writing to express units, for example SI units. Otherwise, abbreviations are generally reserved for note-taking. Thus, avoid: e.g. (for example), i.e. (that is), viz. (namely) in formal work. Acronyms are a kind of abbreviation formed by taking the initial letters of a name of an organisation, a procedure or an apparatus, and then using these letters as words in their own right instead of writing out the title in full. Thus, World Health Organisation becomes WHO. The academic convention is that the first time that you use a title with an abbreviation or acronym alternative, then you should write it in full with the abbreviation in brackets immediately after the full title. Thereafter, within that document you can use the abbreviated form. In some forms of academic writing, for example formal reports, you may be expected to include a list of abbreviations in addition to these first-time-of-use explanations.

Adjective and adverbs
A noun or object may be described using an adjective while verbs may be qualified using an adverb. Many, but not all, adverbs end with the letters 'ly'. Generally adverbs tell how, why, when, where, or under what conditions, something happened. *The patient's face was* **red***.* (The adjective 'red' describes the colour of the face.) *The client* **strongly** *denied this allegation.* (The adverb 'strongly' describes the forceful way in which the denial was made.) Whereas an adjective is usually placed in a fixed position in English ('*the client's red face*', but not '*the red client's face*'), an adverb can be placed in different positions ('*the client strongly denied the allegation*' or '*the client denied the allegation strongly*') to clarify or emphasise a specific meaning. However, an adverb should not split up a verb in its infinitive form. For example, '*to boldly go*' should be cast as '*to go boldly*' ('*to go*' being the infinitive here).

Clichés
Living languages change and develop over time. This means that some expressions come into such frequent usage that they lose their meaning; indeed, they can often be replaced with a much less long-winded expression. For example: **First and foremost** *(first);* **last but not least** *(finally);* **at this point in time** *(now).* *This procedure is the* **gold standard** *of hip replacement methods.* (*This procedure is the best hip replacement method.*) In the second example, 'gold standard' is completely inappropriate; correctly used, it should refer to monetary units, but it has been misused by being introduced into other contexts.

Colloquial language
This term encompasses informal language that is common in speech. Colloquialisms and idiomatic language should not be used in academic writing. This example shows how colloquial language involving cliché and idiom has been misused: **Not to beat about the bush,** *increasing income tax did the Chancellor* **no good at the end of the day** *and he* **was ditched** *at the next Cabinet reshuffle.* (*Increasing income tax did not help the Chancellor and he was replaced at the next Cabinet reshuffle.*)

'Hedging' language

In academic writing, it is important to be cautious about using absolute terms such as: *always* and *never*; *most* and *all*; *least* and *none*.

This is because it is often impossible to state categorically that something is or is not the case. There are verbs that allow you to 'hedge your bets' by not coming down on one side or another of an argument, or which allow you to present a variety of different scenarios without committing yourself to any single position.

seems that   looks as if   suggests that   appears that

This involves using a language construction that leaves the reader with the sense that the evidence presented is simply supporting a hypothetical, or imaginary, case. To emphasise this sense of 'hedging', the use of a special kind of verb is introduced. These modal verbs are:

can/cannot   could/could not   may/may not   might/might not

These can be used with a variety of other verbs to increase the sense of tentativeness. For example:

*These results **suggest** that there has been a decline in herring stocks in the North Sea.*

Even more tentatively, this could be:

*These results **could suggest** that there has been a decline in herring stocks in the North Sea.*

Jargon and specialist terms

Most subjects make use of language in a way that is exclusive to that discipline. It is important, therefore, to explain terms that a general reader might not understand. It is always good practice to define specialist terms or 'regular' words that are being used in a very specific way.

Nouns and pronouns

A noun is the grammar term used to define a person, thing, concept or place. A pronoun is a word that can be used instead of a specific noun. Thus, *I/we*, *you*, *he/she/it* and *they* are all pronouns.

*A **student** carries a special **project** (**student** and **project** are nouns). **They** often carry **it** out in the final year (**they** and **it** are pronouns).*

Pronouns should not be used in formal academic writing until the noun to which they refer has been introduced. Also, care should be taken when a pronoun might refer to more than one noun in the preceding sentence or clause. The personal pronouns 'I' and 'we' are acceptable in some reflective writing but are generally not used in formal academic writing.

Rhetorical questions

Some writers use direct rhetorical questions as a stylistic vehicle to introduce the topic addressed by the question. This is a good strategy if you are making a speech and it can have some power in academic writing, although it should be used sparingly. Such questions can usually be rephrased as statements – for example:

How do plants survive in dry weather? becomes

It is important to understand how plants survive in dry weather. (Note: no question mark needed.)

continued overleaf

Tense of verbs

A verb is a 'doing' word. It can be formed in different ways, depending on the tense it is being used to express. English is complex because for each of the tenses below, there is more than one form.

*The results **indicate** that... The results **are indicating** that...* (Present tenses: the first form is immediate at this moment; the second is continuous, i.e. the results continue to show...)

*The results **indicated** that... The results **were indicating** that... The results **have indicated** that... The results **had indicated** that...* (Past tenses: in order, simple past, past continuous, present perfect and past perfect. Each could be used to indicate a particular set of circumstances that happened in the past.)

*The results **will indicate** that... The results **are going to indicate** that...* (Future tense, indicating what will happen in future.)

In reflective text both present and past tenses may be used. Future tense might be used for an action plan.

Value judgements

These are defined as statements in which the author or speaker is imposing their views or values on to the reader. For example, a writer who states that '*Louis XIV was a rabid nationalist*' without giving supporting evidence for this statement is not making an objective comment in a professional manner. Rewording this statement to: '*Louis XIV was regarded as a rabid nationalist. This is evident in the nature of his foreign policy where he ...*' offers the reader some evidence that explains the claim.

Voice and action

There are two voices: active and passive. In the active voice the subject of the sentence is the actor; in the passive voice, the emphasis is on the action and the actor is not even mentioned. If it is possible to add 'by someone' at the end of a sentence, then it usually indicates the passive voice has been used.

***I decided** to move the chairs to form a circular arrangement around the table.* (Active voice because 'I' is the actor making the decision.)

***The chairs were moved** to form a circular arrangement around the table.* (Passive voice because the chairs are being moved – you could add '*by the participants*' to the end of the sentence.)

The passive voice is favoured in academic writing because it is more objective and impersonal. While reflective writing is usually phrased in the active voice, active and passive can be used in all academic texts at different points, depending on context.

USING LANGUAGE TO EXPRESS YOUR THOUGHTS CLEARLY

As you develop your critical thinking and writing skills, you will need to learn how to 'play' with language. This involves experimenting with each choice of word, each phrase, the order of words, the construction of sentences and the sequence within paragraphs. The ability to manipulate writing in this way is important for a number of reasons:

- it allows you to exploit the flexibility of the English language to express your meaning as clearly and as accurately as possible;
- it demonstrates your ability to group ideas in a logical way;
- it ensures that you maintain the reader's attention and interest.

Table 16.3 provides some examples of ways in which language can be manipulated to improve communication.

Table 16.3 Examples of how 'playing with language' can improve your writing. Writing can often be improved by rearranging the order of words or phrases, by choosing more suitable words or by separating out ideas into independent elements. Examples A–C below illustrate possible techniques that you might adopt.

A. Heads and tails
Sometimes a sentence works better if you experiment by shifting elements around within it. A phrase or clause that is at the tail end of the sentence might be more powerful, and emphasise your meaning more strongly, if it is positioned at the head of the sentence. For example:

*Version A1: The practical application of 'duty to disclose' in relation to the onset of multiple sclerosis was deliberately entrusted to the discretion of the medical profession **because it was seen as impossible to define in policy**.*

could become

*Version A2: **Since it was considered impossible to define 'duty to disclose' in policy** in relation to the onset of multiple sclerosis, the practical application was deliberately entrusted to the medical profession.*

Both instances have validity. However, as a writer, you might wish to place the emphasis on the reason for the failure to define a policy. In that case, Version A2 would be better. However, if you felt the emphasis should rest with the role of the medical profession, then Version A1 would be better. This shows the importance of considering your intention as you construct and review your writing, and it emphasises how important applying logic is to the whole process.

continued overleaf

B. Better word, clearer meaning

Academic writing should, by definition, be both precise and concise. However, sometimes in the process of writing the need to record the ideas overtakes the accuracy and clarity that might be desirable. Consequently, it is worthwhile reviewing your work to identify ways in which you can use words more appropriately to achieve clarity. For example:

> **Version B1:** *The practical application of 'duty to disclose' in relation to the onset of multiple sclerosis was deliberately entrusted to* **the decision-making process operating** *in the medical profession because it was seen as impossible to define in policy.*

could become

> **Version B2:** *The practical application of 'duty to disclose' in relation to the onset of multiple sclerosis was deliberately entrusted to the* **discretion** *of the medical profession because it was seen as impossible to define in policy.*

Not only is Version B2 clearer than Version B1, but it expresses more aptly the leeway that the situation implies.

C. Long and short sentences

Sometimes it is better to split an overly long or complex sentence. For example:

> **Version C1:** *The practical application of 'duty to disclose' in relation to the onset of multiple sclerosis was deliberately entrusted to the discretion of the medical profession* **because it was seen as impossible to define in policy**.

could become

> **Version C2:** *The practical application of 'duty to disclose' in relation to the onset of multiple sclerosis was deliberately entrusted to the discretion of the medical profession.* **This decision was reached because it was seen as impossible to define in policy.**

Version C1 places the reason as a tag on the end of the main clause, whereas Version C2 emphasises the reason by stating it as a separate sentence.

PRACTICAL TIPS FOR ENSURING THAT YOU WRITE IN AN ACADEMIC STYLE

Think about your audience. Your readers should direct the style you adopt for any writing you do. For example, if you were writing to your bank manager asking for a loan, you would not use text-messaging or informal language. For academic writing, you should take into account that your reader(s) will probably be marking your work and, in addition to knowledge and content, they will be looking for evidence of awareness and correct use of specialist terms and structures.

Avoid contractions. In spoken English, shortened forms such as, don't, can't, isn't, it's, I'd and we'll are used all the time. However, in academic written English, they should not be used. Texting contractions are also inappropriate.

Take care with the use of personal pronouns. These are I/me/my and we/us and their possessive forms, my, your and our. For general academic writing, their use is nearly always inappropriate but there are situations in reflective work where this is acceptable. Experiment with language structures (p. 201) to obtain the correct style for your assignment.

 AND NOW ...

16.1 Take steps to improve your grammar. Correct English is essential in academic writing. If you feel this aspect of your work is poor, consider buying a specialist grammar book and try to put its guidance into practice in your assignments. When your lecturers provide feedback that comments on misuse of grammar or of language, look up the point and make sure you understand your error. If you have time, you can consolidate your understanding by doing the exercises provided in such books.

16.2 Ask a friend to work with you on your writing style. Swap a piece of writing and check over your friend's writing style and ask them to do the same for yours. When you have done this, compare the points you have found. Try to explain what you think could be improved. Together, you may be able to clarify some aspects that you were unaware were problematic.

16.3 Make a personal glossary. Especially when starting on a new topic, this will help you to learn the abbreviations, acronyms and jargon of your subject. This could be done as a word-processed file or on a large piece of paper divided into alphabetical sections. Definitions can be obtained from textbooks, lecture notes or online (for example, placing the text 'Define: <word>' in a search engine).

GENERAL WRITING STRUCTURES

How to select and shape your content appropriately

Once you have assembled the information for your assignment and timetabled your efforts, you will need to organise your response to the set writing task. This chapter outlines the main frameworks for written assignments and their structural elements.

KEY TOPICS

→ Standard academic format

→ Representative organisational plans for assignments

→ Adopting a structural model for the main body of text

KEY TERMS

Brainstorm Business report Chronological Citation Hierarchical
Jargon Literature survey Scientific report

Once you have evolved your own response to the task you have been set (Ch 15), you then need to place this within a framework that presents your thinking in a way that is well-structured and flows through a sequence of logic and argument. There are three levels to consider in this context:

1 The standard academic format for writing.

2 The detailed organisational plan for each type of assignment.

3 The internal organisation of the main body of text within the plan.

STANDARD ACADEMIC FORMAT

The basic structure of most academic writing follows the convention of moving from the general (the introduction) through to the specific (the main body) and back to the general (the conclusion).

The introduction

This should consist of three components:

1 A brief explanation of the context of the topic.

2 An outline of the topic as you understand it.

3 An explanation of how you plan to address the topic in this particular text, in effect, a statement of intent.

This section lays down the parameters that you have set yourself for this piece of text. Especially where you have been set a tight word limit, a comprehensive coverage of all aspects of the topic will not be possible. You will therefore need to explain the reasons for covering certain aspects only – and explain why you consider these to be the most important or relevant.

The importance of the Introduction

This is the first contact that your reader makes with you as the author of the text. This means that it has to be well-organised and clear. However, to achieve this it is important to see this introductory section as 'work in progress' because, until you complete the entire text, you cannot really introduce the whole work accurately. Indeed, some people prefer to start writing the main body, move on to the conclusion, and then write the introduction.

Main body

This section lays out your work based on the approach you decide to adopt in organising the content (discussed further in the next section). You will have explained the approach in the introduction and this will mean that you should have mapped out your route for explaining your points. In this section, you may need to generalise, describe, define, or exemplify as part of your analysis. Here it is important to keep this part of the writing as brief, yet as clear, as possible.

May I use subheadings?

In some disciplines, and especially in report writing, sub-headings are acceptable. In others they are not. However, in these cases using sub-headings in drafts can help you maintain the focus of your writing. They help to prevent you digressing into unrelated areas or presenting an apparently rambling paper. If you then 'translate' your sub-heading into a topic sentence (Ch 11), then this will provide a link with the previous paragraph or an introduction to the next theme.

Conclusion

This summarises the whole piece of work. It should review the entire text in three elements:

1 A restatement of the question and what you feel are the important features of the topic.

2 A summary of the specific evidence that you have presented in support of your views.

3 A statement of your overall viewpoint on the topic.

One aspect that distinguishes the conclusion from the introduction is language. In the introduction, your explanation should be given clearly, avoiding jargon or technical words as far as possible. In the conclusion, you can include technical or more sophisticated language because you will have introduced these terms in the main body. You should avoid introducing new ideas in the conclusion that have not already been discussed in the earlier part of the writing.

 Mini-conclusions

As you become immersed in the writing process you will become very familiar with the material and will probably think of 'mini-conclusions' as you progress. By the time you come to write the overall conclusion, this in-depth awareness may be forgotten or diluted. To avoid this, note down separately all the ideas that arise as you write and use this as a resource when considering your conclusion.

REPRESENTATIVE ORGANISATIONAL PLANS FOR ASSIGNMENTS

The three-part structure lies at the heart of most assignment formats, but the precise designs differ in detail according to purpose (Table 17.1). The more formal assignments, classified as reports, include various components, according to subject and purpose, and not always in the same order. Table 17.2 provides some examples, but you should follow closely the guidelines published by your department.

Table 17.1 **Designs of different sorts of assignment.** The essay (a) and literature review (b) have a simple structure. The main body is the largest part, and may be subdivided into sections. The general scientific report (c) has a focus on materials and methods. An undergraduate lab report (d) will probably be a stripped-down, shorter version of (c). A non-scientific style of report (e) would not focus on materials and methods, but might have a larger main body. A typical business report (f) includes the conclusions or recommendations as part of the main body and provides an executive summary for quick reading and often appendices and a glossary for the non-specialist. See Table 17.2 for details of content for each section.

(a) Essay	(b) Literature review	(c) General scientific report	(d) Laboratory report in the sciences	(e) Non-scientific report	(f) Typical business report
Introduction	Title page	Title page	Title page	Title page	Title page
Main body of text	Abstract	Abstract	Introduction	Introduction	Executive summary
Conclusions	Introduction	Abbreviations	Materials and methods	Main body of text	Acknowledgements
References or Bibliography	Main body of text	Introduction	Discussion/Conclusions	Conclusion	Table of contents
	Conclusions	Materials and methods*		References or Bibliography	Main body of text
	References or Literature cited	Results			References/ Bibliography
		Discussion			Appendices
		Acknowledgements			Glossary
		References			

*In some subjects, like Chemistry, the Materials and methods section may appear after the Discussion.

Important aspects of report writing include:

- description – reporting your experiments or summarising facts you have gathered;
- visual summaries – making diagrams, flow charts, graphs or tables to demonstrate your points more clearly;
- analysis – looking at results or facts and possibly working out descriptive or hypothesis-testing statistics;
- discussion – weighing up the pros and cons of a position;
- solution(s) – explaining different options to solve an issue or problem being addressed;
- evaluation – deciding what is important and why;
- recommendation – identifying the best solution and giving evidence to support that choice;
- arriving at a conclusion – stating a position on the basis of your research and thinking.

 Why write reports at university?

Report-writing is regarded as important because it:

- compels you to complete your work, and present it in a neatly organised form for assessment
- records your planning, thinking and research
- helps you to develop important professional skills
- provides a record for future research effort

Table 17.2 Typical components of reports and notes on the expected content of each part. These are arranged alphabetically and would not appear in this order in any report. For representative examples of report formats, see Table 17.1. *Always adopt the precise format specified in your course handbook.*

Section or part	Expected content
Abbreviations	A list of any abbreviations for technical terms used within the text (for example, *DNA: deoxyribonucleic acid*). These are also given within the text at the first point of use, for example '...*deoxyribonucleic acid (DNA)*'.
Abstract	A brief summary of the aims of the experiment or series of observations; the main outcomes (in words) and conclusions. This should allow someone to understand your main findings and what you think they mean. This is normally written last.

Section or part	Expected content
Acknowledgements	A list of people who helped you, sometimes with a brief description of how.
Appendix (plural Appendices)	Includes tabular information, usually, that only an expert would want or need to consult. A section where you can put items such as a questionnaire template, data or results that would otherwise disrupt the flow of the report or make the results section too lengthy.
Bibliography/ References/ Literature cited	An alphabetical list of sources cited in the text, following one of the standard formats (see, e.g. McMillan and Weyers, 2013b).
Discussion (or Conclusions)	*Scientific-style reports*: a commentary on the results and an outline of the main conclusions. This could include any or all of the following: • comments on the methods used • mention of sources of errors • conclusions from any statistical analysis • comparison with other findings or the 'ideal' result • what the result means • how you might improve the experiment • how you might implement the findings (in a business report) • where you would go from here given more time and resources. Sometimes you might combine the results and discussions sections to allow a narrative to develop – to explain, for example, why one result led to the next experiment or approach. Bear in mind that a large proportion of marks may be given for your original thoughts in this section. *Non-scientific-style reports*: in this section you might restate the problem or issue to be addressed, outline the key 'solutions' or responses to the problem, and explain the reason for favouring one over another by providing evidence to support that choice. In some, but not all, instances, a set of recommendations might be appropriate.
Executive summary	In a business report, this takes the place of an abstract. It gives the key points of the report, usually in no more than one A4 page. It should start with a brief statement of the aims of the report, a summary of the main findings and/or conclusions, perhaps given as bullet points, and brief details of the main conclusions and/or recommendations. You would normally write this part last.

continued overleaf

Table 17.2 *continued*

Section or part	Expected content
Experimental	A description of apparatus and method, similar to Materials and methods.
Glossary	A list of terms that might be unfamiliar to the reader, with definitions.
Introduction	*Scientific-style reports*: An outline of the background to the experiment, the aims of the experiment and brief discussion of the techniques to be used. Your goal is to orientate the reader and explain what you have done and why. *Non-scientific-style reports*: The context of the study and an outline of the problem or issue to be addressed, in other words, the aim of the report. This may require reference to the literature or other resource material to be used.
Main body of text	This section includes your appraisal of the topic. It should systematically address solutions or issues in response to the report's purpose and provide an analysis of all pertinent matters. It may be subdivided into sections reflecting different aspects. This part may include tables comparing different approaches or results in different studies. Figures tend to be rare but may be used to summarise concepts or illustrate key findings.
Materials and methods	A description of what was done. You should provide sufficient detail to allow a competent person to repeat the work.
Results	A description of the experiments carried out and the results obtained, usually presented in either tabular or graphic form (never both for the same data). You should point out meaningful aspects of the data, which need not be presented in the same order in which the work was done.
Table of contents	Effectively an index to allow the reader to find parts they are interested in reading more about. May also include a table of diagrams. More likely to be included in a lengthy report.
Title page	The full names of the author or authors, the module title or code and the date. In a business report this may also include the company logo, client details, classification (for example, 'confidential'). *Scientific-style reports*: A descriptive title that indicates what was done, indicates any restrictions, and sometimes describes the 'headline' finding. *Non-scientific-style reports*: A concise but comprehensive title that defines the topic.

The main types of assignment are the following.

Essays
Generally, these follow the simple three-part structure outlined above (Table 17.1a), with the main body generally reflecting one of the approaches shown in Table 17.3. You may be expected to add a list of references at the end (Ch 14).

Literature surveys
These follow the relatively uncomplicated format shown in Table 17.1b, usually with an extensive main body. In a scientific literature review, the approach is often to give a chronological account of developments in the field, quoting key authors and their ideas and findings. Two important formatting aspects to consider are citation of literature references and presenting quotes from your sources (discussed in Ch 14). Aspects of finding appropriate literature are discussed in Chapter 10.

Scientific reports
Representative formats are shown in Table 17.1c and d. These tend to mirror the format of journal articles in the primary literature for each subject area (Ch 10). Aspects you should bear in mind are:

1 Anyone reading your report should be able to assimilate your findings quickly, and should be able to find relevant information in the expected place.
2 Your text should be objective and balanced, considering all possible interpretations of your results.
3 Appropriate statistical analysis should be included (Ch 7).
4 You should provide enough information to allow another competent scientist to repeat your work.

Reports for non-scientific subjects
Increasingly report-writing is becoming a feature in non-scientific subjects. A report-style response could be required for a case study, project or group problem-solving exercise, for example. Table 17.1e shows a representative structure. A good approach for the main body of text in these report-style tasks is to follow the SPSER model (see tip box overleaf). This provides a basic skeleton, but you may wish to tailor the headings and sub-headings to fit the context of the topic or problem that you are addressing.

Taking the analytical approach – the SPSER model

This aid to critical thinking helps you to 'deconstruct' or 'unpack' the topic and involves four (or five) elements, as follows:

- **Situation** – describe the context and brief history
- **Problem** – describe or define the problem
- **Solution** – describe and explain the possible solution(s)
- **Evaluation** – identify the positive and negative features for each solution by giving evidence/reasons to support your viewpoint
- **Recommendation** – identify the best option in your opinion, giving the basis of your reasoning for this. This element is optional, as it may not always be a requirement of your task

This is particularly helpful in the construction of essays, reports, projects and case studies. It is also a useful mode of analysis whenever you feel that you cannot identify themes or trends.

Business-style reports

The main aim of a business report is to provide information that helps decision-making. These reports differ greatly in their style and formality and the chief factor to consider is your audience. Table 17.1f illustrates one possible format. For example, a business plan aimed at an investor or bank manager might be brief and focus on financial projections given in charts and tables, while an academic analysis of a business sector might be relatively lengthy and formal, quoting many sources and views.

ADOPTING A STRUCTURAL MODEL FOR THE MAIN BODY OF TEXT

To decide on a structural model, return to your 'first thoughts' brainstorm (Ch 15) which should have been developed further as you have added key points from your reading and thinking. Consider whether any themes or recurrent issues are evident. It might be helpful to 'colour code' all the items that are related using highlighter pens. Then, you need to reconsider the instruction of the set task to help you construct your strategy, that is, on the basis of description, analysis or argument (Ch 15).

Keep on top of your references

In most disciplines you will be expected to cite recognised authorities within the field you are studying (Ch 14). In Law, this could be cases; in the Arts and Humanities, it could be work of a renowned academic; in the Sciences, it could be reports of new findings or methods. It is best to file the relevant reference details as you go along, otherwise you may be left with a substantial amount of work to do at the end. Adopt the citation and referencing formats that are expected for your discipline or task (Ch 14).

These two activities together should give you some indication of how you can construct the body of your paper as a logical discussion by considering how it would fit into one of several classic structural models or approaches (Table 17.3).

By adopting one of these models, it should be possible to map out the content of your answer in a way that provides a logical and coherent response to the task you have been set. Note that it may sometimes be necessary to nest one of these models within another. For example, within the common denominator approach it may be useful to discuss the chronology of events. Once you have decided what kind of approach is required to cover your written assignment, then you can map this on to the main body of your plan and frame an introduction and conclusion that will 'top and tail' the submission.

When you have completed your first draft it is a good idea to go back to your outline plan and check not only that you have not forgotten any points, but also that you have demonstrated your critical thinking competently over the piece. In this way you can also make sure that the links between sections that you noted in the plan have been achieved in the text.

Table 17.3 Structural models for written assignments

Model and outline	Discussion and examples
Chronological Description of a process or sequence	Each paragraph or section might deal with a specific date or time period. An example of describing a developmental process could be outlining the historical development of the European Union. This kind of text is likely to be entirely descriptive.
Hierarchical Classification of objects or ideas	The material is organised into a logical structure related to properties relevant to the assignment. An example of this approach could be to discuss *'modes of transport'* by subdividing your text into land, sea and air travel. Each of these could be further divided into commercial, military and personal modes of transport. Such classifications are, to some extent, subjective, but the approach provides a framework for making comparisons. It is often applied in scientific disciplines.
Common denominator Identifying a common characteristic or theme	Different examples are considered under headings that apply to all. An example of this approach might be used in answer to the following assignment: *Account for the levels of high infant mortality in developing countries.* This suggests considering a common denominator of deficiency or lack in each country. This could therefore be approached under the headings: 1. Lack of primary healthcare; 2. Lack of health education; 3. Lack of literacy.
Analytical Examining an issue in depth	The issue is 'unpacked' into its components and reconstructed. The SPSER approach might be used to organise your thoughts (see tip box). An example of an assignment that you could tackle in this way might be: *Evaluate potential solutions to the problem of identity theft.* This might result in the following plan: 1. Define identity theft, and perhaps give an example. 2. Explain why identity theft is difficult to control. 3. Outline legal and practical solutions to identity theft. 4. Weigh up the advantages and disadvantages of each. 5. State which solution(s) you would favour and why.

continued below

Phased Identifying short/medium/long term (temporal) aspects of a topic	Aspects are considered in time sequence. An example might arise in answer to a task that instructs: *Discuss the impact of water shortage on flora and fauna along riverbanks.* Short-term factors might be that drying out of the riverbed occurs and annual plants fail to thrive. Medium-term factors might include damage to oxygenating plant life and reduction in wildlife numbers. Long-term factors might include the effect on the water table and falling numbers of certain amphibious species. Note that topics amenable to this treatment do not always prompt this sort of response directly by asking for 'results' or consequences of an event. You could, for example, decide to use it in answer to a question such as: *'Explain why water shortage has deleterious effects on riverbank life.'*
Thematic Commenting on a theme in each aspect of a topic	This is similar to the Phased approach, but, in this case, the topic is considered in a series of themes. Precise details would depend on the nature of the question. For the 'modes of transport' example, this might involve considering passenger-mile efficiency first, then fuel issues and then pollution.
Comparative/contrastive Comparing and contrasting items (often within a theme or themes)	This is a derivative of the themed approach, usually adopted to draw out comparisons and/or contrasts between items (e.g. options or examples). These can be treated in either of two ways. Method 1: introduce the topic then discuss each item separately, focusing on the selected aspects in sequence, then draw conclusions about the merits and demerits of one over the other. Method 2: introduce the topic and then discuss the selected aspects in sequence, making the comparison between the items or examples at each stage, then conclude. Each approach has advantages and disadvantages which would relate to the content and the context of the assignment. For example, in an exam, it might be risky to embark on Method 1 lest you run out of time and fail to complete the discussion of the second item.

Keep the right proportions in your response. Make sure that the three elements within your writing framework are well-balanced in extent. The main body should be the most substantial piece of the writing, whereas the introduction and conclusion should occupy much less space. A common mistake is to devote too much time to outlining the context in the introduction and leave little space to deal with the core part of the assignment and the conclusion (this often occurs under the time pressure of an exam situation).

Pay adequate attention to your conclusion. Often, by the time that you come to write the conclusion, this is done at some speed because of time constraints. Thus, it may not get the attention it deserves in relation to the marks awarded to this section. Try to think about your likely conclusions from an early stage – this may shape both the research you do and the content. However, make sure you keep an open mind if the evidence points you in another direction. Reserve some time to give your conclusion a critical appraisal after a pause in writing.

Review your introduction once you have completed your first draft. Make sure that you have actually done what you set out to do when defining the parameters of your work and in your statement of intent. In some cases, the act of writing may have stimulated new thoughts or a different emphasis and your initial intentions may have altered.

Be ruthless in rejecting irrelevant information. You must keep your report as short and to the point as you can. Especially if you have spent a long time obtaining information or conducting an analysis, you may be tempted to include it for this reason alone. Don't. Relevance must be your sole criterion as it is an indicator of your ability to think critically.

Consider your writing style. Detailed reports can be dense and difficult to read. Try to keep your sentences relatively simple and your paragraphs short. In reports, you can use subheadings and bullet points to break up the text. All of these devices can make the content easier for your reader to assimilate.

AND NOW ...

17.1 Find the correct organisational plan to adopt. This might be given in your course handbook or could be taken from an example that you feel is well organised. If this is dissimilar to those shown in Table 17.2, you may wish to map the expected content to the sections in a similar fashion. Try to learn from the writing style and content of any examples you obtain.

17.2 Compare textual patterns. Look at a chapter in a basic textbook and analyse the structural approach the author has taken. Identify the proportion of space allocated to 'scene-setting' using description and to the analysis/argument/evaluation components of the text. This may indicate the general approach for your subject.

17.3 Practise thinking through organisational plans. Look at some of the essay titles or report assignments you have been set or from past exam papers. Try to identify which of the approaches given in this chapter might best 'fit' each task.

18

WRITING ABOUT REFLECTION

How to structure and report your thoughts

Putting your personal thoughts into words is a difficult skill to master and requires specialised language. Various frameworks and systems are used to record reflection. This chapter describes these main formats and outlines what is expected of you in completing relevant academic exercises. Relevant styles of writing are explored for the different elements of the reflective process.

KEY TOPICS

→ Key aspects of reflective writing

→ Language styles for a general reflective report

→ Writing approaches for specialised reflective tasks

KEY TERMS

Blog   Extra-curricular activity   Learning journal   Objective   Personal development plan   Portfolio   Reflective thinking   Sketchbook   Subjective

Reflection is an activity that can take place outside your academic studies (Ch 1), but when it is expected as a part of your course, you will have to record your thoughts and feelings, and quite possibly have these writings assessed. If you feel that this is a demanding aspect of your studies, you will not be alone. Many people find it difficult to put their reflection into words. Possible reasons are:

● they may have little previous experience of this style of writing;

● they may not fully understand what they are required to write;

● they may not fully understand how they are required to write;

● it may be difficult to express their feelings in words;

● they may fear that others will not understand or value their views;

● they may not wish to put what they regard as provisional or private thoughts 'on the record'.

Some of these difficulties can be overcome by gaining a greater understanding of the rationale and context for reflection (Ch 3). Confidence will also come from practice and a willingness to learn from staff feedback. This chapter provides guidance on the language and expected content for the main forms of reflective assignments.

Why are you reflecting?

If this is for an exercise that is assessed as part of your course, it is essential that you consult the learning outcomes or objectives for this part of the course, so that you understand fully what your lecturers expect you to achieve.

KEY ASPECTS OF REFLECTIVE WRITING

The key differences between reflective writing and other forms of academic writing are:

● the writing style has a personal emphasis, rather than being detached;

● reflective writing is part of a thinking process, rather than being the outcome of that process;

● the subject matter is less controlled: although there will be a purpose to the reflective report, much of the content depends on the writer rather than the title given by a lecturer;

● the inner structure of a reflective report may be laid out under specific headings that are different from the underlying 'introduction/main body/conclusion' structure of an essay or the overt structure of a scientific or business report (Ch 17);

● specific online media may be used for reflective reports, rather than the commonplace printed (or printable) output for a word-processed essay or report.

A common mistake in reflective assignments is to fall back on the 'safe' option of describing events and feelings without offering an interpretation or evaluation of them. This arises because students adopt what is sometimes called a 'reflexive' approach placing emphasis on 'me' and 'my feelings' rather than objective interpretation of 'my perception of a situation I observed or in which I participated'.

LANGUAGE STYLES FOR A GENERAL REFLECTIVE REPORT

Guidance for most academic writing emphasises the use of precise and objective language (Ch 16). Putting your reflection into words, in contrast, requires subjective language, since it is primarily *your* personal responses and views that are sought.

 Objective and subjective writing

Objective writing means that based on a balanced consideration of facts, while subjective writing means based on one person's opinion. Thus, objective writing avoids the use of first person (e.g. '*It has been shown that...*'), whereas subjective writing requires the use of the first person (e.g. '*I felt this was correct...*').

Moreover, when your reflective writing is presented as part of a report, you be expected to change register in different parts of your text. Such assignments may involve, for example, an objective and hence formal description of the activity upon which you have been asked to reflect, contrasting with the necessarily informal style required for describing your feelings in response to events.

Table 18.1 provides an indication of the style of writing required in each component of a piece of reflective writing (consult Table 17.1 if unsure of some of the linguistic terms that are used). The table follows the six subdivisions of the reflective process first outlined in Chapter 3, but, in considering its guidance, you should be sensitive to the expected structure of your report, which may use different headings, or may combine or omit certain elements.

If you are still uncertain about *what* to write, Table 18.2 contains some prompting questions. When considering the reflection section, a combination of brainstorming your feelings using these questions as triggers, while constructing a free-form mind map (Ch 12), might be helpful. Ideas noted during this phase might be transferred to a grid like Table 18.3, which can also be used to organise your thoughts for the evaluation component.

Table 18.1 The language expected in the component elements of a general reflective report. It is assumed that you are asked to reflect on an 'episode' that has taken place as part of your training. Clearly, context is very important here, so the examples provided are not always readily transferrable. They provide instead an indication of acceptable forms of writing that you might use.

Component and type of content expected	Examples of style
Description	
In this section, an accurate and relevant description of the episode is required to set the context for your reflection, analysis and actions. Accuracy is essential because a misplaced perception of events might lead to errors at later stages, while relevance is vital to ensure that your later thoughts are focused in relation of the purpose of the exercise (this is especially important when your reflection is being assessed).	The language required here is self-evidently descriptive and would normally involve the use of the past tense in passive voice: *the patient had previously been diagnosed with xxx syndrome and had been treated with yyy drug at a dose of xxx.* and sometimes in third person: *it was noted that the accused was nervous.* Appropriate (that is, accurate, detailed and relevant) use of adjectives and adverbs is important: *the patient's symptoms included a roseate rash under her left eye which she scratched intermittently.* In some cases the use of the active and personal might be appropriate, as with: *to establish a rapport with the client, I first asked a question about his journey to the office...*
Feelings	
In this section, you will be expected find the correct language to describe personal responses, opinions, emotions and sensations connected to the episode. The feelings you report should be those that are relevant to the exercise. Frankness here is crucial, because masking your true feelings will distort the outcome and lessen the value of the exercise. The statement of your feelings may be closely linked to your evaluation, as in certain of these examples and in that in the row below. Take care not to use idiomatic (colloquial) language or clichés (Table 16.2).	The language used here is necessarily personal and will involve the use of the first person ('I', 'me', 'my'). Verbs in both present and past tenses could be appropriate: *I considered the first part of the meeting went well, because...* *I forgot to let the client know that she had a number of other options, as well as the one I favoured. I acknowledge that this was a mistake, and...* *Looking back on the lesson, I would have changed a number of aspects of my approach to disruptive pupil B.* *My presentation faltered at the start (I was nervous), but once I got into my stride, I started to enjoy things. The most gratifying part was during the questions, when...*

continued overleaf

Component and type of content expected	Examples of style
Evaluation	
This section will require you to see both sides of an episode. It is important to be balanced in your appraisal and to be seen to be even-handed. In so doing, you should feel free to state what you think you did well, as well as what you think you might have improved: don't be too negative. You have a choice in the way you might present this information. You can: 1 present each element separately and discuss positive and negative aspects together. 2 group together the all the positive and negative aspects relating to your reflection. In most cases the first option will be better (assuming you haven't been instructed otherwise) as the reader will be able to focus on the different elements of your discussion separately.	You will probably need to use the first person and past tense in describing your thoughts. For example: *When the client said he didn't like any of my initial drawings, **I was very disappointed** and **didn't know how to react**. However, **I regained my composure and asked him to state** why they didn't meet his expectations. In discussion, it turned out that he didn't appreciate that certain features of the design were dictated (a) by building regulations and (b) by the orientation of the site. **I felt I managed this part of the discussion well**, and as a result **we started to discuss** further options for later designs.*
Analysis	
In this section you will be expected to relate events before, during and after the episode to 'theory' (for examples, models of behaviour) and to quote references relating to the theory. In this way you can demonstrate to your lecturers that you understand the literature of your subject and can apply it to real-life situations. You will	When discussing the literature, you will need to employ the normal academic conventions of citation and referencing (Ch 14), for example, using past tense and third person: *There were only four members of our team so **it was initially difficult to see** how the **nine team personalities of Belbin (2006) might apply**. It seemed to me that each individual took on multiple roles for the exercise, and that we also shifted roles as the project developed. Without doubt, Jane was...*

continued below

probably have been given the theoretical context for the reflective task by your lecturers in the run-up to the exercise, but a visit to the library or relevant websites to do some background reading will be beneficial.	The standard details of Belbin's website which this piece cites would be included in a 'References' or 'Literature cited' section at the end of the report (see Ch 14 for formats – and follow the appropriate discipline conventions). Especially where large numbers of citations are required, the academic style of this section can involve rather dry and scholarly writing which may contrast abruptly with the preceding reflection and evaluation sections. To avoid this, try to refer to a few sources in preceding parts of the report, especially the introductory descriptive parts where you are outlining the aims of the exercise.
Conclusion	
The conclusion should summarise the aims and/or context of the exercise and what you believe to be the important events and outcomes. It should sum up the most important points of reflection, evaluation and analysis, possibly ending with a 'take-home message' from your reflection.	The language will continue in standard academic style, although you should not be afraid of using the first person to echo your reflection. Contrast *In conclusion, the theory of Robson (2005) was validated in this exercise, primarily because...* with *It can be concluded that the theory of Robson (2005) was validated in this exercise, primarily because...*
Action plan	
Without this section, the act of reflection may be considered to be aimless and you won't stand to gain from the experience. To create an effective action plan, your goals should be specific, measurable, achievable, relevant and timely (i.e. 'SMART'). They will indicate clearly how you intend to respond to the episode and your thoughts about it.	If you have a plan, then you might describe this in the present tense: *My plan is to carry out more background reading, so that...* However, in many cases, the future tense will be also appropriate: *I will investigate published case studies to find out more about...*

Table 18.2 Some questions to ask yourself to prompt effective reflection. Not every sub-element of the reflective process may be included in your specific task; furthermore, you do not need to answer all the questions as part of your self-evaluation: they are mainly provided to help to focus your thoughts and responses. In some cases the prompts may equally apply to other aspects – this may depend on the precise details of your task and the instructions provided. Always use the latter as your first point of reference.

Aspect of reflection	Question prompts
Description	• What were the details of the situation I was presented with? • What was my role? • What happened? • What was the 'critical incident' I observed? • What did I do, and what did others do? • What were the outcomes or consequences?
Feelings	• How did I feel personally? • What did I find that was unexpected/interesting/inspiring/deflating/confusing/valuable about the episode, and why? • Why did I respond to events in the way I did? • Did I feel my actions were appropriate? • Were my expectations met, and if not, in which ways? • How might others have responded to the same episode, and why?
Evaluation	• What was positive and what was negative about the episode? • What personal strengths and weaknesses were revealed by the episode? • What did I learn? • Has the episode changed my way of thinking?
Analysis	• How can I explain what happened? • What theory or research is relevant to the situation, and how does what happened relate to this? • How does this relate to other relevant experiences? • How could I have improved in my role? • What alternative actions could have been taken, and what would be the predicted consequences? • In what other ways could people's experience of the episode (or other outcomes) have been improved? • How does the wider context (e.g. ethical, managerial, administrative, social, location/setting) apply to the situation?
Conclusion	• What did I learn from the experience? • How might I respond in future?
Action plan	• What will I do now? • What are my priorities? • When will I complete these activities? • How will I know that I have improved?

Table 18.3 Example of a simple grid for recording feeling and evaluation as part of a reflective exercise. This grid might be used after you have created a mind map to brainstorm your initial thoughts (Ch 12).

Feelings	Evaluation	
	Positive aspects	Negative aspects
I felt sympathetic to the client's situation	This might motivate me to assist them further	This might colour my views of the case, making me unfairly biased in their favour
I considered that the meeting went well	I covered all of the aspects of the case that I wanted to	The meeting over-ran a little, making me late for my next appointment

Finding connections

Reflective writing should show that you can make links between facets of a situation and relate these to the 'bigger picture'. Creating an overview using a mind map or grid could be helpful.

WRITING APPROACHES FOR SPECIALISED REFLECTIVE TASKS

The above principles can be applied to most assignments involving a reflective element, and especially where a structured report is expected. The additional points in Table 18.4 cover both the writing medium and expected style for the specialised reflective tasks first introduced in Chapter 3.

One advantage of online formats is that they allow you to link to websites and files and incorporate images. There is usually no copyright problem with material that you refer to via web links, although you should follow the usual referencing conventions (Ch 14) so that the exact source is recorded. You should beware of including too many links as this may distract the reader from your own message and may be construed as plagiarism (analogous to including too many quotes in an essay, see Ch 13). You should take great care not to use copyright images or other material, especially if your blog is open on the Web, as this is illegal (see Ch 13).

Table 18.4 Writing media and approaches for specialised reflective tasks

Task and format	Expected writing approach
Learning journal	
The journal itself would normally be entered directly into a notebook or developed as a word-processed document.	For each entry, you would normally include the following information: 1 Date and description of the experience 2 Reflection on what happened and what you learned 3 Details of how you intend to follow things up. There is no need to be wordy, nor to produce perfect text. Rather, it is important to focus on the development of your professional skills.
Blog	
Normally, you will be provided with a platform for creating the blog, which may contain sections for relevant information. No particular web programming skills are required.	The amount and type of reflective content should be tailored to the type of blog (see p. 36). It might be a good idea to draft text using a word processor so you can carry out spell checks and make printouts for editing. To take advantage of the medium, images, videos and links to other websites should be incorporated where appropriate. Indeed, these may be critical as a source of material for reflection. Nearly all blogs are presented in reverse date order, with the latest entry first and earlier entries following in sequence. This may present problems as the reader/viewer will have difficulty in following your reflection. It may help to add appropriate cross-references to earlier material so the reader can grasp the developmental sequence of the work.
Sketchbook	
Although notebooks and drawing pads remain popular for sketchbooks, for the obvious reason that they help develop drawing skills, some staff now favour electronic forms of storage for relevant material.	Written annotations in your sketchbook may relate to the origins of the material (dates, places, reminders) or reflections (feelings, ideas, connections). The sequence of entries will allow you to document how a design idea originated. In some cases it may be important to record bibliographic information (Ch 14) as this can help you attribute your influences and differentiate your original work from that of others. If using an online sketchbook, you may need to learn relevant skills of scanning, image manipulation and video capture.

Portfolio/e-portfolio	
An e-portfolio is normally hosted within a specialised programme or virtual learning environment (such as Blackboard® or PebblePad®). These systems are driven via self-explanatory menus and are generally accessible online.	The reflective element in an e-portfolio is likely to be course-specific and defined in the course handbook and/ or task instructions. As with blogs, it may be convenient to write drafts in a word processor, so that you can use specialised editing features such as spell checkers and word counting that may not be included in the e-portfolio program. However, note that some features of documents may not copy through, such as text formatting or tables.
Personal development plan (PDP)	
In many cases, the PDP is collated within a specialised form of e-portfolio that may build up over several years rather than a single term or semester.	The writing in a PDP is likely to be short and to the point. It can be regarded as both a memory aid and personal notebook. Curriculum vitae writing, if part of the PDP, should be treated as a specialised topic and you should approach your Careers Service for advice, or consult McMillan and Weyers, 2013a.

Controlling file sizes

Especially where a large number of images or screenshots are included in reflective blogs or e-portfolios, file size may become an issue due to storage limitations. Use .jpg file format and not .pdf to avoid large file sizes. Even in this format, it may be necessary to reduce the size of images or text-plus-image files. This can be achieved easily in standard image manipulation software such as PaintShop® via *Image > Resize* or similar commands. Where images are embedded in Microsoft Office® files, you can use the *Save as > Tools > Compress Pictures* command and select the appropriate compression setting from the *Options* menu.

 PRACTICAL TIPS FOR REFLECTIVE WRITING

Ensure you have the vocabulary necessary to explain your thoughts and impressions. If a particular word you have chosen doesn't really seem to communicate things exactly, use a thesaurus to search for alternatives and a dictionary or web search 'Define: <word>' function to check your understanding of meaning.

If stuck for material, ask yourself questions. Table 18.2 provides a list of questions to act as prompts.

Re-read your text to check for coherence. Because the style of writing changes in the different elements of reflection, it is easy to produce a disjointed piece of work. This means you should spend extra time reviewing the material. Ask a friend or family member to comment on whether they understand all your points.

AND NOW ...

18.1 Make sure you understand what will be required of you.
Revisit the learning outcomes and marking criteria associated with your current reflective exercise. These are likely to be found in the course handbook. They will help you understand the aims of the exercise as well as the expected structure, content and writing style. Unless otherwise defined, use any word-length limits for the different elements to gauge the relative effort to devote to each.

18.2 Search the Web for similar formats of reflective writing.
If you are uncertain about the content and style of writing to use, it may be beneficial to look at the approaches of others. However, you should not be tempted to follow another's text closely: (a) this amounts to plagiarism (Ch 13); and (b) it would obviate the whole point of reflection, which is meant to be entirely personal to you.

18.3 Take an early opportunity to familiarise yourself with any software you will be expected to use to record your reflection.
If the type of system to be used is new to you, do not let the technical side of things hold you back or distract you when you are ready to commit to writing your feelings down. It may be a good idea to construct a temporary 'nonsense' entry to test out the features.

19

EDITING AND PRESENTING YOUR ASSIGNMENT

How to review your own work and follow academic style conventions

Thinking critically about your own writing is essential if you want to produce work of the highest quality. Editing and proof-reading are opportunities to improve the sense and language of your written assignments. In addition, the presentation of your written work needs care as this can also affect the overall mark.

KEY TOPICS

→ The reviewing, editing and proof-reading process

→ Presenting your work

KEY TERMS

Annotate   Analogy   Assignment   Citation   Legend
Qualitative   Quotation   Typo

The writing process begins with a plan and finishes with reviewing and presenting your work. The review stage involves re-reading your text and thinking in a critical, detached way about what you have written, then editing appropriately and proof-reading for mistakes. Enhancing presentation involves more than attending to layout and use of visual elements; it requires accuracy, consistency and attention to detail. The effort you invest here will improve the quality of your work and hence your assessed mark.

You will need time to get these aspects right. Ideally, you should leave a gap of time between completing the writing and beginning the reviewing process, as this will allow you to 'distance' yourself from your own work and help you look at it as a new reader would. For an assignment such as a lengthy in-course essay, this could mean trying to complete the 'content' phase at least a day ahead of the submission date.

Definitions

Reviewing means appraising critically; that is, examining a task or project to ensure that it meets the requirements and objectives of the task.

Editing means revising and correcting later drafts of an essay, to arrive at a final version. Usually, this involves the smaller rather than larger details, such as details of punctuation, spelling, grammar and layout.

Proof-reading means checking a printed copy for errors of any sort.

THE REVIEWING, EDITING AND PROOF-READING PROCESS

At this stage you are performing the role of editor of your own work. This means looking critically at your text for content, relevance and sense, as well as for flaws in layout, grammar, punctuation and spelling. You should also check for consistency, for example in use of terminology, in spelling, and in presentational features such as font and point size, layout of paragraphs, and labelling of tables or diagrams.

Clearly, there are a lot of aspects to cover, and some degree of overlap in the different aspects of the process. Some people prefer to go through their text in one sweep, amending all types of error as they go; others take a staged approach, reading through their text several times looking at a different aspect each session. A three-stage model you might consider involves three 'sweeps', looking sequentially at:

1 content and relevance

2 grammatical correctness

3 presentation.

Table 19.1 gives some strategies you can adopt when revising your text in this way.

Although the editing process may seem tedious, it is the mix of content, structure and presentation that will gain you marks and anything you can do to increase your 'mark-earning' power will be to your advantage. In the longer term, learning how to edit your work properly will help you to develop a skill of critical analysis that will stand you in good stead throughout your career.

Table 19.1 Editing strategies. The reviewing/editing/proof-reading process can be done in a single 'sweep'. As you become more experienced, you will become adept at doing this. However, initially, it might help you to focus on each of these three broad aspects in a separate 'sweep' of the text.

Content and relevance; clarity, style and coherence	Grammatical correctness, spelling and punctuation	Presentation
• Read text aloud – your ears will help you to identify errors that your eyes have missed.	• Check titles and sub-titles are appropriate to the style of the work and stand out by using bold or underlining (not both).	• Check that you have made good use of white space, that is, not crammed the text into too tight a space, and that your text is neat and legible.
• Revisit the task or question. Check your interpretation against the task as set.	• Consider whether the different parts link together well – if not, introduce signpost words to guide the reader through the text.	• If word processed, check that you have followed standard typing conventions (Table 19.2). Follow any 'house style' rules stipulated by your department.
• Work on a hard copy using proof-reading symbols to correct errors (Figure 20.1).	• Check for fluency in sentence and paragraph structure – remodel as required.	• Check that you have included a reference list, consistently following a recognised method (Ch 14) and that all citations in the text are matched by an entry in the reference list and vice versa.
• Identify that the aims you set out in your introduction have been met.	• Check sentence length – remodel to shorter or longer sentences. Sometimes shorter sentences are more effective than longer ones.	
• Read objectively and assess whether the text makes sense. Look for inconsistencies in argument.	• Ensure that you have been consistent in spelling conventions, for example, following British English rather than American English spelling.	• Ensure all pages are numbered and are stapled or clipped and, if appropriate, ensure that the cover page is included.
• Check that all your facts are correct.	• Spelling errors and typos – use the spell checker but be prepared to double-check in a standard dictionary if you are in doubt or cannot find a spelling within the spell checker facility.	• Check that your name, matriculation number and course number are included. You may wish to add this information as a footnote that appears on each page.
• Insert additional or overlooked evidence that strengthens the whole.		
• Remove anything that is not relevant or alter the text so that it is clear and unambiguous. Reducing text by 10–25% can improve quality considerably.	• Check for cumbersome constructions – divide or restructure sentence(s); consider whether active or passive is more suitable. Consider using vocabulary that might convey your point more eloquently.	• Ensure question number and title are included.
• Assess your material to ensure that you have attributed ideas to the sources, that is, check that you have not committed plagiarism (see Ch 13).		• Check that labelling of diagrams, charts and other visual material is in sequence and consistently presented.
• Remodel any expressions which are too informal for academic contexts.	• Check for use of 'absolute' terms to ensure that you maintain objectivity (Ch 2).	• Ensure that supporting material is added in sequence as appendices, footnotes, endnotes or as a glossary as applicable.
• Eliminate gendered or discriminatory language.		

Using proof-reading symbols

Professional proof-readers have developed a system of symbols to speed up the editing and proof-reading process (you are likely to see some of them on work returned by lecturers). You may wish to adopt some of these yourself, and Figure 20.1 (p. 252) illustrates some of the more commonly used symbols.

PRESENTING YOUR WORK

Most marks for your academic assignments will be awarded for content but some will always be directly or indirectly reserved for presentation, so the final 'production' phase can influence your overall grading. By paying attention to these 'cosmetic' details, you can improve your marks relatively easily.

The overall layout will depend on the type of academic writing you have been asked to produce. An assignment like an essay could have a relatively simple structure: a cover page, the main essay text and a list of references. A laboratory ('lab') report might be more complex, with a title page, abstract, introduction and sections for materials and methods, results, discussion, conclusion and references (Ch 17). Layouts for most types of assignment also vary slightly depending on discipline. You should research this carefully before you start to write up by consulting the course handbook or other regulations.

Other important aspects of presentation relate to text organisation and the conventions for including elements such as figures, tables, numbers and quotes. The key aspects are discussed in Table 19.2.

Why does presentation matter?

- It may be marked for itself as part of the assignment
- It helps the marker understand what you have written
- It shows you can adopt professional standards in your work
- It demonstrates you have acquired important transferable skills that will transfer to other subjects, and, later, employment

Even where presentation does not 'count', it may encourage the marker to take a negative view of your work, feeling that if its appearance is sloppy, then your content may be similarly ill-thought out.

Table 19.2 Key aspects of presentation. This table offers general advice. Always refer to the detailed guidance in your course handbook.

Cover page
This is important to get right because it will create a good first impression. If detailed instructions are not given, include, as appears relevant: • your name and/or matriculation number (where 'anonymous marking' occurs, then your matriculation number only is required) • course title and/or code • title of the assignment • staff member's name • word count. Keep it simple: a cover sheet with fancy graphics will not add to your mark.

Main text

The majority of student assignments are word processed. This makes the drafting and editing phases easier. Consider the following presentational aspects:
 	
• **Font** – There are two main sorts: serif fonts, with extra strokes at the end of the main strokes of each letter (like Times New Roman) and sans-serif fonts (like Arial), without these strokes. The selection is usually left as a matter of personal preference. More likely to be specified is the point size (pt) of the font, which will probably be 11 or 12 pt for ease of reading. Avoid using elaborate font types as they tend not to help the reader assimilate what you have written. For the same reason, you should limit your use of forms of emphasis (*italics* or **bold** or <u>underlined</u>).
 	
• **Margins** – The convention is for left-hand margins to be 4 cm and the right-hand margins 2.5 cm. This ensures that the text can be read if a left-hand binding is used and allows space for the marker's comments.
 	
• **Line-spacing** – It is easier to read text which is spaced at least at 1.5–2 lines apart. This also leaves space for the marker's comments. An exception is where you wish to use long quotations. These should be indented and typed as italics in single-line spacing.
 	
• **Paragraphs** – Lay these out clearly and consistently. Some prefer the indentation method where the paragraph begins on the fourth character space from the left-hand margin. Others prefer the blocked paragraph style, that is, where all paragraphs begin on the left-hand margin. The space between paragraphs should be roughly equivalent to a missing line.
 	
• **Sub-headings** – In some disciplines use of sub-headings is acceptable or even favoured; while in others these 'signpost' strategies are discouraged. It is best to consult your lecturer or course handbook about this if you are uncertain. Usually sub-headings are in bold.
 	
• **'White space'** – This an important aspect of design. Avoid making your text appear too dense by:
  – leaving space (one 'return' space) between paragraphs;
  – justifying only on the left side of the page;
  – leaving space around diagrams, tables and other visual material;
  – leaving reasonable spaces between headings, sub-headings and text.

continued overleaf

Table 19.2 *continued*

Citations and references

The ways in which citations and references should be presented are outlined in Chapter 14. References are usually listed at the end of your text in a separate section, although in some systems they may be positioned at the bottom of the page where the citation occurs.

You must be consistent in the style you adopt and there may be strict subject-specific conventions. If in doubt, consult your course handbook or your lecturer.

Quotes

Quotes can be integrated into the text when short (p. 168), but are usually presented as a 'special' type of paragraph when long.

- **Short quotations** are placed within single inverted commas (British English tradition). Quotations within the quote are in double inverted commas.

- **Long quotations** are usually 30 or more words of prose or more than two lines of poetry. They are indented by five character spaces from the left margin. No quotation marks are necessary unless there are quotation marks used in the text you are quoting.

In both cases, the source and date of publication are provided after the quote. Some disciplines, for example, English Literature or Law, have very specific rules for the way in which quotations are laid out and referenced. In such cases, consult your course handbook or ask for guidance from a lecturer.

Formulae

Short formulae or equations can be included in text, but they are probably better presented on a separate line and indented, thus

$$\frac{a}{x} + \frac{4\beta}{x} / \frac{\eta^2}{x}\frac{\pi}{x} = 0 \qquad \text{(Eqn 1.1)}$$

Where a large number of formulae are included, they can be numbered for ease of cross-reference, as shown above.

Quoting numbers in text

Adopt the following rules:

- In general writing, spell out numbers from one to ten and use figures for 11 and above; in formal writing, spell out numbers from one to a hundred and use figures above this.

- Spell out high numbers that can be written in two words ('six hundred'). With a number like 4,200,000, you also have the choice of writing '4.2 million'.

- Always use figures for dates, times, currency or to give technical details ('5 amp fuse').

- Always spell out numbers that begin sentences, indefinite numbers ('hundreds of soldiers') or fractions ('seven-eighths').

Figures

A wide range of visual material is included under the term 'figure' ('Fig.' for short and usually with an initial capital). This includes graphs, diagrams, charts, sketches, pictures and photographs (sometimes referred to as plates). Quite strict rules apply regarding the way figures are used:

- **All figures should be referred to in the text.** There are 'standard' formulations for doing this, such as *'Figure 4 shows that...'* or *'...results for one treatment were higher than for the other (see Fig. 2)'* that you can imitate from the literature or texts in your subject area.

- **Number the figures in the order they are referred to in the text.** If you are including the figures within the main body of text (usually more convenient for the reader) then they should appear in the text as soon as convenient after the first time of mention.

- **Position your figures at the top or bottom of a page**, rather than sandwiched between blocks of text. This looks neater and makes the text easier to read.

- **Each figure should have a legend** which will include the figure number, a title and some text (often a key to the symbols and line styles used). The convention is for figure legends to appear below each figure. Your aim should be to make each figure self-contained: a reader who knows the general subject area should be able to work out what your figure shows, without reference to other material.

Integrated suites of office-type software allow you to insert graphs produced using the spreadsheet program into text produced with the word processor.

Tables

These are used to summarise large amounts of information, especially where a reader might be interested in the detail. Tables are most often used for numerical data but are also especially useful for qualitative information (this is an example, as is Table 17.1) or mixed data. Tables consist of columns (vertical) and rows (horizontal). By analogy with figures, the convention is to put the controlled or measured variable on the column headers (horizontal) and to place the measured variable or categories of measurement in the rows (vertical). Do not forget to include the units of the information listed if this is relevant. It is quite common to note exceptions and other information as footnotes to tables. The rules for introducing tables in text are very similar to those for figures (see above), with the important exception that a table legend should always appear *above* the table.

PRACTICAL TIPS FOR REVIEWING, EDITING AND PROOF-READING YOUR WORK

Read your work aloud. This is a tried and tested technique to ensure that what you have written actually makes sense. Your ears will pick up the errors that your eyes might miss on a silent reading. This will help you correct grammatical and spelling inconsistencies as well as punctuation omissions.

Work from a hard copy. Reading through your work laid out on paper, which is the format in which your marker will probably see it, will help you identify typos, errors and inconsistencies more readily than might be possible on the screen. A paper version is also easier to annotate (although this can also be done using the 'insert comment' or 'track changes' facility on your word processor). A printout also allows you to see the whole work in overview, to focus on the way the text 'flows' and see some flaws more clearly.

Check frequently for relevance and consistency. Always ensure that you have written and interpreted the question as set and have not 'made up' another title for the task. Whatever you have written will be judged by the terms of the original assignment and not by one that you have created. Ensure that your introduction, examples and conclusion complement and do not contradict each other.

Stick to your word limits/targets. Remember that too few words can be just as bad as too many. The key point is that your writing must be clear to your reader. Sometimes this means giving a longer explanation; sometimes it means simplifying what you have written.

Adopt standard word processing layout conventions. The following guidelines will ensure a neat, well-spaced presentation:

- one character space after the following punctuation – full-stop, comma, colon, semi-colon, closing inverted commas (double and single), question mark and exclamation mark*;
- no character space after apostrophes in a 'medial' position e.g. it's; men's; monkey's;
- no indentation of paragraphs;
- double or 1.5 line spacing;
- one standard line space between paragraphs;
- left-justified text;
- italicised letters for foreign words and titles of books, journals, papers;
- headings in same font size as text, but bold.

*Note that some people prefer two spaces after a full-stop and colon.

19.1 Reflect on a past submission. Look at an assignment that you have already submitted and go through it using the guidance in Table 19.1. Concentrate on two pages and, using a highlighter, mark all flaws, inconsistencies or errors. Look at the overall effect of these errors and reflect on the extent to which this may have lost you marks; then consider how you might allow for more time for the editing/proof-reading phase next time round.

19.2 Practise condensing a piece of text. This is an acknowledged way of improving your work, though you have to bear in mind any word targets that have been set. Look at the text for irrelevant points, wordy phrases, repetitions and excessive examples; if you can reduce its original length by 10–25%, then you will find that you will have created a much tighter, more easily read piece of writing.

19.3 Adopt figure and table styles from the literature. If you have doubts about the precise style or arrangement of figures and tables, and no instructions are published in the course handbook, follow the model shown in texts or journal articles from your subject area. Don't automatically accept the graphical output from spreadsheets and other programs. These are not always in the conventional style. For example, the default output for many charts produced by the Microsoft Excel spreadsheet includes a grey background and horizontal gridlines, neither of which is generally used for academic purposes. It is not difficult to alter these parts of the chart, however, and you should learn how to do this from manuals or the help facility on the program.

FORWARD THINKING

EXPLOITING FEEDBACK

How to learn from what lecturers think of your work

When you receive back assessed work and exam scripts, these are usually annotated by the marker. Careful consideration of these comments is essential. Staff will not only point out minor errors of grammar and spelling, but also flaws in your thinking or the way your thoughts are expressed. This chapter outlines some common annotations and describes how reacting to feedback in the right way can help you to develop your thinking skills further.

KEY TOPICS

→ Types of feedback

→ Examples of feedback comments and what they mean

KEY TERMS

Formative assessment   Summative assessment

There are two principal types of assessment at university: formative and summative. Formative assessments are those in which the grade received does not contribute to your end-of-module mark, or contributes relatively little, but which gives you an indication of the standard of your work. It is often accompanied by a feedback sheet or comments written on the script. Summative assessments contribute directly to your final module mark and include things such as end-of-term/semester exams, project reports or essay submissions.

TYPES OF FEEDBACK

The simplest pointer you will receive from any type of assessment is the grade you receive; if good, you know that you have reached the expected standard; if poor, you know that you should try to improve.

If you feel unsure about the grading system or what standard is expected at each grading level, your course or faculty handbooks will probably include a description of marking or assessment criteria that explain this.

Written feedback may be provided on your scripts and other work. This will often take the form of handwritten comments over your text, and a summary commenting on your work or justifying why it received the mark it did. Sometimes the feedback will be provided separately from your script so that other markers are not influenced by it.

Obtaining informal (preliminary) feedback

Your fellow students or family members can help by reading through your work and commenting. Even though they may lack subject knowledge, they will be able to comment on the clarity of your writing or the logic of your argument.

How well are you performing?

The answer, of course, depends on your goals and expectations, but also on your understanding of degree classifications and their significance. Even in early levels of study, it may be worth relating percentage marks or other forms of grades (descriptors) to the standard degree classes – first, upper second, lower second, third and unclassified. Certain career and advanced degree opportunities will only be open to those with higher-level qualifications, and you should try to gain an understanding of how this operates in your field of study and likely career destination.

Always read your feedback

The comments in your feedback should give you constructive direction for later efforts and are designed to help you to develop the structure and style of your work, as well as encourage you to develop a deeper understanding of the topic. Where students ignore points, especially those about presentation or structure, then they may find themselves heavily penalised in later submissions.

Some feedback may be verbal and informal, for example, a supervisor's comments on your progress with a project or an observation on your contribution during a tutorial. If you feel uncertain about why your work has received the grade it did, or why a particular comment was provided, you may be able to arrange a meeting with the person who marked your work. Normally they will be happy to provide further verbal explanations. However, do not attempt to haggle over your marks, other than to point out politely if part of your work does not appear to have been marked at all, or part marks appear to have been added up wrongly.

EXAMPLES OF FEEDBACK COMMENTS AND WHAT THEY MEAN

Different lecturers use different terms to express similar meanings, and because they mark quickly, their handwritten comments are sometimes untidy and may be difficult to interpret. This means that you may need help in deciphering their meaning. Table 20.1 illustrates feedback comments that are frequently made and explains how you should react to obtain better grades in future. This should be viewed with Figure 20.1 (p. 252) which explains some proof-reading symbols that lecturers may use. If a particular comment or mark does not make sense to you after reading these tables, you may wish to approach the marker for an explanation.

Applying feedback to exam performance

Look at the comments and advice given on written coursework and identify ways in which you can use the feedback constructively in the answers you give in exams. For example, if structure is identified as a weakness, then practise speed–planning answers so that your answers become focused and succinct.

Table 20.1 Common types of feedback annotation and how to act in response. Comments in the margin may be accompanied by underlining of word(s), circling of phrases, sentences or paragraphs.

Types of comment and typical examples	Meaning and potential remedial action
Regarding content	
Relevance Relevance? Importance? Value of example? So?	An example or quotation may not be apt, or you may not have explained its relevance. Think about the logic of your narrative or argument and whether there is a mismatch as implied, or whether you could add further explanation; choose a more appropriate example or quote.
Detail Give more information Example? Too much detail/waffle/padding	You are expected to flesh out your answer with more detail or an example to illustrate your point; or, conversely, you may have provided too much information. It may be that your work lacks substance and you appear to have compensated by putting in too much description rather than analysis.
Specific factual comment or comment on your approach You could have included ... What about ...? Why didn't you ...?	Depends on context, but it should be obvious what is required to accommodate the comment.
Expressions of approval Good! Excellent! ✓(may be repeated)	You got this right or chose a good example. Keep up the good work!
Expressions of disapproval Poor Weak No! ✗(may be repeated)	Sometimes obvious, but may not be clear. The implication is that your examples, logic etc. could be improved.
Regarding structure	
Fault in logic or argument Logic? Non sequitur (does not follow)	Your argument or line of logic is faulty. This may require quite radical changes to your approach to the topic.
Failure to introduce topic clearly Where are you going with this? Unclear	What is your understanding of the task? What parameters will confine your response? How do you intend to tackle the subject?

Failure to construct a logical discussion *Imbalanced discussion* *Weak on pros and cons*	When you have to compare and contrast in any way, then it is important that you give each element in your discussion similar coverage.
Failure to conclude essay clearly *So what?* *Conclusion?*	You have to leave a 'take-home message' that sums up the most salient features of your writing and should not include new material in this section. This is to demonstrate your ability to think critically and define the key aspects.
Heavy dependency on quotations *Watch out for over-quotation* *Too many quotations*	There is a real danger of plagiarism if you include too many direct quotations from text. You have to demonstrate that you can synthesise the information from sources as evidence of your understanding. However, in a subject like English literature or law, quotation may be a key characteristic of writing. In this case, quotation is permitted, provided that it is supported by critical comment.
Move text *Loops and arrows*	Suggestion for changing order of text, usually to enhance the flow or logic.
Regarding presentation	
Minor proofing errors *sp. (usually in margin – spelling)* *⋋ (insert material here)* *⌐ (break paragraph here)* *⁊ (delete this material)* *P (punctuation error)*	A (minor) correction is required. Figure 20.1 provides more detail of likely proof-reading symbols.
Citations *Reference (required)* *Ref?* *Reference list omitted*	You have not supported evidence, argument or quotation with a reference to the original source. This is important in academic work and if you fail to do it, you may be considered guilty of plagiarism. If you omit to attach a reference list, this will lose you marks as it implies a totally unsourced piece of writing, that is, you have done no specialist reading.
Tidiness *Illegible!* *Untidy* *Can't read*	Your handwriting, numerical notation or diagrams may be difficult to decipher. Allocate more time to writing out your work neatly, or use a word processor if allowed.
Failure to follow recommended format *Please follow departmental template for reports* *Order!*	If the department or school provides a template for the submission of reports, you must follow it. There are good reasons, such as the need to follow professional conventions, especially in sciences; you must conform. If you don't, you may lose marks.

Correction mark	Meaning	Example
⌐ (np)	(new) paragraph	*Text* *margin*
≱	change CAPITALS to small letters (lower case)	The correction marks that tutors
~~	change into **bold** type	use in students' texts are generally
≡	change into CAPITALS	made to help identify where there
͡	close up (delete space)	have been errors of spilling or le/lg
/ or ⁊ or ⊢	delete	punctuation. They can ~~often~~ (STET)
⋏	insert a word or letter	indicate where there is lack of
Y	insert space	paragraphing or grammatical
.... or (STET)	leave unchanged	accuracy. If you find that work is (np)
Insert punctuation symbol in a circle (P)	punctuation	returned to you with such
plag.	plagiarism	marks correction, then it is ⊔⊓
⟶	run on (no new paragraph)	worthwhile spending some time
Sp.	spelling	analysing the common errors as ⁊
⊔⊓	transpose text	well as the comments, because this
?	what do you mean?	will help you to improve the
??	text does not seem to make sense	quality of presentation and content
✓	good point/correct	of your work this reviewing can ⊙/≡
×	error	have a positive effect on your
		assessed mark.

In the margin, the error symbols are separated by a slash (/), as in the third example down.

Figure 20.1 **Common proof-reading symbols.** University lecturers and tutors use a variety of symbols on students' assignments to indicate errors, corrections or suggestions. These can apply to punctuation, spelling, presentation or grammar. The symbols provide a kind of 'shorthand' that acts as a code to help you see how you might be able to amend your text so that it reads correctly and fluently. In this table some of the more commonly used correction marks are shown alongside their meanings. The sample text shows how these symbols may be used either in the text or the margin to indicate where a change is recommended.

PRACTICAL TIPS FOR DEALING WITH FEEDBACK

Be mentally prepared to learn from the views of your tutors. You may initially feel that feedback is unfair, harsh or that it misunderstands the approach you were trying to take to the question. A natural reaction might be to dismiss many of the comments. However, you should recognise that tutors probably have a much deeper understanding of the topic than you, and concede that if you want to do well in a subject then you need to gain a better understanding of what makes a good answer from the academic's point of view.

Think about your feedback in relation to your thinking skills. Do any points about your work indicate that the thought processes that are evident are mismatched to the expectations of your lecturers? Consult Chapter 2 and in particular Table 2.3 for an indication of what might be expected, and look again at the marking criteria for your course or the specific marked exercise. If you still don't comprehend why you have been marked down, ask to see a member of staff for an explanation.

Always make sure you understand the feedback. Check with fellow students or with the lecturers involved if you cannot read the comment or do not understand why it has been made.

Respond to feedback. Make a note of common or repeated errors, even in peripheral topics, so that you can avoid them in later assignments.

 AND NOW ...

20.1 Check out your department or faculty's marking criteria. As explained above, these may help you interpret feedback and understand how to reach the standard you want to achieve.

20.2 Decide what to do about feedback comments you frequently receive. For instance, do lecturers always comment about your spelling or grammar; or suggest you should use more examples; or ask for more citations (Ch 13, Ch 14) to be included? If so, look at relevant chapters in this book, to see if you can adjust appropriately.

20.3 Learn to criticise drafts of your own work. This is equivalent to giving feedback to yourself and is an essential academic skill. Annotate drafts of your own work – this is an important way to refine it and improve its quality. Stages you can adopt when reviewing your written work are discussed in Chapter 19.

PREPARING FOR EMPLOYMENT

How to transfer your thinking skills to a career

Well-developed thinking skills are an important outcome of your degree studies, whatever the subject. They are much sought after by employers, but to get on the first step of the career ladder, you will need to communicate your abilities in this and other areas as part of the job application process.

KEY TOPICS

→ Career planning

→ Skills and personal qualities in relation to employment

→ Communicating your skills when applying for a job

KEY TERMS

Employability   Graduateness   Jargon   Transcript   Transferable skills

Moving on from the university experience and fulfilling your professional ambitions is a challenging and exciting step. You need to assess your employability. You need to think about those abilities, traits, motivations and values that distinguish you as an individual. In other words, you need to know yourself before you can hope to convince an employer that you are their ideal candidate.

In relation to thinking skills, this requires that you understand these fully, can summarise them using appropriate language, and can provide examples of their application in your studies and extra-curricular activities. They are a vital component of 'graduateness', that quality which summarises what a future employer will be looking for in job applicants with degree qualifications.

Definitions

Employability – the blend of subject knowledge, subject-specific, generic and career-management skills; and personal qualities, values and motivations that will help a person gain suitable employment and perform effectively throughout their career.

Graduateness – authorities disagree about this term and some even dispute whether there is value in defining it beyond '*having a university degree*'. The concept certainly goes beyond possessing transferable skills, and may involve having subject-related knowledge, the capability to manage tasks and solve problems; being able to communicate well; the ability to work with others; and having self-awareness.

CAREER PLANNING

Career planning involves:

- clear thinking about your long-term goals and aspirations;
- looking for a fit between occupations and your personality and qualifications;
- researching your options, and finding out where the best opportunities lie.

This means that you will need to apply your critical thinking skills to the matter, ideally under guidance from your university's careers service.

Exploring possible career routes at an early stage will provide you with a better idea of the range of options you should be considering. It will also help you to make decisions that will place you in a better position to apply successfully for suitable jobs, for example, about such matters as module options; extra-curricular activities and relevant vacation work experience. The competition for good positions is now so high that this is important whether you are studying for a degree which traditionally leads to a number of potential careers or one with a professional/vocational emphasis.

Take advantage of the expertise and facilities offered by your university careers service

Their advisers can help you with:

- specialist knowledge about relevant job sectors
- facilities for researching research careers options and work positions
- information about careers fairs and seminars by recruiters
- a 'job shop' for vacation employment and internships
- opportunities to practise personality tests
- workshops for CV writing and interview technique

SKILLS AND PERSONAL QUALITIES IN RELATION TO EMPLOYMENT

When employers seek to fill a post by recruiting a university graduate, they assume that applicants come with certain assets that distinguish them from non-graduates. Their main preoccupation lies with the job that needs to be done and appointing the candidate who is best suited to fulfil the role. Your degree and transcript are testimony to your academic ability – but the knowledge-base of your degree may be of less interest to employers faced with numerous similar candidates than the skills and personal qualities that you might bring to the job.

To identify these personal graduate characteristics, your first challenge is to take a frank look at who you are, what your special skills are and what qualities you possess.

Skills and qualities are often confused and the boundary between them can be imprecise.

- **Skills** are things that you can do – sometimes called competences. They can often be learned from scratch and improve as you become more experienced. Table 21.1 provides a list of skills designed to assist with your self-assessment in this area. This will also help you highlight your critical thinking skills as a component of your overall aptitude.

Table 21.1 A list of graduate skills, highlighting those related to critical thinking. The 'thinking element' is classified using a five-star system (***** = high input, * = low input), but this is necessarily a generalisation. Four and five star skills are also emboldened in column 1. The 'personal evidence' column should be used to note situations where you have applied the relevant skill.

Skill	Thinking element	Personal evidence
Analysing problems and tasks	*****	
Communicating in a foreign language	**	
Contributing in meetings	****	
Creative thinking	****	
Critical thinking	*****	
Dealing with data	****	
Designing experiments or surveys	***	
Discussing and debating	*****	
Entrepreneurial skills	***	
Financial management	***	
Information analysis	****	
Information literacy (library skills)	****	
Information and computing skills	**	
Information retrieval	***	
Laboratory skills	**	
Listening to others	**	
Logical approach to problems	*****	
Negotiating skills	***	

continued overleaf

Skill	Thinking element	Personal evidence
Note-taking	**	
Numeracy	***	
Performance under assessment	*	
Performance under stress	*	
Planning your work	****	
Preparing a poster	***	
Project management	****	
Reading for academic purposes	***	
Reflection – self-awareness and self-interrogation	****	
Report writing	***	
Social skills	*	
Speaking in public	**	
Study and revision skills	***	
Teamwork	****	
Thesis or dissertation writing	*****	
Time-management	***	
Writing in standard formats	****	
Writing – organising and presenting	***	
Writing – use of English	**	
Writing letters, memos and emails	**	
Other (specify)		

- **Personal qualities** are innate to you, traits that you are born with and are a reflection of your personality. These natural aptitudes can also develop gradually as you gain experience. Table 21.2 provides a list of relevant personal qualities to consider when appraising the fit between yourself and job descriptions.

Your careers service may be able to offer a range of other personality tests and help you to review the results in relation to potential occupations.

For both skills and personal qualities, employers will be looking for evidence that you have demonstrated these in your studies, vacation work and extra-curricular activities. In relation to critical thinking skills specifically, Table 21.3 shows a possible correspondence between representative skills, university experiences and professional activities. One way of keeping track of your developing expertise is to take part in personal development planning (PDP). This process will have been designed to help you log your achievements and experience; carry out self-assessment; analyse your goals and plan for your future career.

Table 21.2 Assessing your personal qualities. Using the list below, give yourself a mark out of five in the 'rating' column, being appropriately self-critical. You might like to ask a friend or a family member for their opinion too. Circle the relevant number, where 1 = not a strength, 3 = well developed and 5 = very highly developed. If you aren't sure what something means, then look it up – these terms might be valuable to understand for applications and interviews. What evidence can you show to back up your claims?

My personal qualities	Rating	My personal qualities	Rating
Adaptability	1|2|3|4|5	Perseverance	1|2|3|4|5
Crisis management	1|2|3|4|5	Personal fitness and health	1|2|3|4|5
Determination	1|2|3|4|5	Proactive approach	1|2|3|4|5
Energy	1|2|3|4|5	Seeing others' viewpoints	1|2|3|4|5
Enthusiasm	1|2|3|4|5	Self-discipline	1|2|3|4|5
Flexibility	1|2|3|4|5	Sense of purpose	1|2|3|4|5
Honesty	1|2|3|4|5	Staying power/tenacity	1|2|3|4|5
Innovation	1|2|3|4|5	Taking the initiative	1|2|3|4|5
Integrity	1|2|3|4|5	Thoroughness	1|2|3|4|5
Leadership	1|2|3|4|5	Tolerance	1|2|3|4|5
Motivation	1|2|3|4|5	Taking on challenges	1|2|3|4|5
Patience	1|2|3|4|5	Other (specify)	1|2|3|4|5

Table 21.3 How thinking skills can be mapped to the professional context

Thinking skill (and relevant chapter)	Example of relevant typical university activity or experience	Example of related professional activity
Critical thinking (Ch 2)	Analysing a complex academic topic	Analysing problems on a production line or supply chain
Reflective thinking (Ch 3)	Analysing your responses to a learning episode	Thinking about how your actions might affect others at work
Creative thinking (Ch 4)	Coming up with an idea for the design of a poster presentation	Helping to design and market a new product
Arriving at a viewpoint (Ch 5)	Preparing for a tutorial or writing an essay	Presenting a view at a case meeting
Supporting and opposing an argument (Ch 6)	Taking part in a tutorial or committee	Making a presentation to a professional or business meeting
Interpreting data (Ch 7)	Analysing published results for project work and reports	Looking at a business case
Decision-making and work-planning (Ch 8)	Completing academic projects	Completing work-related projects
Group effort and collaboration (Ch 9)	Group project work	Nearly all professional and business activities

COMMUNICATING YOUR SKILLS WHEN APPLYING FOR A JOB

Finding a suitable job is by no means the easiest part of this process, but it is assumed here that, perhaps with the help of your careers service, you have selected an occupation, found a vacant position, and are ready to apply.

Successful applications result, first, from applying for positions for which you are a genuinely suitable applicant and, then, from demonstrating your suitability in an effective way. This means that you need to be watching for and creating opportunities to put across important messages about yourself.

The following are important ways of demonstrating your suitability for a post:

- tailoring your curriculum vitae (CV) so that it makes it clear that you have the necessary qualifications and aptitude;
- providing evidence, both within a CV and covering letter or personal statement, that demonstrates this;
- taking advantage of an interview, should you be selected to attend one.

Definition

Curriculum vitae is a Latin phrase meaning 'the course your life has taken' and is often shortened to CV (pronounced 'see vee'). It is a written summary of your career history and achievements to date.

How can I demonstrate evidence of skills and qualities?

This is perhaps best answered by considering some examples.

1 If a job calls for information gathering and critical thinking skills, you could show you had demonstrated these as part of a study exercise that was a critical review of a research paper, as this involved uncovering the meaning of jargon and tracing other related work by the same author.

2 If the job description indicates that 'staying power', motivation, self-discipline, team playing and leadership skills are important, you could mention how you had shown these qualities in extra-curricular activities, for example, the Duke of Edinburgh's Award scheme, playing as a member of a sports team or performing supervisory responsibilities in your part-time job.

3 If a post requires creativity and originality, you could show that you have demonstrated relevant skills by reference to the formulation of a digital mood board for an assignment, explaining how you had translated your initial ideas into the eventual assessed product.

Analogous connections would exist elsewhere depending on your experience and the specific job requirements.

YOUR CV

The principal aim of a CV is to communicate, in brief, the qualifications, experience and skills you have that might suit you for a job. Your CV may be one of many that a potential employer will scan, and you may only have a few seconds of their attention to make a favourable impression, so its presentation is important. While the essential elements of your CV (Table 21.4) will probably not change for each job you apply for, you should adjust your 'core' version to fit with the requirements of the post, usually to be found in the job description.

APPLICATION FORMS AND LETTERS

In completing an application form, you should take every opportunity to demonstrate that there is a good fit between the job description and your qualifications, experience, qualities and skills, as well as your career enthusiasms. Your letter of application provides an additional chance to impress a potential employer. As with your CV, it should be well-presented and error-free. Use the format and style that you would for a formal business letter. The content should include the following:

- the name of the position you are applying for and any reference number that is given;
- the key qualifications, skills and qualities you feel you can offer;
- if possible, specific links between your CV and the job description;
- reference to your commitment and enthusiasm for the job;
- your career objectives and what you hope to gain from the job; and
- your contact details (postal address, email address and phone numbers).

INTERVIEWS

It is hard enough to be short-listed for a post, but many people find the subsequent interview stage even more of a challenge. This experience is a very real test of your thinking skills. As well as the fact that you will be expected to answer difficult and unseen questions, you will be nervous because your chances of getting a coveted post may depend on your performance.

Table 21.4 Elements of a typical CV

Element, with *alternative headings*	Usual contents
1 Personal details *Name and contact details*	Your full name and address(es), contact phone numbers and email address. You don't have to include your sex or age.
2 Profile *Career aim; Career objective; Personal profile*	A summary of your career plans. Aspects of your goals and aspirations that you would like the employer to focus on.
3 Education *Qualifications; Education and qualifications*	The qualifications you have already achieved including those pending. Most people put current qualifications first, then work backwards. State educational institutions, years of attendance and the academic year in which each qualification or set of qualifications was gained. Include more detail if it is relevant, e.g. aspects of a subject covered in courses.
4 Work experience *Employment*	Details of past and current work (both paid and voluntary). Include dates, employer's name and job title. You may also wish to add major duties if these are not obvious from the job title. These should be arranged in reverse time sequence – from present to past.
5 Skills and personal qualities *Skills and achievements; Skills and competences*	An indication of the match between your abilities and the job description. You may wish to refer to examples and evidence here.
6 Interests and activities *Interests; Leisure activities*	This is a chance to show your character, and perhaps to indicate that you would make an interesting and enthusiastic colleague. Employers will use this section to build a picture of you as a person; however, they may be put off someone who appears quirky or bizarre in their eyes. Also if this section is over-emphasised, they may assume that you have placed greater emphasis on your social life than on your studies. Choose interests which display potentially valuable aspects of your character, e.g. sports activities that indicate you are a good team member.
7 Referees *References*	This is where you provide the names and contact details for those who have agreed to provide a reference for you (make sure you have asked them).

There are various ways in which you can prepare for an interview:

- carry out research on the company and organisation, and the people likely to be on the interview panel;
- think about ways in which you can demonstrate the ability to carry out the duties of the post;
- if the job is professional or technical, revise relevant theory, techniques, practice and law;
- note down questions you may have about the organisation and post;
- ensure you have rehearsed answers to some of the more common interview questions.

Some traditional interview questions

These may be wrapped in subtly different phrasing, or specifically related to the organisation and job description:

- What attracted you to this post?
- What makes you think you are the right person for this job?
- How did your degree and/or work experience prepare you for the challenges of this job?
- What evidence can you provide concerning [a specific skill]
- Please tell me about your experience doing X...
- Tell me about your interest in [a hobby or pastime]...
- What are your strengths?
- What are your weaknesses?
- What would you do if you held this post and the following scenario occurred...?
- How do you see your career here evolving?
- Could you tell me about... [techniques, procedures or legislation related to the role]?
- When would you be able to take up the post, if offered it?
- Seemingly 'off-the-wall' questions, such as 'do you keep a tidy or untidy desk?'
- Would you accept the post if offered and if so, what salary are you looking for?
- Where do you see yourself in 5/10/15 years' time?
- Do you have any questions for us?

At the interview itself, focus on the following:

- when you are introduced to the panel, smile and where appropriate, give a firm, confident handshake;
- adopt confident and relaxed body language and try not to fidget;
- listen carefully to each question, think about it carefully, then address it precisely;
- speak clearly and to the person who asked the question, making occasional eye contact around the panel;
- try to be positive about all questions and make the most of opportunities to mention relevant skills and experiences;
- be genuine, truthful and never waffle;
- remember that the interview is a two-way process and be ready to enter a dialogue and ask questions.

Good luck!

 PRACTICAL TIPS FOR CAREER PLANNING

Keep your CV up-to-date. A professionally presented CV will always be required when you apply for a post, and it is time-consuming to produce this from scratch. Also, it is easy to forget the fine detail that you will need to include in it. Tailoring your CV for every position you apply for will be easier if you create a generic 'core' version that includes all relevant details. Drafting a CV will put you in a better position to view yourself as a potential employer would and may help you plan activities to enhance your profile.

Research different CV models and designs. There are many websites dealing with this. Learn from the different designs and templates you see, and choose aspects you like. Try to be original in your own design without being eccentric. However, avoid US websites, because 'résumés' in that country are formatted differently from a standard UK curriculum vitae – only use this style if you are applying for a position in the USA or Canada.

Discuss your draft CV with a university careers adviser. They will be pleased to comment on its structure and content, and will be able to give advice about ways you might develop it in relation to your career goals and subject area. You should do this even if you are doing a vocational degree with a standard route of entry. Careers in the professions offer many different options and specialities. If you are studying for a degree like these, you need to be just as clued-up about these possibilities as if you were studying for a non-vocational degree and looking at a wide range of potential graduate occupations.

Aim for progression. University is a unique experience and you will not leave higher education as the same person who started out. Evaluate yourself using Tables 21.2 and 21.3 to highlight where you might focus your activities for maximum benefit. Recognise your strengths and play to them. Recognise your weak areas and develop strategies to counter them.

 AND NOW ...

21.1 Organise your CV-related information. If you haven't already done so, create files where you can store the different CV versions you produce and other relevant information for them. These will include physical files, where you can store diplomas, certificates and examples of your work, and computer files, where you can keep word processed documents. This information is so important to your future, so it is a good idea to make appropriate back-ups of electronic files.

21.2 Map evidence for your skills and qualities. Find out which skills are likely to be important in occupations which interest you. Next, write down where you have demonstrated those skills and what associated evidence you might be able to provide about them. Do the same for personal qualities.

21.3 Make an appointment to speak to a careers adviser at your careers service. Even though you may have only vague ideas about future options, the adviser will be experienced at helping you to create a short-list to consider, and will be able to point you in the direction of tools such as personality tests that can help in this process.

REFERENCES AND FURTHER READING

BBC English dictionary, 1992. London: BBC Worldwide Publishing.

Belbin® team roles [online], 2006, Belbin Associates, Cambridge UK. Available at: *www.belbin.com/belbin-team-roles.htm* [Accessed 19 January 2006].

Bloom, B. S., Englehart, M. D., Furst, E. J., Hill, W. H. and Krathwohl, D. R., 1956. *Taxonomy of educational objectives: cognitive domain*. New York: McKay.

Briggs Myers, I. and Myers, P. B., 1995. *Gifts differing: understanding personality types*. Palo Alto, California: Davis-Black Publishers.

Chambers dictionary, 2003. Edinburgh: Chambers Harrap Publishers Ltd.

Chicago manual of style, 15th ed., 2003. Chicago: University of Chicago Press.

CILIP, 2012. Chartered Institute of Library and Information Professionals: Information literacy: definition. Available at: *http://www.cilip.org.uk/ get-involved/advocacy/information-literacy/Pages/definition.aspx* [Accessed 9 March 2012].

De Bono, E., *Edward de Bono's authorised website*. Available at: *http:// www.edwdebono.com/* [Accessed 1 March 2012].

Fleming, N., *VARK—A guide to learning skills*. Available at: http://www. vark-learn.com [Accessed 1 March 2012].

Foley, M. and Hall, D., 2003. *Longman advanced learner's grammar*. Harlow: Longman.

Fowler, H. and Winchester, S., 2002. *Fowler's modern English usage*. Oxford: Oxford University Press.

Gibbs, G., 1988. *Learning by doing: a guide to teaching and learning methods*. Further Education Unit. Oxford Polytechnic: Oxford.

Graham, B., 2006. *The role of minerals and vitamins in mental health*. Available at: *www.nutritional-healing.com.au* [Accessed 16 January 2007].

Information Literacy Group, 2009. *Information literacy*. Available at: *www. informationliteracy.org.uk* [Accessed 14 January 2009].

Intellectual Property Office, 2009. Copyright. Available at: *www.ipo.gov.uk/ types/copy.htm* [Accessed 17 March 2012].

Jones, A. M., Reed, R. and Weyers, J. D. B., 2003. *Practical skills in biology*, 3rd ed. London: Pearson Education.

Krueger, R. A. and Casey, M. A., 2000. *Focus groups: a practical guide for applied research*, 3rd ed. Thousand Oaks, California: Sage Publications.

Longman dictionary of contemporary English, 2003. Harlow: Longman.

Luft, J. and Ingham, H., 1955. The Johari window, a graphic model of interpersonal awareness. *Proceedings of the Western Training Laboratory in Group Development*. Los Angeles: University of California, LA.

Magistretti, P. J., Pellerin, L. and Martin J.-L., 2000. Brain energy metabolism: an integrated cellular perspective. *Psychopharmacology: The Fourth Generation of Progress*. American Society of Neuropsychopharmocology. Available at: *www.acnp.org/Default. aspx?Page_4thGenerationChapters* [Accessed 14 May 2007].

McKenna, P., 2006. Make a new you with Paul McKenna: sleep. Available at: *www.timesonline.co.uk/article/0,,32769-2540709,00.htm* [Accessed 16 January 2007].

McMillan, K. M. and Weyers, J. D. B., 2013a. *The study skills book*, 3rd ed. Harlow: Pearson Education.

McMillan, K. M. and Weyers, J. D. B., 2013b. *How to cite, reference and avoid plagiarism at university*. Harlow: Pearson Education.

Morris, D., 2002. *Peoplewatching: the Desmond Morris guide to body language*. London: Vintage.

Patents Office, 2005. *Basic facts about copyright* [online]. Available at: *www.patent.gov.uk/copy/indetail/basicfacts.htm* [Accessed 17 March 2012].

Penguin A–Z thesaurus, 1986. Harmondsworth: Penguin Books.

Ritter, R. M., 2005. *New Hart's rules: the handbook of style for writers and editors*. Oxford: Oxford University Press.

Rutherford, D., 2002. *Vitamins and minerals: what do they do?* Available at: *www.netdoctor.co.uk/health_advice/facts/vitamins_which.htm* [Accessed 16 January 2007].

Sana, L., 2002. *Textbook of research ethics: theory and practice*. New York: Kluwer Academic.

Schön, D. A., 1983. *The reflective practitioner: how professionals think in action*. Ashgate Publishing Limited: Aldershot (also new edition 1991).

SCONUL, 2011. Society of College, National and University Libraries: The seven pillars of information literacy model. Available at: *http://www. sconul.ac.uk/groups/information_literacy/sp/publications/coremodel.pdf* [Accessed 9 March 2012].

Shamoo, A. E. and Resnik, D. B., 2003. *Responsible conduct of research*. Oxford: Oxford University Press.

Thompson Reuters, 2012. *Web of knowledge*. Available at: *http://wokinfo. com/* [Accessed 9 March 2012].

Trask, R. L., 2004. *Penguin guide to punctuation*. London: Penguin Books.

University of Dundee, 2005. *Code of practice on plagiarism and academic dishonesty* [online]. Available at: *www.somis.dundee.ac.uk/academic/ Plagiarism.htm* [Accessed 20 June 2012].

GLOSSARY OF KEY TERMS

Acronym An abbreviation formed from the first letter of words to form a word in itself, e.g. radar, NATO.

Analogy A comparison; a similar case from which parallels can be drawn.

Analyse To look at all sides of an issue, break a topic down into parts and explain how these components fit together.

Annotate To expand on given notes or text, e.g. to write extra notes on a printout of a PowerPoint presentation or a photocopied section of a book.

Argue To make statements or introduce facts to establish or refute a proposition; to discuss and reason.

Argument Discussion centered on a disagreement; also, reasoning aimed at demonstrating truth or untruth.

Assignment Coursework, usually completed in own (i.e. non-contact) time.

Bias A view or description of evidence that is not balanced, promoting one conclusion or viewpoint.

Bibliography A list of all the resources used in preparing for a piece of written work. The bibliography is usually placed at the end of a document. Compare with **Reference** list.

Blog Sequential online record of experiences and/or opinions (short for 'web-log').

Blurb A piece of writing used as publicity, typically for a book, and appearing on the jacket or cover.

Brainstorm An intensive search for ideas, often carried out and recorded in a free-form or diagrammatic way.

Brainstorming Act of creating a **brainstorm**, often carried out as a group activity.

Business report A report produced to provide information that helps decision-making in a commercial context. It often follows a formulaic or 'house' style.

Chronological Arranged sequentially, in order of time.

Citation (1) The act of making reference to another source in one's own writing. (2) A passage or a quotation from another source provided word for word within a text. See References.

Citing Quoting a reference. See **Citation**.

Colloquial Informal words and phrases used in everyday speech (e.g. slang), and generally inappropriate for formal and academic writing.

Copyright A legally enforceable restriction of the copying and publishing of original works, allowing the author(s) or assignee(s) or their agents alone to sell copies.

Creative thinking Act of producing original ideas, both as an artistic endeavor and in solution to a problem.

Creativity The ability to carry out creative thinking, often with a material product.

Critical thinking The examination of facts, concepts and ideas in an objective manner. The ability to evaluate opinion and information systematically, clearly and with purpose.

Criticism The act of evaluating or judging the qualities of something (both positive and negative).

Curriculum vitae (Latin) A standard document for assisting a possible employer to find out who you are and what experience, skills and qualities you have to offer.

CV (abbr.) The abbreviated form of **curriculum vitae**.

Debate The act of discussing an issue (verb); also, a formal process where teams discuss a topic (noun).

Describe To state how something looks, happens or works.

Descriptive statistics Numerical descriptions of a data set, e.g. the average value (mean) of an array of numbers.

Devil's advocate Someone who deliberately argues from a particular point of view, while not necessarily personally holding that point of view.

Dispersion In statistics, a measure of the spread of values within a data set or frequency distribution, e.g. standard deviation.

Ellipsis The replacement of words deliberately omitted from the text by three dots, e.g. 'A range of online ... methods of delivering materials and resources for learning'.

Employability That blend of subject knowledge, subject-specific, generic and career-management skills, personal qualities, values and motivations that will help a student gain suitable employment and perform effectively throughout their career. See also **Graduateness**.

Error bars Lines extending from a symbol on a graph that indicate a (specified) error of a mean value (or other statistic of location).

Evidence Information that provides the basis for a point of view.

Extra-curricular activity Pursuit or interest carried out while at university that is not, strictly, a part of the academic content of the course (the curriculum).

Extrapolation In graphing, the act of creating an assumed line or relationship outside the limits of the available data points, assuming the line will follow trends identified using those points.

Fact Statement generally acknowledged as valid.

Fallacy A logically erroneous argument used in reasoning or debate.

Falsifiability Of a **fact** or **hypothesis**, capable of being shown to be invalid or untrue.

Finger tracing The act of running your finger immediately below the line of text being read to follow your eyes' path across a page, starting and stopping a word or two from either side.

Formative assessment An assessment or exercise with the primary aim of providing feedback on performance, not just from the grade given, but also from comments provided by the examiner. Strictly, a formative assessment does not count towards a module or degree grade, although some marks are often allocated as an inducement to perform well. See **Summative assessment**.

Freewriting Method of generating ideas which involves rapid, 'stream of consciousness' writing about a topic without preconceived ideas about structure or content.

Frequency distribution Representation of the variability in data. In graph forms, usually showing classes of a measured variable on the x-axis and frequency-within-classes on the y-axis.

Gantt chart Coded graphing method showing the schedule of activity on a project, the relationships between elements of the task, and progress achieved to date.

Gist The essence of something, e.g. a summary or a list of key ideas from a piece of writing or a talk.

Graduateness A term that summarises the skills and personal characteristics expected of someone who possesses a university degree. The concept goes beyond the possession of transferable skills, and may involve having subject-related knowledge; the capability to manage tasks and solve problems; being able to communicate well;

the ability to work with others; and having self-awareness. See also **Employability**.

Hierarchical Division of objects or (ideas) into a logical classification system.

Hypothesis A testable theory (pl. hypotheses).

Hypothesis testing In statistics, a form of analysis that allows a numerical probability to be assigned to the outcomes of a hypothesis.

ibid. **(abbr., Latin)** Short for *ibidem*, meaning 'in the same place'; especially used in some referencing systems, e.g. Chicago method, when referring to the immediately previous source mentioned.

Idiom A form of language used in everyday speech and understood by native speakers, but whose meaning is not immediately apparent from the actual words used, e.g. to 'pull someone's leg' (make them believe something that is not true).

Indentation In text layout, the positioning of text (usually three to five character spaces in) from the margin to indicate a new paragraph.

Instruction words The words indicating what should be done; in an exam question or instruction, the verbs and associated words that define what the examiner expects of the person answering.

Interdisciplinary Involving one or more disciplines (subjects) or crossing boundaries between them.

Interpolation In graphing, the assumed trend or relationship between adjacent data points. Compare with **Extrapolation**.

Jargon The specialised vocabulary of a group of people with a common occupation or profession, often impenetrable to outsiders.

Landscape orientation The positioning of paper so that the 'long' side is horizontal. See also **Portrait orientation**.

Lateral thinking New thinking that does not follow the apparent logical course of past thinking and presents a new perspective on an issue or problem.

Learning journal Sequential set of notes (or diary) recording what a student has learnt, and how.

Learning outcome Similar to a learning objective, often focusing on some product that a student should be able to demonstrate, possibly under examination.

Legend The key to a diagram, chart or graph, e.g. showing which lines and symbols refer to which quantities.

Literature survey A report on the literature on a defined area, usually specified in the title. May include the author's independent conclusions based on the sources consulted.

Location In statistics, an estimate of the 'centre' of a data set or frequency distribution, e.g. the mean.

Marking criteria A set of 'descriptors' that explain the qualities of answers falling within the differing grade bands used in assessment; used by markers to assign grades, especially where there may be more than one marker, and to allow students to see what level of answer is required to attain specific grades.

Metacognition Understanding how you think and how you make use of thinking processes.

Metaphor Figure of speech in which a name or description is applied to an object to which it would not usually be applied, usually with the intention of drawing attention of a particular quality in the object.

Mnemonic An aid to memory involving a sequence of letters or associations, e.g. 'Richard of York goes battling in vain', to remember the colours of the rainbow: red, orange, yellow, green, blue, indigo, violet.

Mood board Poster-sized area such as a pin-board on which items are attached to create feelings or atmosphere regarding a project.

Moot Form of legal **debate**, usually centered on a point of law.

Noun A word denoting a person, place or thing.

Objective Regarding language and thinking, that which has an impersonal tone and avoids personal expressions or feelings (contrast **subjective**).

op. cit. **(abbr. Latin)** Short for *opus citatum*, meaning 'from the work cited'. In some forms of citation this term is used to refer to a previous citation of the same text or article.

Opinion View belonging to a person or group, often **subjective** and based on incomplete evidence.

Opportunity cost The benefits you would lose out on if you take a particular path of action where choice is involved.

Originality Quality of being new, fresh in nature or in style.

Outlier Value which is isolated or distant from the main body of a set of data; a datum at the extremes of a **frequency distribution**.

Paradigm Theoretical framework which is confirmed by numerous observations or experiments and which has proved resistant to challenge and which is therefore generally accepted.

Parametric In a statistical context, involving the assumption that data follow a specific mathematically described population distribution.

Paraphrase To quote ideas indirectly by expressing them in other words.

Paraphrasing Restating text, giving the sense, idea or meaning, but in other words.

Peer review Process whereby research papers (and research grant applications) are reviewed by colleagues of equal standing, known as referees with a view to their acceptance for publication (or funding).

Perfectionism The personal quality of wanting to produce the best possible product or outcome, sometimes regardless of other factors involved.

Personal development plan (PDP) A reflective analysis of who you are, what you've done and what you plan to do.

Phrasal verb An idiomatic verbal phrase consisting of a verb and adverb or a verb and preposition. See **Idiom**.

Plagiarism Copying the work of others and passing it off as one's own, without acknowledgement.

Portfolio Collection of materials (usually written) either as work samples, papers or electronic files (hence eportfolio), sometimes in support of a qualification.

Portrait orientation The positioning of paper so that the 'short' side is horizontal. See also **Landscape orientation**.

Primary source The source in which ideas and data are first communicated.

Priority Ranking in relation to importance, urgency or both. High priority is very important, urgent or both.

Procrastination Putting off a task to another occasion.

Pronoun A word that may replace a **noun**: I, you, he, she, it, we, they. For example, 'Traffic lights are red, green and amber. *They* light in a particular sequence.'

Proof In science, evidence that indicates a hypothesis is true. The word 'proof' should be used cautiously when applied to quantitative research – the term implies 100 per cent certainty, whereas this is very rarely justified owing to the ambiguity inherent in statistical analysis and experimental design.

Propaganda Skewed or biased reporting of the facts to favour a particular outcome or point of view.

Provenance Regarding a source of information, who and where it originated from, and why.

Qualitative Data (information) that cannot be expressed in numbers, e.g. the colour of the lecturer's tie or the quality of life of elderly patients.

Quantitative Data (information) that can be expressed in numbers, e.g. the width of the lecturer's tie or the number of elderly patients included in a survey.

Quotation Words directly lifted from a source, e.g. a journal article or book, usually placed between inverted commas (quotation marks), i.e. '...' or '...'

Quoting The lifting of text word for word from another work for inclusion in your own – signified by the use of quotation marks and a reference to the original. Style guides may require quoted material to be indented or italicised and indented.

Reference list A list of sources referred to in a piece of writing, usually provided at the end of the document. Compare with **Bibliography**.

Reflective thinking Act of looking back over past events; analysing how you have learned and developed as a person and your feelings about this; evaluating your experience; and thinking about future approaches or actions in the light of your thoughts.

Register The style of language and grammar used in written or spoken form as appropriate to the context, often distinguishing formal from informal usage, for example.

Restriction The limits or bounds set on a task.

Rhetoric Speech or writing intended to persuade.

Rhetorical question A question asked as part of a talk or written work where an answer from the audience or reader is not required or expected, and indeed where the answer is usually subsequently provided by the speaker or author. Used as a device to direct the attention and thoughts of the audience or reader, e.g. 'Why is this important? I'll tell you why ...'

Scenario A particular situation or event, real or imagined, usually described in outline, and often used for training purposes.

Scientific method The scientific approach to a problem, involving the creation of a hypothesis and testing it using evidence obtained in experiments or by observation.

Scientific report A report on a piece of scientific observation or experiment that follows a generic format, with subdivisions (e.g. abstract, introduction, materials and methods, etc.) in a particular order.

Secondary reference A reference where the original text is not available and the reference relates to a citation in a text which you have read.

Secondary source A source that quotes, adapts, interprets, translates, develops or otherwise uses information drawn from primary sources.

Simile Figure of speech where one thing is compared to another.

Sketchbook Artists' notepad, usually with thick cartridge paper suitable for drawing and painting.

Skewed In statistics, term used to describe a **frequency distribution** that is not symmetrical about the mean value.

Study group A set of students who meet to study together, often informally.

Subjective In relation to language and thinking, that which concerns personal matters, opinions and feelings (contrast **objective**).

Summarising The act of creating a broad overview of an original piece of text, briefly stating the main points from the original but expressing ideas using your own words (other than for technical words with precise meanings).

Summative assessment An exam or course assessment exercise that counts towards the final module or degree mark. Generally, no formal feedback is provided. See **Formative assessment**.

Superscript Text, including numerals, above the line of normal text, usually in a smaller font, e.g. ^{2}. Contrast with subscript, which is text or numerals below the line, thus $_a$.

Synonym A word with the same meaning as another.

Team role The role of a team member within a team situation, e.g. leader, worker, creative person.

Terminator paragraph The paragraph that brings a piece or section of writing to an ending or conclusion.

Topic An area within a study; the focus of a title in a written assignment.

Topic paragraph The paragraph, usually the first, that indicates or points to the topic of a section or piece of writing and how it can be expected to develop.

Topic sentence The sentence, usually the first, that indicates or points to the topic of a paragraph and how it can be expected to develop.

Transcript The certified details of a student's academic record, e.g. modules taken, performance in exams and modules, as recorded by a university.

Transferable skills Skills gained in one situation that can be used in another.

Truth Statement that is consistent with known **facts**.

Tutorial A small-group meeting to discuss an academic topic, led by a tutor.

Typo Short for typographical error – a typing mistake or, less commonly, a typesetting error.

Value judgement A statement that reflects the views and values of the speaker or writer rather than the objective reality of what is being assessed or considered.

Verb The 'doing' word(s) in a sentence. A part of speech by which action or state of being is indicated, serving to connect a subject with a predicate. A verb also shows, for example, time shifts by changes in tense, e.g. past, present or future.

Verbatim From Latin, meaning word for word, e.g. verbatim notes are word-for-word copies (transcriptions) of a lecture or text.